D1563595

Cambridge studies in medieval life and thought

Edited *by* WALTER ULLMANN, LITT.D., F.B.A.
Professor of Medieval History in the
University of Cambridge

Third series, vol. 12

UNIVERSITIES, ACADEMICS AND THE GREAT SCHISM

CAMBRIDGE STUDIES IN
MEDIEVAL LIFE AND THOUGHT

THIRD SERIES

UNIVERSITIES, ACADEMICS AND THE GREAT SCHISM

R. N. SWANSON

Assistant Archivist
Borthwick Institute of Historical Research
University of York

CAMBRIDGE UNIVERSITY PRESS

CAMBRIDGE

LONDON · NEW YORK · MELBOURNE

Published by the Syndics of the Cambridge University Press
The Pitt Building, Trumpington Street, Cambridge CB2 1RP
Bentley House, 200 Euston Road, London NW1 2DB
32 East 57th Street, New York, NY 10022, USA
296 Beaconsfield Parade, Middle Park, Melbourne 3206, Australia

First published 1979

Printed in Great Britain by
The Eastern Press Limited
London and Reading

Library of Congress Cataloguing in Publication Data
Swanson, Robert Norman
Universities, academics, and the Great Schism

(Cambridge studies in medieval life and thought; 3d ser., v. 12.)

Bibliography: p.

Includes index.

1. Schism, The Great Western, 1378–1417.
2. Universities and colleges – Europe – History.
I. Title. II. Series.
BX1301.S95   270.5   78-56764
ISBN 0 521 22127 7

270.5
S97z

FOR MY PARENTS

CONTENTS

MAPS

All three maps are based on maps 119 and 123b in *Grosser Historischer Weltatlas*, Bayerischer Schulbuch-Verlag, 1970.

PREFACE

This book is a revised and partially rewritten version of a dissertation of the same title submitted for the degree of PhD at the University of Cambridge in 1976. In bringing the work to its present state I owe much – including the original suggestion of the topic – to Professor Walter Ullmann. His constant enthusiasm and interest have been a great encouragement over the years. Professor Howard Kaminsky of the Florida International University and Dr Margaret Harvey of the University of Durham have both offered advice and debated various matters with me, the former also generously allowing me to consult unpublished material. Professor Barrie Dobson of the University of York read through a preliminary draft of the book and offered constructive and valuable criticism. Responsibility for the final product, and for any errors it may contain, remains entirely my own.

My debt to the libraries which allowed me to consult material in their keeping, particularly manuscripts, will emerge clearly from the notes and quotations, and the inclusion of a full list here would be both lengthy and tedious. Nevertheless, I would like to express my thanks to them for their ready assistance. I have received much stimulus from my contemporaries as research students at Cambridge, and during the final preparation of the book have been greatly encouraged by my colleagues at the University of York. I am also deeply grateful for the ready hospitality offered by friends in Rome, Cambridge and London, without which the travelling involved to consult sources would have proved impossible. I am also grateful for financial assistance from Christ's College, Cambridge, the Board of Graduate Studies, Cambridge, and the British Academy's Small Grants Research Fund in the Humanities (UGC), which helped cover the cost of microfilms. Finally, there are the two people to whom my debt is

ix

too great to be adequately acknowledged in a preface. The book is for my parents, to whom I dedicate it as a small token of my thanks.

R. N. S.

October 1977

ABBREVIATIONS

ASV	Archivio Segreto Vaticano.
Auct. Ch.	H. S. Denifle and E. Chatelain, *Auctarium chartularii universitatis Parisiensis*, vols. 1–3: *Liber procuratorum nationis Anglicanae (Alemanniae) in universitate Parisiensi*, 2nd edn (3 vols., Paris, 1937).
BN	Bibliothèque nationale, Paris.
Bulaeus	C. E. Bulaeus, *Historia universitatis Parisiensis* (6 vols., Paris, 1665–73).
Ch. Paris.	H. S. Denifle and E. Chatelain, *Chartularium universitatis Parisiensis* (4 vols., Paris, 1891–9).
Chron. S. Den.	M. L. Bellaguet, *Chronique du religieux de St Denys* (6 vols., Paris, 1839–52).
Glorieux	P. Glorieux, *Jean Gerson, oeuvres complètes* (10 vols. in 11, Tournai, 1960–73).
Hardt	H. von der Hardt, *Magnum oecumenicum Constantiense concilium* (6 vols., Frankfurt and Leipzig, 1697–1700).
Raynaldus	A. Theiner, *Caesaris S. R. E. Card. Baronii, Od. Raynaldi, et Jac. Laderchii . . . annales ecclesiastici*, vols. 26–7 (Bar-le-Duc, 1872–74).
Thes. Nov. Anec.	E. Martène and U. Durand, *Thesaurus novus anecdotorum* (5 vols., Paris, 1717), vol. 2 only.
Valois	N. Valois, *La France et le grand schisme d'occident* (4 vols., Paris, 1896–1902).

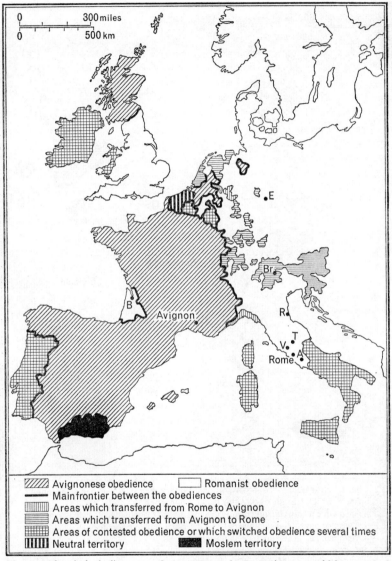

Map 1. The rival obediences, 1378–1409. Towns in Romanist areas which recognised the Avignon pope: A=Anagni (to 1386); Br=Brixen (to 1389); E=Erfurt (to 1380); R=Ravenna (to 1386); T=Todi (to 1386); V=Viterbo (to 1386). B=Bordeaux, which accepted the Avignon papacy from 1380 onwards. N.B. Portugal was Romanist after 1385; Naples was Romanist from 1400.

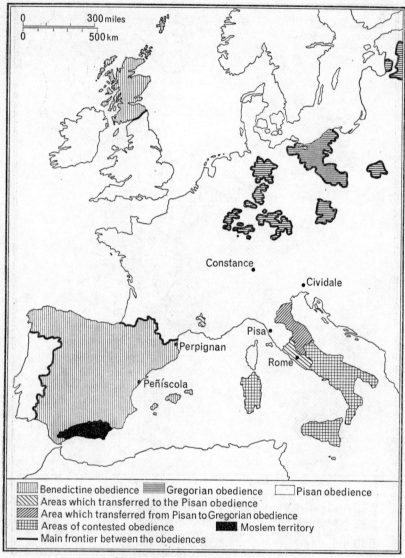

Map 2. The rival obediences, 1409–18.

Benedictine obedience   Gregorian obedience   Pisan obedience
Areas which transferred to the Pisan obedience
Area which transferred from Pisan to Gregorian obedience
Areas of contested obedience   Moslem territory
Main frontier between the obediences

0   300 miles
0   500 km

Constance
Cividale
Pisa
Perpignan
Rome
Peñíscola

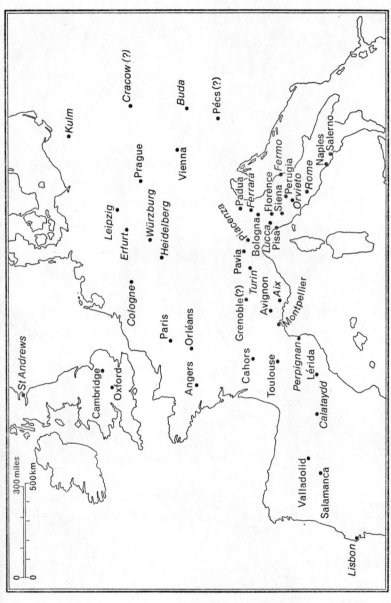

Map 3. The universities of Europe, 1378–1418. '?' after a name indicates that the existence of this university in 1378 is uncertain; names in italics are those universities founded between 1378 and 1415. All other names are universities that were in existence in 1378.

INTRODUCTION

The schism which rent the Roman church in the years between 1378 and 1418 was a crisis of truly massive proportions. As a division within what claimed to be a universalist cosmology, it could obviously be settled only in similarly universalist terms. But, whilst dealing with many of the political and intellectual facets of the response to the crisis generated by the rival elections of Bartholomew Prignano and Cardinal Robert of Geneva to the papacy in 1378, and with the more personal involvement of the leading individuals of the period, the historiography of the great schism has not so far paid much attention to this universalist question throughout the entire period, particularly the involvement of those institutions specifically intended to be concerned with the issues raised by the dispute. Thus, although the administrative and institutional development of the medieval universities has been much dissected, little attention has been given to their activities when confronted with an ecclesiological issue of such dimensions as the schism. The purpose of this book is to attempt to redress the balance, by considering the participation of the European universities and their members in the debates which were generated as a result of the events of 1378.

Regardless of the stage of development by that date of an ecclesiology capable of offering an effective challenge to the papal monarchy, when the double election did occur and Europe reacted by dividing into rival camps there was no machinery in existence which could be immediately invoked to settle the problem. Some acceptable ecclesiological formula had therefore to be devised to permit the imposition of a solution, and that formula had to be produced by a body whose competence to act in such matters was universally recognised. Clearly, with the papacy itself divided, there was no chance of the rivals acting together, and, as the cardinals were blamed for having caused the problem in the first place, it was most unlikely that they would be given the authority or the trust to end the dispute. In 1378, therefore, the most obvious alternative jurisdiction was that of the emperor: but with the death of Charles IV in 1378 and the accession of his son Wenceslas, that possibility was also destroyed. For a number of reasons the empire under Wenceslas proved incapable of acting in the dispute, an incapacity compounded in 1400 by the counter-election of Rupert III of the Palatinate as King of the Romans, thereby causing a schism in the empire as well as the papacy. The imperial authority to intervene in the search for an end to the papal schism was also limited and challenged by the rise of Gallicanism and the territorial monarchies, which claimed 'imperial' jurisdiction within their own frontiers. Only with the decay of this opposition and the reunification of the empire under Sigismund of Hungary after 1410 was the imperial jurisdiction recognised as capable of becoming effectively involved in the search for ecclesiastical reunification. But by that date the ecclesiology which would permit the imposition of a solution had already been devised. It is the contention of this book that the solutions had been produced within the universities, the academics having been accepted as the only remaining universal grouping capable of involving itself in the issues and arriving at the necessary ecclesiological remedy. Even though developments within the universities themselves, with growing diversification and fragmentation, progressive laicisation and a general transformation of the institutions, meant that the universality of the academic community was more imaginary than real; nevertheless the lingering notion of the international status of the universities as representatives of the supra-national community of learning meant that they could be conceded the authority to debate and pronounce on the means of attaining the reunification of the divided church. Not, admittedly, that they could do this with impunity, but nevertheless with a good deal of independence. The theories which were produced within the academic milieu during the period eventually resulted, after a number of false starts, in the ecclesiology of the Councils of Pisa and Constance and the restoration of a united papacy with the election of Martin V.

The geographical and temporal scope of the subject have imposed their own necessary limitations of the amount of material I have been able to consider, and I make no claims for this to be more than a preliminary statement on academic involvement in the debates occasioned by the schism. Almost of necessity, the whole picture in the years to 1403 is dominated by events within the University of Paris, a situation for which there are three main reasons. The first is the pre-eminence attained (or, at least, sought) by the French in the attempt to resolve the schism by political methods, and even though his arguments have been modified during the course of the present century no historian of the schism can fail to be influenced by the ever-present shade of Noel Valois. For the University of Paris itself the sheer mass of available source material – whether published or still in manuscript form, and whether as official records or personal tracts and statements – virtually forces that corporation to the forefront of any consideration of academic involvement in the debates on the schism. Finally, however, the pre-eminence of the Parisian masters in the intellectual response to the schism prior to 1403 is also justified by the university's central position within the framework of the European discussions of the issue. This centrality was not only geographical, in that Paris was at the centre of the web of inter-university contacts which spread across the continent during this period, but it was also figurative, as it was the Parisian pronouncements on the various possible solutions to the division of the church which generally stimulated the formulation of declarations and statements on the issue by other bodies and institutions, both favouring and opposing the Parisian standpoint. A good deal of material doubtless remains to be discovered relating to academic reaction to the schism, but although this may diminish the quantitative preponderance of the Parisian masters in the debates, it seems unlikely that it will reduce their qualitative dominance. Indeed, it seems probable that it will tend to emphasise the central position of the University of Paris in the inter-academic debates.

This centrality became much less important after 1403, when Parisian dominance of the discussions declined. Correspondingly, the importance of other universities increased, although the

3

removal of the unifying influence of Paris meant that the developments became more fragmentary. The complexities of the situation thereafter grew until, almost unexpectedly, the Council of Constance cut the Gordian knot and, with a blithe disregard for anything other than the reunification of the church, ended the schism almost (but not quite) as rapidly as the division had itself begun, after the death, forty years previously, of Pope Gregory XI.

Chapter 1

THE CONTEXT

When Pope Gregory XI entered Rome for the first time in January 1377, the results of his simple desire to return the papacy to its nominal see could not have been guessed at. His predecessor, Urban V, had himself made an attempt to end the so-called Babylonish Captivity, the exile of the Roman papacy in its enclave at Avignon, which had begun during the pontificate of Clement V at the beginning of the fourteenth century. But Urban's stay in Rome had proved to be no more than a temporary sojourn. He had returned to Avignon to die, and it was there that Gregory XI, a Frenchman, had been duly elected as his successor in 1370. Gregory had made no secret of his determination to travel to Rome when the opportunity arose, but this proved impossible until 1376. And, by late 1377, it seemed likely that this re-establishment of the papacy at Rome might be as temporary as that under Urban V. For Gregory XI, however, the stay proved permanent: he died in Rome on 27 March 1378, at the age of 48.

In the uncertainties of the situation which followed the death of Gregory XI, the conclave which elected his successor proved to be very much a struggle for control of the papacy between the various factions within the College of Cardinals. This was the first conclave held in Italy since Clement V had removed the papacy to France, and on its outcome would depend the location of the centre of the Roman church, deciding whether the papacy should return to Avignon, or be firmly re-established at Rome. The majority of the cardinals apparently desired the former course. But they were divided on other matters, both politically and geographically. Only sixteen cardinals were at Rome to elect the successor to Gregory XI; the others had either remained at Avignon to continue the routine government of the church during the pope's absence or were engaged on diplomatic business elsewhere. The sixteen at Rome were divided politically into French, Limousin and Italian factions, each of which was anxious to have its own candidate elected pope. This situation in itself augured badly for the conclave, but a further complexity was added by the Roman people, who were also determined to try to influence events, as they saw the prospect of recovering the financial benefits which went with accommodating the papal court threatening to evaporate back to France. When the conclave began, it was to the accompaniment of mob violence outside, as the Roman populace shouted for the election of a Roman or Italian as pope, threatening to massacre the cardinals if a foreigner was chosen.

On 8 April 1378 the new pope was elected – but the Roman mob invaded the conclave before the election could be proclaimed and the cardinals fled for their lives, having robed the octogenarian Cardinal Tebaldeschi in the papal regalia in the hope of thereby deluding the crowd. On the following day, after a majority of the cardinals had reconvened to confirm their choice, the truly elected pope was finally proclaimed, and on Easter Sunday, 1378, Bartholomew Prignano, a Neapolitan and formerly Archbishop of Bari, was enthroned as pope with full ceremony, with the name of Urban VI.

The election of Prignano had been very much a compromise: he was not a cardinal, and was not attached to any of the factions in the college. However, he was by no means a newcomer to ecclesiastical politics, his career having involved him at the highest levels of the government of the church. But in this probably lay the foundations of the future difficulties which Urban had to face, for the new pope was a bureaucrat, his experience limiting his outlook. Although imbued with the theory of papal power, he had no practical experience of the limitations thereon which had developed at Avignon as the cardinals established their oligarchic hold on the ecclesiastical government. Prignano's view of the papacy made no concessions to such developments – his theory of the papacy was almost that of Boniface VIII, if not of Gregory VII, and would not permit him to share power with the cardinals.

In such circumstances, relations between the pope and the cardinals soon deteriorated. The latter, apart from disliking Urban's intention to be papal monarch in fact as well as name,

6

were also upset by his treatment of them in other ways. It seems clear that, whatever his administrative qualities, Prignano was personally unfitted to be pope. By the end of his reign, there can be little doubt that he had been driven insane by the impossibility of reconciling his political theories to actuality, and there may be signs of this incipient insanity in his early dealings with the cardinals, as the sudden access of power transformed a mere archbishop into an autocrat. He attacked the extravagance of the cardinals in a singularly tactless manner (although this 'reformist' zeal was welcomed in some sectors) and, perhaps most damaging of all as far as they were concerned, made it obvious that he had no intention of returning to Avignon. By June 1378, the rift between the pope and his electors was becoming obvious. Taking advantage of the riotous background to the April election to argue that their choice had been made under duress, and taking advantage also of the antagonism which had arisen between the pope and some of his most powerful temporal neighbours as a result of a series of almost deliberate and politically naive rebuffs which he had offered them, the dissident cardinals left Rome and placed themselves under the protection of the Count of Fundi. In July they formally challenged the election of Urban VI as pope, proceeding in the following month to declare it null. On 20 September 1378, at Anagni, the cardinals elected one of their own number, Cardinal Robert of Geneva, to be their new pope as successor to Gregory XI. He took the name of Clement VII.[1]

Thus the great schism began. By 1380 there were two distinct papacies: one at Rome, the other at Avignon. At Rome, Urban VI reigned until 1389, being succeeded in turn by Boniface IX (1389–1404), Innocent VII (1404–6), and Gregory XII. At Avignon, Clement VII held sway until 1394, when he was followed by Benedict XIII. In 1409, by which time most of Europe was thoroughly exasperated by the continuance of the schism, the rebellious cardinals of both obediences summoned the Council of

[1] For the events between April and September 1378 see *Valois*, vol. 1, pp. 3–83; M. Souchon, *Die Papstwahlen von Bonifaz VIII bis Urban VI und die Entstehung des Schismas, 1378* (Brunswick, 1888), pp. 109–58; W. Ullmann, *Origins of the great schism*, 2nd edn (Hamden, Conn., 1972), pp. 9–56; L. Gayet, *Le grand schisme d'occident d'après les documents contemporains déposés aux archives secrètes du Vatican* (2 vols., Florence and Berlin, 1889), vol. 1, pp. 41–426, vol. 2, pp. 1–282.

Pisa, which sought to terminate the dispute by deposing the then rivals. It merely added the further complication of another papacy, with the election of the short-lived Alexander V. On his death in 1410, Balthasar Cossa was chosen his successor, as Pope John XXIII. A further attempt to end the schism was made at the Council of Constance (1414–18), at which both John XXIII and Gregory XII were removed. The assembly also declared Benedict XIII deposed again, but, as in 1409, he refused to accept the council's decision, and remained aloof in his Spanish stronghold of Peñíscola. Meanwhile, in 1417, Martin V was elected pope at Constance, and rapidly secured almost universal recognition. However, Benedict XIII continued to head a fragment of the church until his death in 1423, but even then the schism was not finally terminated. Following Benedict's death, his recently created cardinals divided into two parties, the majority electing Clement VIII as their pope, while Jean Carrier carried out an election on his own, and chose a certain Benedict XIV. Clement VIII at last submitted to Martin V in 1429; Benedict XIV's pontificate is quite obscure.

Despite these lingering remnants of the schism, the dispute was to all intents and purposes over by 1419. Between its inception and this effective termination, the simple existence of a division within the church gives some sort of unity to what was one of the most complex and crucial periods of European history, as the middle ages ended and the Europe of the Renaissance developed to replace them. But the coherence thus imparted is scarcely more than superficial, and is very much imposed. For one thing, the schism itself was not one crisis, but a combination of many. And the crises of the schism were merely some of those affecting Europe at this time, generally extending beyond the years 1378–1419 to envelop the whole century between the Black Death in 1349–50 and the fall of Constantinople in 1453. Contemporary commentators themselves began the process of exploiting the schism to impose coherence on their world, as is evident from the causal view adopted by Ludolf of Sagan in his complaint that, because of the schism, 'surrexit regnum contra regnum, provincia contra provinciam, clerus contra clerum, doctores contra doctores, parentes in filios et filii in parentes'.[2] It cannot be denied that such

2 J. Loserth, 'Beiträge zur Geschichte der husitischen Bewegung, III: Der Tractatus de

8

conflicts did occur, but whether their cause can be so exclusively identified with the schism is highly dubious. They were rather the result of the political exploitation of the division within the church, to legitimise pre-existing international rivalries and aspirations, as France, Scotland and most of the Iberian peninsula gave their loyalty to Clement VII, while England, most of Italy and much of the rest of Europe remained true to Urban VI.[3]

These political rivalries were only some of the contemporary problems. There were also theoretical political difficulties, the secular counterparts of the constitutional difficulties which the church was also experiencing. Succession disputes were common: besides the running sore of the Neapolitan succession – which during the schism was perhaps something of a special case, because of the intimate involvement of the popes in the politics of what was nominally a papal fief – almost every other monarchy in Europe suffered some sort of dynastic upheaval. These crises provoked considerable constitutional debate which, as in the case of the church, frequently concentrated on the interrelationships of the constituent parts of the body politic, and the mutual responsibilities of head and members. These issues were perhaps most explicitly raised in the English solution to the problem of the transference of power from Richard II to Henry IV in 1399, but similar crises affected other states including – in the 1390s – the Holy Roman Empire itself.

All these problems were in turn only part of a wider circle of difficulties. The whole ethos of the century from 1350 to 1450 was one of change, of reformation and alteration, and frequently of frustration. Within the church, for example, there is evidence of a widespread desire for reformation, usually involving the fragmentation of the papal monarchy into a number of smaller, semi-independent national churches, and the adoption of a simpler, more 'apostolic', ecclesiastical system. This latter desire, welling up from the lower orders of the church, spawned numerous heretical and semi-heretical movements, most obviously in England and Bohemia. The economic difficulties of the period, combined with the aspirations arising from the efflorescence of a barely controllable popular piety, provided ready tinder for any

longevo schismate des Abtes Ludolf von Sagan', *Archiv für Österreichische Geschichte*, **60** (1880), 404. [3] For these territorial divisions, see Map 1.

9

spark of social disorder, compounding dissensions which were already sufficiently serious in isolation.

The pervading crisis which affected all facets of European society between the mid-fourteenth and mid-fifteenth centuries had its most obvious impact on institutions, especially the more 'artificial' institutions such as the universities. Along with the rest of Europe, these experienced a basic transformation during the period, a transformation in which the great schism played a major role as a catalyst. But the crises which affected the universities were older than the schism. The most vital, and most lasting, was that of patronage, not only to sustain the students in the schools, but also to provide employment for graduates. This whole question was to be much debated during the years of the schism, as the generalised economic crisis of the period took its toll on the incomes from ecclesiastical benefices and the revenues of the endowed colleges. Attempts to solve the problem internally, by such methods as the establishment of more endowed colleges or (as in England) the economic subjection of the university town to the university authorities, frequently did no more than increase rivalries, both between groupings within the university and between town and gown. The transference of university financing to the state budget, a policy adopted in Florence and other Italian universities, naturally resulted in increased dependence on the state and, as the financing remained to some extent a matter of whim, did not make for academic security. This loss of independence because of financial control was part of the process of changing relationships between the universities and the higher, generally secular, authorities, which occurred as ecclesiastical power within the universities was reduced, laicisation set in and the princes and governments sought more effective control over their academics, subjecting the universities to increasing restrictions on individual movement and independence. To all these developments the schism added its own complications, generally hastening the transformation. Even before the outbreak of the schism, however, the increasing pressures on the universities had produced difficulties, with considerable uncertainty not only over their future development, but also over their very existence. The number of such institutions in existence in the years immediately preceding the start of the schism had fluctuated wildly, and continued to do so after the division of 1378, which made the whole situation more complex and provided the background for a complete overhaul of the educational map of Europe.

Although there had been many attempts to establish new universities throughout Europe from the middle of the fourteenth century onwards, very few of these foundations had survived through to 1378.[4] An intellectual *Drang nach Osten* had first foundered, and by 1378 had all but died out: although universities had been erected at Pécs, Cracow, Vienna and Prague, only the last remained a flourishing institution in 1378. The others may not have been quite extinct, but the evidence available for any continuing and effective existence is decidedly meagre. A number of other charters of foundation granted for universities by the emperor Charles IV had proved virtually meaningless.[5] But it has to be recognised that the movement for university expansion already existed, the impetus being eventually transformed into reality under the catalytic influence of the great schism. This was especially to prove the case in areas where universities had formerly been scarce or decadent. Scotland acquired its first university at St Andrews, while in Wales the independence movement led by Owain Glyndŵr aspired to academic as well as political separation from England.[6] In the Iberian peninsula the foundation at Lisbon was regularised, Perpignan revived, and an attempt was made to establish a university at Calataydd.[7] The most dramatic transformation occurred in the north and east of continental Europe. Although the University of Pécs was probably extinct by 1418, and the importance of Prague had declined significantly because of the Hussite controversy,

[4] For the basic information on the foundation and character of the universities at this time, see H. Rashdall [ed. F. M. Powicke and A. B. Emden], *The universities of Europe in the middle ages*, 2nd edn (3 vols., Oxford, 1936). A more thematic approach is given in A. B. Cobban, *The medieval universities: their development and organization* (London, 1975).

[5] See the list of his charters in R. Salomon, 'Eine vergessene Universitätsgründung', *Neues Archiv der Gesellschaft für ältere deutsche Geschichtskunde*, **37** (1911–12), 814–17.

[6] On this Welsh activity, see below, p. 148.

[7] For this project, see V. Beltrán de Heredia, 'El estudio general de Calatayud, documentos referentes a su institucion', *Miscelánea Beltrán de Heredia*, ed. V. Beltrán de Heredia, vol. 1, Biblioteca de teologos españoles, vol. 25 (Salamanca, 1971), pp. 235–55.

these failures were more than compensated for by the revival of the Universities of Cracow and Vienna, and the firm establishment of new foundations at Cologne and Heidelberg. After false starts at Erfurt and Buda, those places also acquired flourishing universities, while another was established at Leipzig in 1409. There had also been two attempts at foundations which had proved unsuccessful: the university at Würzburg had collapsed in 1413 after an existence of eleven years, and the University of Kulm, while nominally established in 1386, never appears to have been active at all, although there is mention of an intended revival there in 1403.[8]

Elsewhere in Europe, the changes in the educational map were to be less marked. The situation in England was unaltered, while in France the only sign of expansion is a reference to a projected foundation at Nantes in 1414.[9] However, the nominal foundation of Aix-en-Provence took place in 1409. Italy experienced greater changes but these were mainly in the relative importance of existing *studia*, as Bologna declined while Pavia rose, and Pisa and Siena revived while Florence suffered. However, there was a successful foundation at Turin in 1412 which followed an abortive attempt to establish a university there in 1405. At Ferrara the stabilisation of an attempted foundation was prevented by endemic civil war, while Pope Innocent VII's plans to revive the urban University of Rome died with him in 1406.[10]

Just as the schism acted as a catalyst in the general proliferation of universities, starting a movement which was to continue throughout the fifteenth century, so too was it influential in the spread of faculties of theology. Although there had been signs of a growing desire for more such faculties in Europe prior to the schism, the popes were generally reluctant to permit such diffu-

[8] On the attempted foundation at Kulm, see B. Kürbis, 'Une université manquée: Chelmno entre le XIVe et le XVIe siècle', in *Les universités européennes du XIVe au XVIIIe siècle, aspects et problèmes: actes du colloque internationale à l'occasion du VIe centenaire de l'université Jagellone de Cracovie, 6–8 Mai 1964*, Etudes et documents publiés par l'Institut d'histoire de la faculté des lettres de l'université de Genève, vol. 4 (Geneva, 1967), pp. 133–4.

[9] H. Diener, 'Zur Geschichte der Universitätsgründungen in Alt-Öfen (1395) und Nantes (1423)', *Quellen und Forschungen aus italienischen Archiven und Bibliotheken*, **42–43** (1963), 279.

[10] *Raynaldus, ann.* 1406, no. 2; G. Griffiths, 'Leonardo Bruni and the restoration of the university of Rome (1406)', *Renaissance Quarterly*, **26** (1973), 1–10.

sion. This reluctance, however, disappeared during the schism, as
the older universities were augmented and it became the custom
to include a faculty of theology in the initial foundation. Clement
VII, however, retained the caution of his predecessors: he specifically excluded the study of theology from the revived university
at Perpignan, and despite royal petitions Lérida also remained
without such a faculty.[11]

This spread of faculties of theology is merely one aspect of a
claim which was being increasingly advanced by universities and
their members, that they had a right to participate in church
affairs. This demand reached its peak during the Council of
Constance, when the University of Paris claimed to pronounce
definitive sentence on such issues as tyrannicide, Jean Gerson
declaring that all who repudiated the Parisian decision that
tyrannicide was heretical were themselves guilty of heresy.[12]
Similar claims for the universities as pillars of orthodoxy within
the church were expressed by Heinrich von Oyta in 1388, in a
sermon delivered before the Bishop of Passau.[13] Oyta's views
were echoed at the Council of Constance, when the assembly
expressed its shock at the expansion of Hussitism in Prague.[14]
Even Wyclif, although occasionally antipathetic to universities,[15]
seems to have shared the view that they enjoyed a special position
within the church, and attacked the appropriations of churches
to monasteries because of their detrimental effects on university
finances.[16] The self-esteem which academics occasionally revealed,
and which derived from their sense of having a special purpose
within the church, at times reached ludicrous proportions. In
1409, for example, in a sermon preached after the conclusion of
the Council of Pisa, Jean Gerson drew extensively on French

[11] Some of the documents are in A. Rubió y Lluch, *Documents per l'historia de la
cultura Catalana mig-eval* (2 vols., Barcelona, 1908–21), vol. 1, pp. 396–7; vol. 2,
pp. 253–4, 317.

[12] L. E. Dupin, *Johannis Gersonii . . . opera omnia* (5 vols., Antwerp, 1706), vol. 5,
p. 362; A. Coville, *Jean Petit; la question du tyrannicide au commencement du XVe
siècle* (Paris, 1932), p. 516.

[13] G. Sommerfeldt, 'Zwei politische Sermone des Heinrich von Oyta und des Nikolaus
von Dinkelsbühl (1388 und 1417)', *Historisches Jahrbuch*, **26** (1905), 321.

[14] *Hardt*, vol. 3, p. 590.

[15] A. W. Pollard, *Johannis Wyclif Dialogus, sive Speculum ecclesie militantis* (London,
1886), pp. 53–4.

[16] J. Loserth, *Johannis Wyclif Tractatus de ecclesia* (London, 1886), pp. 373–5.

national mythology not merely to justify claims for French leadership in the process which was hoped would reunite the Greek
and Latin churches under the Greek-born Pope Alexander V, but
also to claim for the University of Paris itself the role of mentor
to the King of France in fulfilling this policy.[17]

Taken in isolation, such claims could be dismissed as incredible;
yet the major political forces of Europe were apparently prepared
to concede a good deal of their substance. This especially applied
within the church itself, where the papacy seems to have intended
that the universities should from the start be involved in theological and legal activities on behalf of the church. To this end,
successive popes had sought to control the previously spontaneous
growth of universities by judicious grants of the various privileges
which they claimed that they alone could confer, until the theory
developed that only popes could create such *studia generalia*.
Certainly, in the course of time, collections of decretals were
customarily sent to the universities as the appropriate places for
their study and dissemination.[18] The universities were also seen
as institutions with a vital role for evangelising the infidel, to
which end the Council of Vienne in 1311 prescribed the establishment of chairs in oriental languages in some of the leading universities [19] – although it is doubtful if this decree and the theory
behind it were actually implemented. The universities were
intended to combat heresy, but their intellectual activities made
them also centres from which heresy was just as likely to spread,
a paradoxical situation of which Wyclif provides perhaps the
supreme example.

But the universities refused to see their role as constrained
within the papally defined limits, and constantly struggled to
divest themselves of the restrictions imposed by the papal view.
Thus, despite decrees aimed at its prohibition, Aristotelianism
spread inexorably through the universities, which also became

[17] *Glorieux*, no. 365.
[18] *Ch. Paris.*, nos. 104, 153, 608, 755; E. Friedberg, *Corpus iuris canonici* (2 vols., Leipzig, 1879), vol. 2, pp. 933–6, 1129–32; M. Fournier, *Les statuts et privilèges des universités françaises depuis leur fondation jusqu'en 1789* (4 vols., Paris, 1890–94), nos. 16, 43, 538, 1246, 1901; W. Ullmann, *Law and politics in the middle ages* (London, 1975), pp. 169–70.
[19] *Ch. Paris.*, no. 695; W. Ullmann, *A short history of the papacy in the middle ages*, 2nd edn (London, 1974), p. 241.

involved in secular matters through the study of civil law. The universities became the training schools for the bureaucrats of both secular and ecclesiastical chanceries; in France from the beginning of the thirteenth century the law graduates of the French provincial universities dominated the personnel of the French chancery. Papal realisation of the potential effects of such developments was clear in attempts to limit the spread of civil law studies, particularly their prohibition at Paris by Pope Honorius III in 1219.[20] Such activity was probably motivated by a desire to secure academic loyalty to the church if the universities ever became involved in the conflicts between the papacy and the cardinals, or between church and state. Such involvement did occur at the end of the thirteenth century: in their dispute with Boniface VIII the Colonna cardinals sought the support of the Parisian masters,[21] while several of the French universities became embroiled in the harsher subsequent conflict between the pope and King Philip IV.[22]

Nor were appeals to the universities confined to issues which, although obviously political, might still be considered as falling within the 'ecclesiastical' sphere. Academics, with their increasing involvement in secular matters, were also consulted on non-ecclesiastical matters. In 1368, when the precarious peace established between England and France by the Treaty of Brétigny was visibly cracking, King Charles V of France appealed for theoretical support of his stance not only from the relatively tame native Universities of Montpellier, Toulouse and Orléans, but also from the foreign doctors of Bologna.[23] The latter were again

[20] The struggle on Aristotelianism is summarised in W. Ullmann, 'Boniface VIII and his contemporary scholarship', *Journal of Theological Studies*, N.S. **27** (1976), 61–70. On Roman law, see M. Fournier, 'L'église et le droit romain au XIII⁰ siècle, à propos de l'interprétation de la bulle *Super speculum* d'Honorius III, qui interdit l'enseignement du droit romain à Paris', *Nouvelle revue historique de droit français et étranger*, **14** (1890), 80–119, and also the literature cited in Ullmann, *Law and politics*, p. 103 n. 1.

[21] H.-X. Arquillière, 'L'appel au concile sous Philippe le Bel et la genèse des théories conciliaires', *Revue des questions historiques*, 89 (1911), 32–7.

[22] For documents reflecting university involvement in this struggle, see P. Dupuy, *Histoire du differend d'entre le pape Boniface VIII et Philippes le Bel, roy de France* (Paris, 1655), *preuves*, pp. 53–4, 117–18, 155–7, 163; *Ch. Paris.*, nos. 604, 604a, 621–3, 630, 633–6.

[23] P. Chaplais, 'Some documents regarding the fulfilment and interpretation of the Treaty of Brétigny (1360–1369)', in *Camden Miscellany*, vol. 19, Camden Society Publications, 3rd series, vol. 80 (London, 1952), p. 53.

consulted, more privately, on the same issue in 1369. Among the doctors offering their opinions on this occasion was Johannes de Legnano, who was to play an important part in the academic contribution to the debates surrounding the opening of the great schism.[24] In both instances the appeal to the universities was made on points of law, but the influential position attained by the universities in secular matters was only partly dependent on their teaching of civil law. Much more significant was the use made of their knowledge by graduates who became involved in politics after leaving the strictly academic life – or, indeed, while still engaged on university activities. In this respect, a definition which confines membership of a medieval university to periods of study or regency (although that definition will, of necessity, be the one chiefly adopted throughout this work) is not strictly valid. Medieval universities were perpetual corporations, of which the member remained a member for life. Of this he could be made well aware if he ever acted against what the university considered to be its own interests, the masters being as anxious to respond to the misdeeds of their fellows as to any other challenge.[25]

A side effect of the growing status of the universities was their increasing importance as instruments for shaping and directing 'public opinion'. It was in this context that they had been dragged into the dispute between Boniface VIII and Philip the Fair, and it was this function which reached its zenith during the great schism. The wave of foundations, the struggles between factions to dominate the universities, and the actions of popes against any universities which opposed them (including attempts at closure) all testify to the role of the academics in these debates. Gilles Bellemere, a supporter of Clement VII, included the universities amongst the institutions which were to be informed of the events of September 1378,[26] while in May 1379, Urban VI listed a number of universities which he claimed were his sup-

24 ibid., p. 55, with the opinions of the doctors at pp. 61–78.
25 For this broad definition of a university, see V. Martin, *Les origines du Gallicanisme* (2 vols., Paris, 1939), vol. 1, p. 342. For instances of universities acting against 'disobedient' members, see Fournier, *Statuts*, no. 231; H. E. Salter, *Snappe's formulary and other records*, Publications of the Oxford Historical Society, vol. 80 (Oxford, 1924), pp. 161–2.
26 F. J. P. Bliemetzrieder, 'Ein Aktenstück zu Beginn des abendländischen Schismas', *Studien und Mitteilungen aus dem Benedictiner- und dem Cistercienser-Orden*, **28** (1907), 33.

porters (although several of them had already declared for his opponent).[27] The extensive manuscript traditions of tracts by individual academics and corporate statements by the universities also reflect the general acceptance of their importance in the debates.

Moreover, it seems clear that the appeal to the universities during the schism was addressed to them as representatives of some sort of supra-national community, which was the intellectual equivalent of the secular and ecclesiastical supra-nationality theoretically enjoyed by emperor and pope, respectively. Obviously, this community existed more in theory than in fact: the rather cavalier attitude of several universities to the theoretical privileges conferred by the *ius ubique docendi* (the right of graduates of a university to lecture elsewhere without further examination, the power to confer that right being almost part of the definition of a medieval university), and the frequent conflicts which erupted as a result, all testify to that aspect of the situation.[28] Moreover, the theoretical similarity between the institutions which was implied not only by the existence of the *ius ubique docendi*, but also by the use of the generic term *studia generalia*, could not obscure growing actual differences between the universities, each at different stages of development. Apart from the basic constitutional differentiation between the magisterial northern universities based on the model of Paris, and the rather more decadent student universities based on the model of Bologna, there were many more variations. The Italian universities were well advanced on the road to laicisation, Bologna already exhibiting signs of academic dynasticism. The degree of secular influence also varied, as did the concentration on a particular branch of study (Paris being considered as the leading theological university, whereas Bologna held the leadership as far as law was concerned), the number of resident members, and the cosmopolitan character of different institutions. With these manifold differences, the idea of community cannot have been much more than theoretical; nevertheless during the schism, with the

27 M. Seidlmayer, *Die Anfänge des grossen abendländischen Schismas*, Spanische Forschungen der Görresgesellschaft, zweite Reihe, vol. 5 (Münster, 1940), p. 343.
28 Cobban, *The medieval universities*, pp. 27–35.

17

supra-national authority of the papacy obviously non-existent, and that of the empire undermined not only by the personal incompetence of Wenceslas (and, after 1400, by the appearance of Rupert of the Palatinate as rival King of the Romans), but also by the rise of the territorial monarchies which claimed imperial rights within their own frontiers and thus some sort of jurisdiction over the church, the universities remained the only surviving supra-national community to which any sort of appeal could be made for a solution to what was, essentially, a problem of universalist dimensions. That the members of the universities felt themselves to be part of an academic community which extended beyond the limits of the individual university is clear from their own contributions to the debates stimulated by the schism.

Clearly, however, any expression of academic supra-nationality made by academics themselves has to be treated with some degree of reserve, as being based partly on self-interest. But the most significant reflection of the influence ascribed to the universities as institutions and their members as individuals during the schism derives from two aspects of the contemporary literature on the subject: the ascription of fictional opinions to some thinkers, and the works of anti-university publicists. Thus, the Italian lawyers Johannes de Legnano, Baldus de Ubaldis and Antonius de Butrio – all of whom made significant contributions to the debates on the schism – were all at times said to have adopted loyalties diametrically opposed to those advocated in their works.[29] Such claims were naturally made by individuals supporting the fictional cause, and to prevent counter-charges all the statements were made after the lawyer concerned had died. The suggestions nevertheless provide a strong indication of the importance attached during the schism to gaining the adherence of the more influential academics, an importance often recognised also by the rivals for the papacy, who were anxious to purchase support by judicious promotions, a policy which (particularly during the pontificate of

---

[29] Seidlmayer, *Anfänge*, p. 340; *Thes. Nov. Anec.*, p. 1469; Ullmann, *Origins*, pp. 146–7; J. Weizsäcker, *Deutsche Reichstagsakten unter König Ruprecht*, Deutsche Reichstagsakten, vols. 4–6 (3 vols., Gotha, 1882–88), vol. 3, pp. 401–2; L. Schmitz, 'Die Quellen zur Geschichte des Konzils von Cividale, 1409', *Römische Quartalschrift*, **8** (1894), 227.

Benedict XIII) was at times to prove a source of friction within the universities themselves.

The second type of literature reveals contemporary attitudes towards the position of the universities as institutions, and is to some extent the opposite of that mentioned above: attempts to belittle the universities and their members and thereby undermine their influence. Thus, one anonymous writer dismissed the academics as mere puppets of their local tyrants,[30] an accusation which was repeated by Boniface Ferrer in his lengthy and virulent defence of Benedict XIII, produced after the termination of the Council of Pisa.[31] In this tract, academics were generally accused of intellectual dishonesty, Ferrer claiming that they had tailored their arguments to suit political and personal expediencies.[32] Individual academics – especially members of the University of Paris – were the objects of especially vitriolic attacks, with Simon de Cramaud (one of the leading figures at Paris) being twice called an heresiarch.[33]

These attacks by Ferrer, and the claims put forward by the universities themselves (and frequently conceded) that they could judge theological matters, lead on to consideration of a major influence on the universities of the period in general: the context within which they had to exist, in intellectual rather than political or economic terms. During the period of the schism, this concerns not so much the clashes between rival philosophical standpoints, important though these were, but rather the more general outlook of contemporary society. In this respect, perhaps the most important feature of the schism was its chronological proximity to the Black Death. The ravages of the plague had left a profound scar: death's dance had bequeathed a totally new atmosphere of fatalism and mysticism, apparent in the contemporary iconography of death, the growing artistic concentration on the Passion and its Instruments and the rise of pietistic sects such as the Flagellants. These barely healed wounds were suddenly reopened by the schism, producing a further outpouring of mysticism which, in

---

[30] Weizsäcker, *Reichstagsakten*, vol. 3, p. 695.
[31] *Thes. Nov. Anec.*, pp. 1435–1529, with the charge appearing at p. 1469.
[32] ibid., pp. 1472, 1493–4.
[33] ibid., pp. 1453, 1521. Pierre d'Ailly was also singled out for attack; see L. Salembier, *Le cardinal Pierre d'Ailly* (Tourcoing, 1932), pp. 255–7.

the case of individuals such as Jean Gerson, spilled over to affect their thinking on university matters and other major contemporary issues such as ecclesiastical reformation.[34] The widespread desire for such reform of the church, and the great contemporary concern with superstition and sorcery,[35] are all important indications of the general trend, while it can be no accident that one of the major literary controversies of the period centred not on a practical matter, but the mystical and essentially intangible subject of the Immaculate Conception.[36] This mysticism also affected the literature on the schism, adding an eschatalogical layer to several tracts. This appears most frequently in the works of the Parisian academic Pierre d'Ailly. Allusions to an apocalyptic interpretation of the schism appear in tracts produced by him throughout the dispute, from his *Sermo de B. Bernardo*[37] and undated second tract *De falsis prophetis*,[38] both composed in the early stages of the schism, through to his *De persecutionibus ecclesiae*, written in 1418.[39] Besides being a highly sarcastic attack on the cardinals, it is also possible that his *Epistola diaboli Leviathan*,[40] produced in 1381, may have been intended to convey some apocalyptic sentiments. D'Ailly was not the only Parisian master to reveal such an outlook: Jean Courtecuisse, in one of his sermons, expressed the opinion that unless the problem of the schism was rapidly resolved the church faced the danger of complete collapse.[41] In England, John Wyclif occasionally offered an eschatological interpretation of events in his works,[42] while in Spain the influence of prophecy at the start of the schism is reflected in the writings of Nicholas

[34] J. L. Connolly, *John Gerson, reformer and mystic* (Louvain, 1928); S. E. Ozment, 'The university and the church; patterns of reform in Jean Gerson', *Medievalia et Humanistica*, N.S. 1 (1970), 111–26; L. B. Pascoe, 'Jean Gerson: mysticism, conciliarism, and reform', *Annuarium Historiae Conciliorum*, 6 (1974), 135–53.

[35] F. Bonney, 'Autour de Jean Gerson: opinions de théologiens sur les superstitions et la sorcellerie au début du XVᵉ siècle', *Moyen Age*, **77** (1971), 85–98.

[36] I. Brady, 'The development of the doctrine on the Immaculate Conception in the C14 after Aureoli', *Franciscan Studies*, **15** (1955), 194–202.

[37] Emmanuel College, Cambridge, MS 9, fos 136v–137r.

[38] Dupin, *Gersonii opera*, vol. 1, p. 517.

[39] N. Valois, 'Un ouvrage inédit de Pierre d'Ailly, le *De persecutionibus ecclesiae*', *Bibliothèque de l'Ecole des chartes*, **66** (1904), 557–74.

[40] P. Tschackert, *Peter von Ailli* (Gotha, 1877), pp. [15]–[21].

[41] G. di Stefano, *L'oeuvre oratoire française de Jean Courtecuisse*, Università di Torino, facoltà di lettere e filosofia: filologica moderna, vol. 3 (Turin, 1969), p. 370.

[42] For example, in his *De dissensione paparum*: see R. Buddensieg, *John Wyclif's polemical works in Latin* (2 vols., London, 1883), vol. 2, p. 570.

Eymeric, which included attacks on contemporary references to Jean de Roquetaillade, Merlin and others.[43] Later, in Germany, Henry of Langenstein also showed a concern for prophecy when he interpreted the prophecies ascribed to Hildegard of Bingen as presaging the controversy.[44] The great involvement of prophecy in the debates of the schism was, however, only partly due to the mysticism of the period. It must also have received considerable stimulation from the unfortunate coincidence that the double election of 1378 occurred in precisely the year specified by Arnold of Villanova and other seers as that in which Antichrist would make known his presence on earth.[45]

The revival of the fatalism originally fostered by the Black Death contributed immensely to the shock produced throughout Europe by the outbreak of the schism in 1378, coinciding as it did with the social and economic consequences of the plague. It was in these potentially traumatic circumstances that the universities and their members began their involvement in the debates resulting from the schism, first to determine which of the contestants was the legitimate pope, and secondly to try to find some means of breaking through the barriers of partisan rigidity and apocalyptic fatalism in order to re-establish the integrity of the Roman church.

[43] H. Finke, 'Drei spanische Publizisten aus den Anfängen des grossen Schismas: Matthäus Clementis, Nikolaus Eymeric, der hl. Vicente Ferrer', in *Gesammelte Aufsätze zur Kulturgeschichte Spaniens*, ed. H. Finke, K. Beyerle and G. Schreiber, Spanische Forschungen der Görresgesellschaft, erste Reihe, vol. 1 (Münster, 1928), p. 185 and n. 13.
[44] G. Sommerfeldt, 'Die Prophetien der hl. Hildegard von Bingen in einem Schreiben des Magisters Heinrich v. Langenstein (1381) und Langensteins Trostbrief über den Tod eines Bruders des Wormser Bischofs Eckard von Ders (um 1384)', *Historisches Jahrbuch*, **30** (1909), 46–61. On the general issue of prophecy and the schism, see M. Reeves, *The influence of prophecy in the later middle ages* (Oxford, 1969), pp. 418, 422–7.
[45] Reeves, *Prophecy*, pp. 323–4, 417–18; G. Leff, *Heresy in the later middle ages* (2 vols., Manchester, 1967), vol. 1, p. 180.

Chapter 2

A MATTER OF LOYALTY

With the election of Clement VII and the creation of the double papacy, the rest of the church was faced with the dilemma of deciding which of the claimants deserved to be recognised as head of the church. The determination of allegiances was no simple matter. In normal circumstances, the rest of the church was merely required to accept as pope the man whom the cardinals declared they had elected. Initially, the situation following the election of Urban VI had accorded with this pattern and, on the authority of the cardinals' letters proclaiming the election of the new pontiff, Urban had secured wide and immediate acceptance. But the later election of Clement VII forced an actual decision on allegiance, an examination of the rival cases to determine whether to remain true to the originally proclaimed pope or to accept the version of events offered by the cardinals and transfer to their party and pope. It was a choice which confronted the universities as harshly as it faced any other body. At Paris, the process of developing uncertainty about the situation can be traced even before the formalisation of the schism. Immediately on hearing of the death of Gregory XI, the Parisian masters had begun their preparations for the recognition of his successor. The English nation within the university started the procedure for sending a *rotulus*, the by now traditional roll of petitions for benefices drawn up by the universities (and other institutions, as well as major prelates and princes) for presentation at the *curia* on the accession of a new pope and other special occasions.[1] When the university received notification of the election of Urban VI, the event was duly celebrated with a *Te Deum*.[2] By Easter the preparation of the

[1] *Auct. Ch.*, vol. 1, pp. 538–9. On *rotuli* in general, see D. E. R. Watt, 'University clerks and rolls of petitions for benefices', *Speculum*, **34** (1959), 213–24; J. Verger, 'Le recrutement géographique des universités françaises au début du XVᵉ siècle d'après les *Suppliques* de 1403', *Mélanges d'archéologie et d'histoire*, **82** (1970), 855–72.

[2] *Ch. Paris.*, no. 1605; *Valois*, vol. 1, pp. 120–1.

rotulus was well under way,[3] although not quickly enough to satisfy the English nation.[4] On completion, the roll was sent to Avignon, where the envoys had expected to find the pope. He was not there, and the envoys split up in confusion. It was by now mid-July.[5] One of the members of the embassy with the *rotulus*, William of Oesterzele, then went on to Italy, where he joined the dissident cardinals at Anagni.[6] Meanwhile, other Parisian academics were at Rome, among them Marsilius of Inghen and Henry de Thenis.[7] The concern of the University of Paris for the progress of the *rotulus* had provoked a letter to the former of these, to which he replied on 27 July, reporting among other things the growing controversy about the circumstances of the election of Urban VI.[8] From this point onwards, both sides sought to persuade the Parisian masters of the veracity of their interpretation of the events of the conclave, the university being subjected to a veritable barrage of propaganda.[9]

The basic problem posed by the crisis within the church was one of law. Both before the election of Clement VII and after, the cardinals based their case on the hazy agglomeration of canon law which passed for the ecclesiastical constitution, so that the schism, when it occurred, was totally unlike any previous division within the church.[10] Earlier dual papacies had been the results of conflicts between rival factions within the College of Cardinals – such as that between Innocent II and Anacletus II in the early twelfth century, which was frequently to be cited as a precedent by commentators on the great schism itself – or else had been caused by rivalries between popes and emperors (or would-be emperors), such as had preceded the elevation of Nicholas V in opposition to John XXII in the 1330s. The division which began in 1378 fitted neither of these patterns: there was only one party, the cardinals, who claimed that their own earlier actions at the

3 *Ch. Paris.*, no. 1419.
4 *Auct. Ch.*, vol. 1, pp. 553–4.
5 The envoys are listed in *Ch. Paris.*, vol. 3, p. 236 n. 1.
6 ibid.
7 ibid., vol. 3, p. 555; *Auct. Ch.*, vol. 1, pp. 558 n. 2, 559.
8 *Ch. Paris.*, no. 1608; G. Ritter, *Studien zur Spätscholastik, I: Marsilius von Inghen und die okkamistische Schule in Deutschland*, Sitzungsberichte der Heidelberger Akademie der Wissenschaften, vol. 12, part 4 (Heidelberg, 1921), pp. 23–5.
9 *Ch. Paris.*, nos. 1607, 1609–11.
10 On the definition as a schism, see Salembier, *Pierre d'Ailly*, p. 49; and on the legal aspect, Ullmann, *Origins*, pp. xi–xiii.

election of Urban VI had been illegal, that the papacy was therefore vacant, and that Clement VII (when elected) was the only
true successor to Gregory XI.

Faced with this situation, the only possible reaction to the
question of legitimacy and allegiance was to consider it in legal
terms. It was an Italian academic, Baldus de Ubaldis, at the time
lecturing at Padua, who provided the first such legal statement on
the merits of the case proposed by the cardinals. His *Allegationes
primae* [11] were written in response to the *factum* of the cardinals,
which had been passed on to him by one of the neutral Italians
in the college, probably Orsini.[12] On 20 July 1378 the dissidents
had called on the Italians to join them, but on 6 August the
Italians had replied with a demand for a general council to decide
the issues,[13] a call which almost certainly owed much to the
conclusions reached by Baldus de Ubaldis.

The immediate effect of the Italians' appeal to Baldus was to
render the uncertainties of the ecclesiastical constitution a legitimate topic of scholarly discussion, with the possibility that something practical and concrete might develop from the academic
considerations. This transformation of the problem was apparent
not only in the wide circulation which the *Allegationes primae*
enjoyed, but also in the general proliferation of writings on the
ecclesiastical constitution which occurred during the period of the
schism. However, the academic contribution to these discussions
was to be by no means unanimous: to quote Ludolf of Sagan,
the doctors wrote 'non tam diversa vel plurima, quam contraria et
adversa'.[14]

Baldus' *Allegationes* fall into two distinct sections; one offering
general remarks on the constitution of the church, the other con-
centrating on the specific dispute over the election of Urban VI.
In the first part, the cardinals' case was immediately denied: a
pope cannot be pope in name without being pope in fact;[15] while

[11] Printed in *Raynaldus, ann.* 1378, nos. 36–7; A. Bzovius, *Annalium ecclesiasticorum*,
vol. 15 (Cologne, 1622), pp. 62–70. See also J. A. Wahl, 'Baldus de Ubaldis; a study
in reluctant conciliarism', *Manuscripta*, **18** (1974), 22–4.

[12] N. del Re, 'Il "Consilium pro Urbano VI" di Bartolomeo da Saliceto', in *Collectanea Vaticana in honorem Anselmi M. Card. Albareda*, Studi e Testi, vol. 219
(Vatican City, 1962), pp. 219 n. 2, 226 n. 3.

[13] *Raynaldus, ann.* 1378, no. 42.

[14] Loserth, 'Beiträge', p. 404.   [15] Bzovius, *Annalium ecclesiasticorum*, p. 65.

the claim by the cardinals that they had never actually intended that Urban should behave as pope was considered to be more a reflection on them than on him.[16] In the second part of the tract, the cardinals' own actions were cited to disprove their claims: their failure to protest against the first 'forced' election, their re-election of Urban the following day, and the letters proclaiming the fact of the election were all referred to, together with the cardinals' acceptance of Urban's authority and munificence (which Baldus, despite their claims to the contrary, throughout considered as having been voluntary). All in all, given that the cardinals had not actively opposed or denounced the election from the start, the only possible conclusion was that they had, at the time, truly wanted Urban as their pope.[17] In addition to all this, Baldus also considered the specific issue of the degree of free choice enjoyed by the cardinals in the riotous circumstances of the election. He concluded that, despite the Roman efforts to force the cardinals to elect a Roman or Italian as pope, the cardinals had retained a free choice among those nationalities – and in any case had actually chosen a sort of Franco-Italian, who might well have been unacceptable to the Roman people.[18]

Given these conclusions, it is hardly surprising that the *Allegationes primae*, and the supplementary arguments included in Baldus' *Allegationes secundae*,[19] were soon adopted as the basis of the Urbanist case throughout the schism. To these were frequently added other arguments derived from the works of Johannes de Legnano of the University of Bologna. His *De fletu ecclesiae*[20] was directed at a wide audience and provoked considerable discussion and criticism, to which he replied in 1380 with his *Tractatus secundus*.[21] Typical of the criticism to which Legnano was subjected was the bitter attack on him launched by

16 ibid., p. 66.   17 ibid., p. 67.
18 ibid., p. 69.
19 *Raynaldus*, vol. 26, pp. 581–99.
20 Extracts are in *Raynaldus*, ann. 1378, nos. 31–5; *Bulaeus*, vol. 4, pp. 482–5. See also Seidlmayer, *Anfänge*, pp. 122–5; F. Ehrle, *Martin de Alpartils Chronica actitatorum temporibus domini Benedicti XIII*, Quellen und Forschungen aus dem Gebiete der Geschichte, vol. 12 (Paderborn, 1906), pp. 433–9; F. J. P. Bliemetzrieder, *Literarische Polemik zu Beginn des grossen abendländischen Schismas*, Publikationen des Österreichischen Historischen Instituts in Rom, vol. 1 (Vienna, 1910), pp. 47*–53*. The juristic aspect of the works of Legnano and de Ubaldis is examined in Ullmann, *Origins*, pp. 143–60.   21 The second work is in *Raynaldus*, vol. 26, pp. 599–613.

Robertus Gervasius, Bishop of Senez, in his *Libellus vocatus Mirra electa*, in which Legnano was accused of heresy and was likened to one of the beasts of the Apocalypse.[22] Like Baldus, Legnano had laid great emphasis on the legitimising effects of the cardinals' actions after the original election,[23] a point also made by Bartholomaeus de Saliceto in his *Consilium pro Urbano VI*,[24] a work completed between September 1378 and August 1379.[25] Like Johannes de Legnano, Saliceto too was a member of the University of Bologna, and a lawyer. His attitudes towards the two rival elections were characteristic, for although the Urbanist lawyers were prepared to admit the possibility that they had been insufficiently informed of facts and events when preparing their statements[26] nevertheless for them the second election, and the cardinals' subsequent acceptance of Urban VI, were both undeniable and unavoidable obstacles to recognition of Clement VII.[27]

The tracts produced by Baldus de Ubaldis, Johannes de Legnano and Bartholomaeus de Saliceto were all indicative of the views of their writers as individuals, but at the same time the question of allegiance was also being decided by academic corporations, with declarations being produced either by individual faculties or by whole universities. At Padua the main evidence for debate on the issues is provided by a *consilium* produced by the lawyers Angelus de Aretino and Ubertinus de Lampugnano, which was subsequently approved by the whole college of lawyers within the university.[28] The date of the statement is uncertain, but it may well predate the election of Clement VII. Closely following the theories advanced by Baldus de Ubaldis – and almost certainly swayed by his arguments – the lawyers again proposed that, even if the initial election was rendered null by the force implicit in

[22] *BN*, MS Lat. 1467, fos 12r–v, 19v–36r.   [23] *Raynaldus, ann.* 1378, nos. 33–5.
[24] Printed in del Re, 'Il "Consilium" ', pp. 234–63.   [25] ibid., p. 221.
[26] Thus, in August 1378, Johannes de Legnano requested further information from Pedro de Luna on the events of 8 April (*Raynaldus, ann.* 1378, no. 30). In 1380 he announced that he was prepared to change his views if sufficient convincing evidence was produced (Seidlmayer, *Anfänge*, p. 235).
[27] Saliceto referred to these events in his *consilium* (del Re, 'Il "Consilium" ', p. 256), while in 1380 Baldus de Ubaldis reiterated the point about the second election to the Castilian envoys who were then at Rome (Seidlmayer, *Anfänge*, p. 237).
[28] Printed in F. J. P. Bliemetzrieder, 'Gutachten der juristischen Fakultät zu Padua über Urbans VI Wahl (Sommer 1378)', *Studien und Mitteilungen aus dem Benedictiner- und dem Cistercienser-Orden*, **30** (1909), 97–111.

the riotous behaviour of the Romans (a suggestion which the
Paduans in any case challenged, as three of the cardinals had
throughout refused to vote for Urban), the second election and the
subsequent behaviour of the cardinals gave retrospective valida-
tion.[29] But the lawyers did not comprise the whole of the
university, and evidence of continuing indecision among the
academics there is provided by jottings made by the Augustinian
lector, Ludovicus de Padua, in December 1378. In these he
recorded his uncertainty on the truth or otherwise of the cardinals'
claim that the original election in April had been carried out
under duress.[30]

Evidence also exists for the Oxonian debates on the problems
of allegiance, but this is difficult to interpret. Although it is
possible that a member of the University of Oxford produced both
the letter written in England as a reply to the cardinals' statement, and the Urbanist *Rationes Anglorum*,[31] uncertainties
surrounding their precise authorship make them effectively worth-
less for present purposes. It is therefore necessary to turn to the
statements of the university's most vocal member at this time,
John Wyclif. Although his individual statements from the early
years of the schism were profoundly Urbanist in tone, it is only in
his *De potestate pape* that there appears anything which may
relate strictly to the rest of the university – and even this information is minimal, and in all probability tempered by Wyclif's
own views. While there is some indication that the second election
and the passive acceptance of Urban VI by the cardinals validated
the original election, the ultimate decision – possibly implying a
rejection of the appeal to law as the deciding factor in the issue –
seems to rest solely on the personal qualities of the rivals: Urban
VI was a better man than Clement VII, therefore Urban was truly
pope and his rival a usurper excluded from the body of the
church.[32]

[29] ibid., pp. 100, 105-6, 111.
[30] L. Gargan, 'Libri di teologi agostiniani a Padova nel trecento', *Quaderni per la storia dell'Università di Padova*, 6 (1973), 19–20.
[31] On the letter, see Ullmann, *Origins*, pp. 120-2, while for the *Rationes Anglorum* see A. O. Gwynn, *The English Austin friars in the time of Wyclif* (Oxford, 1940), pp. 240-1, 245-7.
[32] J. Loserth, *Johannis Wyclif Tractatus de potestate pape* (London, 1907), pp. 254-5, and also the introduction thereto, pp. xxix-xxx.

Although vague, the evidence of the debates at Oxford is both quantitatively and qualitatively greater than that available for many other universities. Almost nothing remains from the Spanish universities or the majority of those in Italy, even though it was against their Urbanist theologians and philosophers that Robertus Gervasius aimed the second part of his *Libellus vocatus Mirra electa*.[33] Where there is any evidence, it is generally scanty. The early Clementist determination of the University of Naples is hidden behind the vague declaration by Queen Joanna I that she had accepted Clement VII on the advice of unidentified theologians and lawyers, from within and without the kingdom.[34] This skeleton does, however, acquire some flesh from the apparent purge of Clementist academics which followed Charles III's successful conquest of the kingdom,[35] while even before this invasion took place Pope Urban VI had sought to replace certain of the university's officials, which would suggest that they were adherents of Clement VII.[36] For contemporary Cambridge, the only sign of an official Urbanist decision is the refusal of the Aragonese Nicholas da Costa to take the oath of loyalty to Urban which was apparently being imposed at the university as a condition of inception.[37]

In occasional instances, however, the agglomeration of evidence does provide a fuller picture. The Bolognese declaration favouring Urban VI in 1381 apparently followed Clementist attempts to gain the university's support,[38] but there had been many earlier indications of Urbanist leanings. These included the individual statements such as those made by Johannes de Legnano and Bartholomaeus de Saliceto, and Urban's ready promotion of Bolognese academics, such as his appointment of Michael Ayguano as General of the Carmelites in 1380.[39] Moreover, even

33 *BN*, MSS Lat. 1467, fos 92r–123r, Lat. 1468, fos 1r–22v. The specific reference to the Spaniards and Italians occurs in MS Lat. 1467, fo. 93r.
34 S. Fodale, *La politica napoletana di Urbano VI*, Collezione viaggi e studi, vol. 13 (Rome, 1973), p. 32 n. 45.
35 *Valois*, vol. 2, p. 13 n. 3.   36 Fodale, *La politica*, pp. 56–7.
37 A. B. Emden, *A biographical register of the University of Cambridge to 1500* (Cambridge, 1963), p. 501 (entered as 'Sacosta'), Rubió y Lluch, *Documents*, vol. 1, pp. 282–3.
38 C. Ghirardacci, *Della historia di Bologna, parte seconda* (Bologna, 1657), p. 382.
39 B. M. Xiberta, *De scriptoribus scholasticis saeculi XIV ex ordine Carmelitarum*, Bibliothèque de la Revue d'histoire ecclésiastique, vol. 6 (Louvain, 1931), pp. 329–30.

before the university's official declaration of support for Urban, its loyalties had been obvious. In the summer of 1379, when asked for advice by the Count of Flanders, the academics had stated that, until the issue was resolved by a general council of the church, they intended to remain loyal to Urban VI.[40]

The details of activities at Prague are rather less clear than for Bologna, but a strong Urbanist tendency is apparent not only in the signs of the exclusion of some Clementists, but also in Clement VII's attempts to decree the closure of the university.[41] The loyalty to Urban may have been stimulated by John of Jenstein, Archbishop of Prague and chancellor to King Wenceslas, whose influence was much felt within the university in succeeding years.[42] It may even have been at his instigation that the Augustinian theologian Johannes de Braculis produced his *Determinatio quaestionis de canonica electione Urbani sexti* in 1379, the work being offered to the archbishop for correction.[43] The most extraordinary aspect of this work is its structure: an elaborate allegory, likening the election of Urban VI to the papacy to the election of Saul as king over Israel,[44] and apparently unique as the basis for considering the issues of the schism. The arrangement of the tract, stressing the national divisions within the Christian community, reduces the work to a lengthy consideration of the impact of the Roman crowd on the election, with their demands for a Roman or Italian pope, and the overt threat of death if the cardinals did not comply. Whether an election superficially concluded in accordance with this demand was actually performed under duress, allowing the cardinals to declare it null and form themselves into another conclave, was therefore the issue with which Braculis was most concerned.[45] Throughout his treatment of the

---

40 *Valois*, vol. 1, pp. 258–9.

41 ibid., vol. 1, pp. 290–1.

42 R. E. Weltsch, *Archbishop John of Jenstein (1348–1400)*, Studies in European history, vol. 8 (The Hague, 1968), pp. 157–61.

43 Universitní knihova, Prague, MSS XIV.C.16, fos 156r–170v, XIV.D.19, fos 45r–50v, 52r–60r. References are given to the first of these, which alone names the author (fos 156r, 170v). It is also the only one to give the date of completion, at fo. 170v. The submission of the work to Jenstein's correction appears at fo. 156r.

44 MS cit., fo. 156r.

45 ibid., fo. 156r: 'An Samuel et populi circumcisi carnaliter numerus, elector Saulis in regem, potuisset coniunctim vel divisim prefatum Saulem, dum Saul electioni consenserat ac inunctus et coronatus fuerat more regio, nulla culpa iuste degradacionis vel refutacionis ex parte Saulis ymmo nulla causa legitima qualitercumque previa, et

issue, however, he revealed a clear Urbanist bias, and it is obvious that he, like several others, believed Urban VI to be the pope who would carry through the much needed reforms within the church. Braculis therefore took every opportunity to reject the arguments of the cardinals. He recognised the conflicting national forces at work in the dispute, but was convinced that there had been no force involved in the April election. Urban VI had been elected as a compromise candidate, and that in itself – he being a Neapolitan rather than a Roman or Limousin – was adduced to be sufficient proof of the lack of duress.[46] Urban therefore ought not to resign.[47] The claims of the cardinals were utterly invalid: they had elected Urban VI quite willingly, not as a result of force, but because they had considered him the man best capable of carrying on the government of the church.[48]

Elsewhere in Europe, the Spanish realms proved especially dilatory in declaring their allegiance, each of them going through a phase of official neutrality. In Castile this lasted until 1381;[49] in Aragon a decision was delayed until after the death of Peter IV in 1387;[50] while Navarre succeeded in postponing a declaration until 1390.[51] Yet, although these kingdoms did not recognise any pope, it was nevertheless expected that a pope would take care of their academics. The shorter period of neutrality means that signs of the duplicity which this situation generated are less evident in Castile than in Aragon or Navarre, where there was *de facto* recognition of the Avignonese pope throughout the period of official non-alignment. Thus, Peter IV of Aragon appealed to Clement VII for the re-establishment of the university at Perpig-

ipso Saule contradicente, tamquam non regem iuste, decenter et irreprehensibiliter refutasse, ac alium regem Israel elegisse'.

[46] The consequences of a Limousin election are only implied, but Braculis' recognition of the need for compromise is clear on several occasions, for example ibid., fo. 165v: 'credendum fore, quod electores Saulis utiliter attenderunt, si ipse non circumcisum carnaliter populis cirmcisis prefecissent in regem multa scandala, multa spretiis, multa pericula, et multe rebelliones inter caput et suum corpus politicum succrevissent'.

[47] ibid., fo. 166r: 'Saul non debebat hanc electionem per impressionem celebratam nec nullam nec nephandam reputare, nec eam iam per conssensum per se acceptatam resignare'.

[48] ibid., fo. 167r: 'non ob furentis populi metum mendose, sed ob utilitatis regni firmamentum et augmentum amorose'.

[49] Seidlmayer, *Anfänge*, pp. 25–64; *Valois*, vol. 1, pp. 198–211, vol. 2, pp. 202–6.

[50] Seidlmayer, *Anfänge*, pp. 65–117; *Valois*, vol. 1, pp. 212–25, vol. 2, pp. 211–13.

[51] *Valois*, vol. 1, pp. 211–12, vol. 2, pp. 215–16.

nan,[52] and both that university and the University of Lérida sent *rotuli* to Avignon during these years.[53] The lack of a national university in Navarre made the problem of the academics more complicated, but the College of Navarre at Paris certainly recognised Clement VII in the years before 1390, while Navarrese students at the southern French universities appeared on the rolls sent to Avignon from those institutions, as well as on private *rotuli* such as that sent to Clement VII by Martin de Salva in 1378.[54]

Besides this evidence of a positive acceptance of Clement VII in the Spanish kingdoms, there are also signs of persecution of those Spaniards who wished to be loyal to Urban VI. One victim of such attacks was Matthew de Clementis, who was for a time a master at Perpignan, possibly having accepted the position in the hope of converting the university there to his own Urbanist views.[55] In this he failed dismally, the only result being to arouse the antipathy of the Clementist Infante John of Aragon. The latter's hostility increased in intensity when it was rumoured that Urban VI had promoted Clementis to the archbishopric of Saragossa.[56] Clementis was finally forced to flee the country when John succeeded his father as King of Aragon in 1387; thereafter he appears among the masters of the newly established university at Heidelberg.[57]

However, although the Spanish academics had effectively decided in favour of Clement VII, there is little sign of their participation in the various national deliberations which eventually determined the official allegiances of the states. Clement VII gave extensive powers for the reformation of the Castilian universities to his envoy Pedro de Luna, in the deliberate hope that this

---

[52] Fournier, *Statuts*, no. 1483.

[53] The Lérida *rotulus* (dated for December 1378, but mistakenly ascribed to Clement VI) is printed in A. Griera Gaja (ed.), *Miscelánea Mons. J. Rius Serra*, Biblioteca filológica-histórica, vol. 15 (2 vols., Abadiá de San Cugat das Valles, 1964), vol. 1, pp. 184–224. The Perpignan roll, which apparently predates the official foundation by Clement VII, is in H. S. Denifle, *Les universités françaises au moyen-âge: avis à M. Marcel Fournier* (Paris, 1892), pp. 92–3.

[54] J. Goñi Gaztambide, 'Los obispos de Pamplona del siglo XIV', *Principe de Viana*, **23** (1962), 318.

[55] F. J. P. Bliemetzrieder, 'Ein Bericht des Matthäus Clementis an Urban VI (ca. 1381) über seine Arbeiten zu dessen Gunsten in Aragonien', *Studien und Mitteilungen aus dem Benedictiner- und dem Cistercienser-Orden*, **29** (1908), 584–6.

[56] Finke, 'Drei spanische Publizisten', pp. 193–4.   [57] ibid., p. 181.

would induce them to support his cause at the assembly held at
Medina del Campo in 1381 to declare which pope Castile would
thenceforth recognise officially,[58] but there is little sign of academic
involvement in the deliberations of that gathering. Almost the
only hint came in the king's statement that graduates had been
among those assisting him to reach his decision [59] – but this reference is somewhat ambiguous, for there were many Parisian
graduates among the French representatives at the council, including Evrard de Tremaugen, Pierre de Thury and Jean d'Aramon,
all of whom presented Clementist statements.[60] The only named
academic who can be immediately connected with a Spanish
university and who attended these proceedings was, paradoxically,
Aragonese: Ferrarius de Vergos, identified as a *lector* at the
University of Lérida.[61] Precisely which pope he supported is uncertain, as he apparently produced two discussions of the events
of April 1378, one of which favoured Clement VII, while the
other supported Urban VI.[62]

Despite the general paucity of evidence from the Spanish universities, one surviving tract may still illustrate the nature of the
debates there. This is the work of an anonymous Clementist
doctor of the University of Salamanca, which may possibly have
been concocted for the assembly at Medina del Campo.[63] Although
the work is Clementist in intention, it is essentially fair in its
treatment of Urban VI: even if his election was rendered invalid
because the Romans had deprived the cardinals of their *libertas in
eligendo*, this did not reflect on Urban's personal suitability for
the papacy.[64] Basing his arguments on those put forward in a

58 L. Suárez Fernández, *Castilla, el cisma, y la crisis conciliar (1378-1440)*, Estudios del consejo superior de investigaciones científicas, escuela de estudios medievales, vol. 33 (Madrid, 1960), p. 8 n. 22.
59 ibid., p. 155; S. Baluzius [ed. G. Mollat], *Vitae paparum Avenionensium . . . ab anno Christi MCCCV usque ad annum MCCCXCIV* (4 vols., Paris, 1914-22), vol. 4, p. 255.
60 Their tracts are in *BN*, MSS Lat. 1469, 1470.
61 Seidlmayer, *Anfänge*, p. 220.
62 These are mentioned in the index to *ASV.*, Arm. LIV. 48, on fos 2r, 3r. I have not been able to find the originals.
63 *ASV.*, Arm. LIV. 18, fos 48r-51r: *Allegationes cuiusdam doctoris Salamantini*.
64 ibid., fo. 50v: 'Concludo quod licet persona electa sit bona et valens et scientifica persona, quia tamen in eius electionem intervenerunt multa vicia provocata (quod non fuit ex culpa electa sed romanorum), dicta eleccio non tenet de juris rigore nec de bona equitate'.

tract by Cardinal Pierre Flandrin, the Salamancan doctor claimed that, even if the first election was technically correct, its forced nature made it invalid, and necessarily prevented any possibility of subsequent legitimisation by the cardinals,[65] an argument further supplemented by appeals to metaphysics.[66]

In contrast with the other Iberian realms, the evidence for Portuguese action on the question of allegiances is much more dramatic. During the later years of Ferdinand I, recognition of the pope was a matter of foreign policy rather than conviction; apart from the period of the English alliance, the country accepted Clement VII until 1382. But it was only after the revolution of 1385, when John of Aviz acquired the throne and the Clementist–Castilian connection was utterly rejected, that any definite decision was taken, in favour of the Roman line.[67]

The evidence of academic participation in these events is rather sparse. Initially the members of the University of Lisbon accepted Clement VII as pope, the king having applied to him for the foundation of the *studium*.[68] They sent a *rotulus*[69] and other petitions,[70] but thereafter there is little sign of activity until the declaration made at Santarem in favour of Urban VI in February 1383.[71] Although *letrados* were present at the national assembly at which the declaration was made,[72] with Gil do Sem replying 'pro parte doctorum' to the Clementist arguments advanced by Pedro de Luna,[73] there is no evidence of any official university involvement.

[65] ibid., fo. 48v: 'Queritur si ex istis actibus eleccionis coronationis subsequentur censseatur purgatum vicium quod in prima eleccioni intervenit. Et est dicendum quod non, ex eo quod tales actas subsecutas celebrando Cardinales ellectores erant sub potestate Romanorum'. This issue was considered elsewhere in the work, fos 48v–49r, 50r–v. Flandrin's tract is in Bliemetzrieder, *Literarische Polemik*, pp. 3–71.

[66] MS cit., fo. 49r: 'coronacio facta de domino Urbano est accidens sine subiecto, cum coronacio presuponat precedere eleccionem canonicam, quod non precessit . . . ergo talis coronacio nulla'.

[67] *Valois*, vol. 1, pp. 225–38, vol. 2, pp. 207–9; J. C. Baptista, 'Portugal e o cisma de ocidente', *Lusitania Sacra*, 1 (1956), 65–203.

[68] Baptista, 'Portugal', p. 104, with the bull at pp. 189–90. It also appears in A. Moreira de Sá, *Chartularium universitatis Portugalensis, 1288–1537* (Lisbon, 1966–), no. 351; V. Beltrán de Heredia, *Bulario de la universidad de Salamanca*, Acta Salmanticensia, vols. 12–14 (3 vols., Salamanca, 1966–67), no. 1374.

[69] Beltrán de Heredia, *Bulario*, no. 1372; Moreira de Sá, *Chartularium*, no. 314.

[70] Moreira de Sá, *Chartularium*, nos. 315–50 *passim*.

[71] Baptista, 'Portugal', pp. 143–4.

[72] ibid., p. 144.   [73] Biblioteca Apostolica Vaticana, MS Barb. Lat. 872, fos 113r–116r.

With the revolution which followed the death of Ferdinand I, activity on the schism increased. Although only four members of the university are specifically mentioned among the *letrados* present at the Cortes of Coimbra in 1385 [74] (all of them adherents of John of Aviz, of whom one later became his chancellor, and another acquired a bishopric), it seems a reasonable assumption that they represented a large section of academic opinion. The speech supporting John of Aviz in his candidature for the throne, made by the lawyer John das Regras, is especially important as a statement of the opinions of an Urbanist academic. Das Regras asserted that Ferdinand I would have remained true to Urban VI if the Castilians had not pressurised him to defect at the start of the schism.[75] He denounced the Castilian candidate to the Portuguese throne as a schismatic heretic,[76] while championing John of Aviz as one who was loyal to Urban VI, and whose elevation to the kingship would honour both the pope and the Apostolic See.[77] No other members of the university appear to have revealed their intellectual attitudes to the schism, but there is a strong possibility that some Lisbon students gave quite decisive proof of their allegiance to Clement VII by voting with their feet and following the retreating Castilian forces into exile.[78]

A similar exodus – this time of Urbanists – marked the culmination of the French process of deciding the question of allegiance. Among the provincial universities, this procedure is even more obscure than in Portugal. It may be assumed that, on hearing of the original election of Urban VI, the provincial universities had automatically accepted him as pope. The University of Montpellier seems to have rivalled that of Paris in the speed with which it prepared a *rotulus* and sent it to Avignon,[79] but the process of changing allegiance is hidden. It may have been to this period of initial, almost unthinking, acceptance of him as pope that Urban VI himself referred in 1379, when he claimed that Toulouse and

[74] Moreira de Sá, vol. 2, p. 129; F. Lopes [ed. M. Lopes de Almeida and A. de Magalhães Basto], *Crónica de D. João I* (2 vols., Oporto, 1945–49), vol. 2, p. 5.
[75] Lopes, *Crónica*, vol. 1, p. 401.
[76] ibid.   [77] ibid., vol. 1, p. 423.
[78] Several exiled academics appear on the *rotulus* to Clement VII dated for 1388 which is printed in Moreira de Sá, *Chartularium*, no. 413.
[79] *Cartulaire de l'université de Montpellier* (2 vols. and supplement, Montpellier, 1890–1912), vol. 1, p. 580.

Orléans (as well as Paris) had declared for him against Clement VII,[80] but it seems more probable that the Roman pope was actually referring to the not inconsiderable number of supporters which he retained at least in Orléans and Paris during the first years of the dispute. However, although both Orléans and Angers sent representatives to the meeting held at Paris in September 1378, where the schism was discussed and the king advised to declare neutrality,[81] there is no sign of further provincial activity before the universities sent their *rotuli* to Clement VII.[82] Whatever debate there was in the provincial universities must have been brief: the Universities of Angers, Cahors and Orléans apparently sent their rolls to Clement even before he left Italy.[83] This ready transfer to his obedience probably reflects a combination of French royal influence and local factors – Orléans, for example, had never really recovered its independence following a conflict with Philip IV at the beginning of the fourteenth century, and as the main centre of civil law studies in France was peculiarly dependent on the secular authorities for providing employment for its graduates, while Angers was at the centre of the appanage of Louis I, Duke of Anjou, who was later to reveal himself as perhaps the staunchest of Clement VII's political supporters. Moreover, in none of the provincial universities was there a sufficiently large contingent of foreign students equivalent to the Anglo-German nation at Paris, which could provide the focus for opposition to Clement VII.

Whatever the reasons for the provincial haste in transferring allegiance to the more recently elected pope, this precociousness contrasted markedly with the attitude of the University of Paris, which did not declare its support for Clement VII until 26 May 1379. This declaration came at the end of a period of considerable activity, especially literary, marked by numerous external attempts to influence the academics, and considerable pamphleteering.

Although the Parisian masters had been aware of the situation in Rome and its potential developments from as early as July

---

[80] Seidlmayer, *Anfänge*, p. 343.

[81] *Valois*, vol. 1, pp. 103-4.

[82] Fournier, *Statuts*, nos. 188, 403, 697, 1021-3, 1443, 1888, 1896-7. The Montpellier rolls are printed in *Cartulaire de l'université de Montpellier*, vol. 1, pp. 578-607.

[83] *Valois*, vol. 1, p. 116 and nn. 5-6.

1378, the university was apparently inactive until September, when it was represented at the meeting which discussed the growing difficulty, and urged neutrality.[84] King Charles V, however, favoured his cousin, Clement VII, and in the subsequent events there were clear signs of the emergence of the principle of *cuius regio, eius religio*, a view which was to bedevil French activity on the schism right through to 1418. Until the formal decision on allegiance was taken in May 1379, the conflict between the French crown and the University of Paris over the latter's right to discuss the matter was to be a major cause of contention.

But even before the king had begun to exert his influence on the academics, some of them were beginning to waver in their loyalty to Urban VI. By November 1378 the English nation was considering the possibility that another *rotulus* might have to be prepared,[85] the formalities for which were initiated at a rather confused congregation held in December.[86] The first detailed discussions on the schism appear to have taken place in January 1379, when the university issued a declaration of neutrality on 8 January.[87] This should perhaps be interpreted as an evasive attempt to postpone an actual choice between the claimants for the papacy rather than as a true declaration of policy. It is clear that the statement reflected a stalemate within the university, where the discussions had made it obvious that a consensus was out of the question.[88]

Evidence of the contemporary arguments within the University of Paris is provided by the *Allegationes quorundum magistrorum Parisiensium*, compiled by the lawyer Jean de Bournazel.[89] All aspects of the dispute had obviously been discussed: the notoriety of the 'force' in the election of Urban VI, the credibility of the cardinals, the validity or otherwise of the election held in April 1378, whether Urban should be obeyed and his administration tolerated, and the legality or otherwise of the election of his rival.

---

[84] ibid., vol. 1, pp. 103–4, 121 n. 7. See also the statements of Jean le Fèvre (*Bulaeus*, vol. 4, pp. 523–4) and Guillaume de Salvarvilla (Baluzius, *Vitae paparum*, vol. 1, pp. 533–4).

[85] *Auct. Ch.*, vol. 1, p. 567.

[86] *Ch. Paris.*, vol. 3, p. 235; *Bulaeus*, vol. 4, p. 480.

[87] *Ch. Paris.*, no. 1616; *Bulaeus*, vol. 4, pp. 565–6; *Valois*, vol. 1, p. 122.

[88] *Ch. Paris.*, vol. 3, p. 561.

[89] ibid., no. 1617; printed in *Bulaeus*, vol. 4, pp. 555–64. For the date see *Valois*, vol. 1, p. 128 n. 1.

To the evidence provided by this compilation can be added that derived from other tracts produced within the university at this time, the style and content of which varies markedly. Some of them were openly biassed, such as the ultra-Clementist tract produced by Raoul d'Oulmont (who was to appear as a constant adherent of the Avignonese line, even in the crises which beset the obedience in the earlier years of Benedict XIII). His tract, despite its mass of legal citations, added nothing to the development of the debates.[90] Much more sober consideration of the issues was contained in a very lengthy anonymous work completed in August 1380, but which seems never to have been officially published. This drew extensively on previous contributions to the debates from both sides, and was especially aware of the national rivalry between the French and the Italians which was at the heart of the struggle for control of the papacy.[91] Many other writers were also aware of this national antagonism, which was most commonly reflected in the production of tracts in dialogue form, a form in any case admirably suited to the circumstances of the debates. Typical of these works were the *De planctu bonorum* of Jean le Fèvre [92] and the *Epistola pacis* of Henry of Langenstein.[93] Both tracts dealt with the problem of the double election and both saw the conflict between the papacies, even at this stage, as one between countries, nationalities and universities, as well as being a straightforward legal dispute.

Le Fèvre's work indeed fitted into the dialogue form of the debates in more than one sense. For the *De planctu bonorum* was meant to be considered as a response to Johannes de Legnano's

---

[90] BN, MS Lat. 1463, fos 73v–74r.

[91] ASV., Arm. LIV. 39. See also Ehrle, *Alpartils Chronica*, pp. 414–25.

[92] BN, MS Lat. 1469, fos 42r–66v. On the date see *Valois*, vol. 1, p. 127 n. 2; *Ch. Paris.*, no. 1632; A. Coville, *La vie intellectuelle dans les domaines d'Anjou-Provence de 1380 à 1435* (Paris, 1941), pp. 108–10.

[93] BN, MS Lat. 14644, fos 142r–161v (misbound). The only printed edition is *Henrici de Hassia de Langenstein . . . Epistola pacis scripta 1379 . . . pro Urbano papa . . . programma . . . in academia Iulia Carolina* (Helmstadt, 1778–79). The work is summarised in F. J. Scheuffgen, *Beiträge zu der Geschichte des grossen Schismas* (Freiburg-im-Breisgau, 1889), pp. 43–58. See also A. Kneer, *Die Entstehung der konziliaren Theorie: zur Geschichte des Schismas und der Kirchenpolitischen Schriftsteller Konrad von Gelnhausen (†1390) und Heinrich von Langenstein (†1397)* (Rome, 1893), pp. 66–70, 72–4; F. J. P. Bliemetzrieder, *Das Generalkonzil im grossen abendländischen Schisma* (Paderborn, 1904), pp. 45–54. The conciliarist aspects of the tract will be considered below, pp. 59–61.

De fletu ecclesiae: it is therefore hardly surprising that the protagonists in the tract were characterised respectively as *Parisiensis* and *Bononiensis*. The tract was intended principally for Charles V, although the author obviously meant it to reach a wider audience as well, in order to convince them of the validity of the Clementist case. The dialogue itself, however, contained little of novelty to the discussions.[94] Of far greater significance was the final section of the work, which considered the behaviour of the cardinals after the election of Urban VI.[95] Le Fèvre admitted that the cardinals deserved to be blamed for giving the impression that the original election had been validly performed, but sought to excuse their actions by an appeal to the canonistic version of the doctrine of necessity, their peculiar situation and the threat to their personal security being adduced in justification of their actions.[96] The use of the concept of necessity appears nowhere else in the academic debate on allegiances, although both it and the related Aristotelian concept of *epieikeia* were to be frequently cited in the search for a means to end the schism by methods which would not normally have been countenanced.

The *De planctu bonorum* was an unashamedly Clementist work; the tract produced by Langenstein considered the issue from the opposing, Urbanist, standpoint; at one point the Clementist advocate in his dialogue was bluntly accused of arguing 'pueriliter'.[97] Langenstein identified the root cause of the schism as Urban VI's desire for ecclesiastical reformation, which had gained him the enmity of the cardinals when he sought to reduce the luxury with which they were surrounded.[98] As in most tracts dealing with the matter of allegiance, it was the actions of the cardinals after the election of Urban VI which received most attention. The nationalistic aspect of the crisis was also revealed, the Clementist emphasising the Roman mob's insistence on the election of either a Roman or Italian as pope. This argument was simply dismissed by his opponent: Urban VI was neither a Roman nor an Italian, but a Neapolitan, and his election had not been exactly welcomed by the mob, as popular murmurings had

[94] *BN*, MS Lat. 1469, fos 42v–64r.
[95] ibid., fos 64r–65v.
[96] ibid., fo. 64v.
[97] *BN*, MS Lat. 14644, fo. 158v.   [98] ibid., fos 145r, 148v.

made manifest.[99] Although the arguments for both sides followed a pattern which was by now becoming fairly standard, the work did give some indication of possible future developments. An appeal by the Clementist to the University of Paris revealed the influence which that institution was already attempting to exert,[100] but at the same time the Clementist also called for support from Charles V as tutor and defender of the church.[101] This appeal was an overt demand for secular intervention, and a clear reference to the potential royal power of dictating the question of allegiance within the state, a power which was soon to come into conflict with the aspirations of the university.

While this rather individual pamphleteering continued, the university and its constituent corporations were also active, the debates throughout early 1379 being reflected in the *Acta* of the English nation. During February that body was a consistent opponent of royal attempts to achieve a rapid declaration in favour of Clement VII. On 12 February the members of the nation agreed to protest against royal suggestions that they were deliberately hindering the completion of the *rotulus* destined for Avignon – a sure indication of the wavering of Urbanist resolve.[102] But presumably some Urbanists must have been suggesting just such an obstructionist course. In any case, preparations for the roll continued, with a refusal to permit the enrolment of a proctor who had falsified his accounts being decreed as part of the attempt to coerce him into repaying the money he had embezzled.[103] Although the nation in all probability contained staunch adherents of both pontiffs, it may well be the case that neutralism retained considerable support: a member about to leave Paris petitioned that if a roll were constructed he might be included on it as though present – pragmatically asking that he be enrolled regardless of which pope the *rotulus* might actually be sent to.[104]

Clearly any attempt to determine just which claimant enjoyed majority support within the University of Paris at this time would

[99] ibid., fo. 158v: 'Romanum vel ytalicum volumus, gallicum noluimus, et miserum neapolitanum habemus'.
[100] ibid., fos 153v–154r.
[101] ibid., fo. 154r.   [102] *Auct. Ch.*, vol. I, p. 569.
[103] ibid., vol. I, p. 571.   [104] ibid.

be an impossibility, but there were several individuals besides the tractarians who openly revealed their loyalties. Attendance at the meetings with Charles V in November 1378 and on 7 May 1379, at which the Clementist party held the ascendancy, revealed several of the supporters of the Avignon pope.[105] On the *rotulus* sent to Avignon by the lawyers, Raoul d'Oulmont claimed that he had supported the cardinals even before they had elected Clement VII,[106] while his fellow lawyer Robertus de Grignonneria also gave them his support, defending them against accusations of falsehood in their statements about the election of Urban VI.[107] More generally the French nation and the faculty of medicine revealed their loyalty to Clement VII in May 1379, when they sent their own *rotulus* to Avignon, with Pierre d'Ailly acting as their envoy.[108] From evidence dating from the mid-1380s it also appears that Gilles des Champs – later one of the leaders of university opinion at Paris – had adhered to Clement VII from the outset.[109] On the Urbanist side overt declarations of loyalty were somewhat rarer, but the refusal of Gerard de Kalkar to participate in an embassy to deliver a roll to Avignon in 1379 made his feelings sufficiently clear.[110]

The formal process of deciding allegiances finally ended in May 1379. On the 21st the king sent a letter to the university which, although worded as a request, was very much an order to recognise Clement VII or face royal displeasure.[111] The debates of the following day revealed the divisions within the university: the French and Norman nations immediately declared for Clement, as did the faculties of medicine and law. But the theologians and the Picard and English nations sought further time for discussion.[112] Another royal letter[113] and a further congrega-

105 *Valois*, vol. 1, pp. 113–14, 132 and nn.
106 *Ch. Paris.*, vol. 3, p. 254.
107 His Clementist opinions are twice cited in *ASV.*, Arm. LIV. 39, at fos 37v–38r and 53v–54r. In the latter instance, he is described as having asserted that 'dicti cardinales nec arguendi nec accusandi sunt de dissimulacione, quin videlicet in toto isto negocio puram dixerint veritatem absque admixtione falsitatis'. On the identification as Grignonneria, see Ehrle, *Alpartils Chronica*, p. 417.
108 *Ch. Paris.*, no. 1622.
109 ibid., vol. 3, p. 387. Des Champs had acted as envoy of the Norman nation on an early *rotulus* to Clement VII: ibid., vol. 3, p. 264.
110 *Auct. Ch.*, vol. 1, pp. 578–9.
111 *Bulaeus*, vol. 4, p. 568; *Ch. Paris.*, no. 1623; *Valois*, vol. 1, p. 137.
112 *Valois*, vol. 1, p. 138.   113 *Bulaeus*, vol. 4, p. 570.

tion on 24 May induced the theologians to recognise Clement, but the Picard and English nations continued their opposition.[114] This, however, was simply ignored: the formal acceptance of the legitimacy of the Avignon papacy was decreed in the name of the whole university on 26 May, the statement being repeated before the king on 30 May.[115]

But the declaration reflected royal pressure rather than conviction: a considerable section of the university was still undecided as to which pope it wished to recognise – the Norman nation, for example, may still have wished to accept Urban VI, despite its pronouncements to the contrary.[116] Therefore, although the declaration of 26 May pleased Clement,[117] the debates continued within the university. The definitive acceptance of Clement VII was delayed until February 1383, after Louis of Anjou had intervened, cowed the native academics, and forced his opponents into exile.[118]

In the meantime any attempt to discuss the question of allegiance openly was rapidly crushed, thanks to concerted activity by the crown and the faculty of law.[119] The only signs of continuing debate are provided by the activities of the faculty of arts and its constituent nations, although this evidence has to be treated with caution. The faculty of arts, containing a large number of foreigners whose opinions were not subject to French governmental control, was chiefly concerned to establish and maintain a *modus vivendi* between the adherents of the rival obediences. Much of the apparent opposition to Clement VII which was voiced in university debates between 1379 and 1383 really reflected attempts to maintain the original neutralist stance of the university rather than loyalty to Urban VI.[120] The English were especially concerned not to be provocative: even in May 1381 they did not reject the *via concilii*, although their acceptance

---

[114] *Ch. Paris.*, no. 1624, records all the debates of this week. See also *Valois*, vol. 1, p. 138; Bliemetzrieder, *Das Generalkonzil*, pp. 54–5.

[115] *Bulaeus*, vol. 4, pp. 572–3; *Ch. Paris.*, no. 1627; *Valois*, vol. 1, p. 139.

[116] G. A. van Asseldonk, *De Neerlanden en het westers Schisma (tot 1398)* (Utrecht, 1955), p. 248.

[117] *Bulaeus*, vol. 4, pp. 578–9; *Ch. Paris.*, no. 1630; *Valois*, vol. 1, p. 139.

[118] *Ch. Paris.*, no. 1650; *Valois*, vol. 1, p. 365.

[119] *Valois*, vol. 1, p. 140.

[120] ibid., vol. 1, pp. 139–40; *Bulaeus*, vol. 4, pp. 579–80; *Ch. Paris.*, no. 1424.

of it was limited by the proviso that the nation 'non intenderet recedere a mandatis, jussionibus et obediencia superiorum suorum, sed eis firmiter insistere et obedire'.[121]

But the situation within the university was rapidly being overtaken by events. In September 1380 the spirit of compromise had suffered a major setback with the death of King Charles V, and the transfer of the effective government of France to his brother Louis of Anjou. Anjou's political ambitions in Italy, as Clement VII's candidate for the succession to the throne of Naples after the death of Joanna I, forced him into a partisan position which clashed with the university's attempts to find a solution to the schism. The real conflict was, however, delayed until after the only real difficulty over the problem of allegiance which troubled the university during this first phase of the schism. This was the dispute over the existence of two rival chancellors which lasted throughout much of 1381–82.

This conflict began on 17 May 1381, when the Bishop of Paris declared that all opponents of Clement VII were automatically 'schismatic heretics'. The university discussed his remarks, but a final decision that so simplistic a viewpoint was untenable was not produced until 15 June.[122] This statement reflected the conciliatory – almost neutralist – attitude prevailing within the university at this time, but came too late. Clement VII had already authorised the bishop to deprive all Urbanists within the university, and transfer their benefices to his own adherents.[123] On 15 July he further ordered the installation of Jean Blanchart as chancellor, with instructions not to admit Urbanists to degrees.[124] Nevertheless, the Urbanists continued to graduate, taking their degrees from the Chancellor of Ste Geneviève, while on 1 April 1382 the Urbanist majority within the English nation secured revenge on the Clementist members of the nation by ordering the expulsion of all those who had received degrees from Blanchart.[125] Despite continuing attacks on the Urbanists, which included the purging of the officials of Ste Geneviève and the annulment of degrees

[121] *Auct. Ch.*, vol. 1, pp. 607–8.
[122] *Ch. Paris.*, no. 1639; *Valois*, vol. 1, pp. 342–3.
[123] *Ch. Paris.*, no. 1638; *Valois*, vol. 1, p. 345.
[124] *Ch. Paris.*, vol. 3, pp. 301, 358, 371; *Valois*, vol. 1, p. 345.
[125] *Auct. Ch.*, vol. 1, pp. 618–25, 629–30, 632–3; *Valois*, vol. 1, pp. 345–6.

conferred there, they continued their opposition.[126] New Clement-ist officials were appointed to Ste Geneviève on 25 April 1382, their nomination being immediately challenged by the English nation, which denied the validity of the papal letters of appoint-ment.[127] Only in July did the Parisian Parlement settle the issue, declaring in favour of Blanchart, but the English nation did not cease its opposition until November 1382.[128]

This was to prove the only major clash on the recognition of the rival popes to occur at Paris during this period, its most striking feature being its usefulness as a reflection of the tensions between the rival groups within the English nation. Compromise was necessary not merely within the university as a whole, but within its constituent corporations. But the painful process of achieving a *modus vivendi* was not confined solely to Paris. Several universities experienced conflicts between official policy and individual conscience, as is revealed in cases such as those already noted of Nicholas da Costa and Matthew de Clementis at Cambridge and Perpignan.[129] In most cases a successful compro-mise seems to have been achieved, but apart from the Parisian example only the Universities of Oxford and Bologna provide any evidence for these developments as they affected whole institutions.

In the case of Bologna, the compromise seems to have been arrived at without conflict. The Spanish College, or rather its non-Portuguese members, remained Clementist throughout, and apparently sent *rotuli* to Avignon without hindrance.[130] The loyalties of the Portuguese members are less certain, but presum-ably reflected the vacillations and tensions of Portuguese royal policy, with additional complications being introduced in 1385. After the successful rejection of Castilian influence in Portugal it seems probable that the relationship of the Portguese to the other members of the college resembled that of the Clementists within the English nation at Paris.

At the University of Oxford, it was the Scots who formed a

---

[126] Clement VII's letter deposing the officials of Ste Geneviève is in *Valois*, vol. 1, p. 346 n. 3.
[127] ibid., vol. 1, pp. 347–8.
[128] ibid., vol. 1, p. 348; *Ch. Paris.*, no. 1468.
[129] See above, pp. 28, 31.
[130] Beltrán de Heredia, *Bulario*, no. 154. This is the first of a succession of rolls sent throughout the period of the schism.

distinctive Clementist contingent within the generally Urbanist whole. By 5 December 1382 the tensions between the adherents of the two popes had become so great that Richard II sent a mandate to the chancellor of the university instructing him to treat the Scots as though they were under royal protection, provided that they did not seek converts to Clement VII.[131] The king had acted purely pragmatically, to defend his foreign policy of peace with his northern neighbour. The order seems to have been effective, and Scots continued to attend the university under this royal protection through to the last years of the schism, being also able to arrange for sending petitions to Avignon through third parties.[132]

By 1383 the spirit of compromise reflected in these arrangements seems to have been generally accepted throughout the European universities. Official allegiances had been decided, but the universities accepted that they would not be able to eradicate a small but persistent internal opposition to that decision. There had, of course, been casualties along the route – most notably in the exiles from Lisbon and Paris – but both of these were special cases, with their own special explanations. The case of Paris was particularly important, as there the exiles were not really opponents of Clement VII, but individuals who had advocated means of ending the schism which were at the time politically inexpedient for the French. For, concurrently with the debates on recognition of the popes, another debate had been in progress within the universities, on just how to dispose of the apparently insoluble problem of the existence of a dual papacy.

131 A. F. Steuart, 'Scotland and the papacy during the great schism', *Scottish Historical Review*, **4** (1906–7), 147; E. Perroy, *L'Angleterre et le grand schisme d'occident* (Paris, 1933), p. 69. Richard II's letter is in *Rotuli Scotiae in turri Londiniensi et domo capitulari Westmonsteriensi asservati*, vol. 2 (London, 1819), pp. 45–6, and (an undated copy) in H. E. Salter, W. A. Pantin and H. G. Richardson, *Formularies which bear on the history of Oxford, c. 1204–1420*, vol. 1, Publications of the Oxford Historical Society, N.S., vol. 4 (Oxford, 1942), pp. 249–50.
132 For example, the petition of Thomas Butill, in W. H. Bliss, *Calendar of entries in the papal registers relating to Great Britain and Ireland: petitions to the pope*, vol. 1 (London, 1896), p. 570.

Chapter 3

DE SCHISMATE EXTINGUENDO

The discussions as to the validity of the rival papal elections were a necessary prelude to the debates on the means of ending the schism, which could really be achieved only by a definitive judgement of the conflicting claims. However, by declaring allegiance and committing themselves to specific popes, the academics of Europe ensured that their debates on a solution to the problem would be inconsequential: they could not discuss the matter impartially without prejudicing their already proclaimed allegiances. In general, unless the individuals and corporations concerned were prepared to reject their earlier declarations of obedience, discussions on ending the schism could not proceed beyond the realms of theory.

Despite this difficulty, however, there was almost continuous interest in the search for a means of terminating the schism through to 1383, particularly within the University of Paris. The Parisian masters soon recognised their situation, and tried to overthrow their earlier declaration for Clement VII, seeking also to persuade Charles V to change his policy. Their attitude was perhaps best expressed by Conrad of Gelnhausen in his *Epistola concordiae*, where he discussed the problems of a solution while specifically excluding the issue of allegiance and legitimacy.[1] Guillaume de Salvarvilla also seems to have realised that proposing a solution necessitated rejection of both contenders,[2] while the most striking contrast between this attitude and the determined views of a declared adherent of one of the claimants was revealed in a poetical debate which broke out within the University of Paris in 1381. A conciliarist participant maintained the

[1] Bliemetzrieder, *Literarische Polemik*, p. 117.
[2] F. J. P. Bliemetzrieder, 'Conclusions de Guillaume de Salvarvilla, maître en théologie à Paris, sur la question du concile général pendant le grand schisme d'occident (1381)', *Revue d'histoire ecclésiastique*, 11 (1910), 54-5.

45

need for neutrality, claiming that discussion was a necessary pre-condition for a decision, while his replicant considered that there was no problem – for him Clement VII was pope, and that was all that mattered.[3]

In such circumstances it is not surprising that this first phase of the schism passed without any solution being achieved, despite the fact that the period from June 1378 to the forcible imposition of obedience to Clement VII on the University of Paris in 1383 was replete with suggestions for ending the division within the church.

Among the people preparing such schemes, the academics proved especially productive. The extent of their interest is most obviously revealed in Pierre d'Ailly's disputation of 1381, *Utrum indoctus in jure divino posset juste praeesse in Ecclesiae regno*.[4] Although d'Ailly did refuse to declare which of the solutions he listed had his own approval or preference,[5] the tract contained a lengthy summary of the arguments for and against each of the possible solutions then under consideration.[6] For the first time the alternatives were properly presented, in the basic form in which they were to be discussed throughout the schism. D'Ailly declared that

Ad sedationem hujus scandalosi schismatis, in genere duae viae tan-guntur. Una est via rigoris, alia est via amoris. Prima via est illorum qui dicunt, quod in hac casu procedendum est contra schismaticos per excommunicationes et bellorum impugnationes: secundum via est dicentium contrarium; et ista est tripartita. Prima via ponit quod istud schisma convenientius potest terminari per concilii generalis determi-nationem: secunda, quod per compromissi sive concilii particularis arbitrarium ordinationem: tertia, quod per alterius vel utriusque electorum voluntariam cessionem, et nova electionem.[7]

Of these alternative types of solution the first, the way of force and warfare (generally known as the *via facti*), gained least academic support. However, it cannot have been without its advo-cates, otherwise it would not have been included in d'Ailly's list, and it was suggested in a Clementist poem which circulated

---

[3] These poems will be discussed more fully towards the end of this chapter.

[4] Printed in Dupin, *Gersonii opera*, vol. 1, pp. 646–62.

[5] ibid., vol. 1, p. 657.

[6] ibid., vol. 1, pp. 657–62.   [7] ibid., vol. 1, p. 657.

within the University of Paris in 1381.[8] The *via facti* was certainly
a tempting prospect at this stage of the dispute, for it appeared to
offer the most straightforward means of settling the issue, even
though only the secular princes possessed the military strength
necessary to put it into operation. Nevertheless, it seemed the
clearest solution in an already divided Europe: it would prove
unquestionably that God was on the side of the eventual victor –
and at this point neither party was prepared to contemplate the
possibility of defeat. Force was therefore readily adopted by both
sides in their attempts to increase the territorial limits of their
obediences, and in the hope of driving their opponents into submission. It made its most blatant appearance in the struggle for
the Neapolitan succession, with Urban VI supporting Charles of
Durazzo against Joanna I and her Clementist adopted heir,
Louis I of Anjou.[9] It was also to be seen in the conflicts in the
Low Countries, with the crusade of the Bishop of Norwich,[10]
and in the Castilian attempts to conquer Portugal after the death
of Ferdinand I in 1383. Attempts to implement the *via facti* also
appeared intermittently in French policy on the schism through
to the 1390s.

But although it seemed straightforward, the *via facti* had
several major drawbacks. It embroiled the peculiar problems of
the schism in the political rivalries of the European powers; and
it also gave the secular princes an excuse and mask of legitimacy
to cover their increasing interference in ecclesiastical matters.
This interference in time led to intervention in attempts to
terminate the schism, as the princes sought to extend their powers
within the church at the expense of the proper ecclesiastical authorities, and frequently in opposition to academic aspirations. In
any case, the possibility of the *via facti* proving effective in ending
the schism was very remote. For one thing, the balance of forces
within Europe meant that it was impossible for either side to gain
a total military victory; and certainly no single prince or dynasty

---

[8] N. Valois, 'Un poème de circonstance composé par un clerc de l'université de Paris
(1381)', *Annuaire-bulletin de la société de l'histoire de France*, **31** (1894), 237, lines
455–8.

[9] See M. Rothbarth, *Urban VI and Neapel*, Abhandlungen zur mittleren und neueren
Geschichte, vol. 49 (Berlin and Leipzig, 1913), pp. 49–61; *Valois*, vol. 1, pp. 182–90,
vol. 2, pp. 8–89.

[10] Perroy, *L'Angleterre*, pp. 166–209; *Valois*, vol. 2, pp. 224–32.

possessed sufficient strength to force the opposing obedience to submit. Moreover, even if the nominal victory were gained, whether the peace thereby imposed would prove lasting was highly dubious: in a battle of arguments, mere brute force was not the best of weapons. Finally, there would be the problem of the effects on the church of a full-scale war between the rival obediences. Even a minor expedition such as that of the Bishop of Norwich to the Low Countries stirred up a major reaction, and may in part have contributed to the general Lollard policy of rejecting the papacy as an institution.

Despite this, however, the *via facti* did gain the support of a minority within the universities. But in general, it was the second, peaceful type of solution (especially in its forms as the *via concilii* and *via cessionis*, the ways of a council or resignation) which was to dominate the discussions throughout the years of the crisis. But there is little evidence for the consideration of cession in these early stages, other than at Paris, and even that university gives no real indication of the nature of the arguments advanced, as d'Ailly excised the appropriate section from his *Utrum indoctus* when he re-edited the tract after the Council of Pisa.[11] The attraction of abdication, especially when a state of neutrality was in force, was nevertheless revealed in the Parisian declaration of 8 January 1379. In this instance, voluntary or induced cession seems to have been the only policy on which the university could reach any agreement.[12] Indeed, the masters may have been prepared to adopt the call for abdication as their official policy; but royal interference to force a declaration of allegiance killed any hopes of defining a programme which might have ended the schism before it became entrenched.

For, unfortunately, the third means of ending the schism which was then being considered, the *via concilii*, could not provide an effective solution in the form in which it was then advanced. At this point, the function of the council was seen as purely determinative: it was generally accepted that one of the rival claimants had been legitimately elected to the papacy; the role of the council

---

[11] Dupin, *Gersonii opera*, vol. 2, p. 662; see also G. Ouy, *Le receuil épistolaire autographe de Pierre d'Ailly, et les notes d'Italie de Jean de Montreuil*, Umbrae codicum occidentalium, vol. 9 (Amsterdam, 1966), pp. xii–xiii.

[12] *Ch. Paris.*, no. 1616.

would be to examine the facts and declare just which of the contenders was actually pope. Superficially it appeared to be a simple answer to the problem, but it was unlikely to prove effective because of the basic obstacle of allegiance which remained to check any progress. The difficulty was first highlighted by Baldus de Ubaldis in July 1378, his conciliarism at a time when the dispute had not yet developed into a schism being undermined by his insistence that any council could only be legitimately summoned by Urban VI.[13] This problem of the issue of a summons was the chief obstacle to conciliarism in its early form, compounding the weaknesses revealed in the ecclesiastical constitution by the schism itself. A general council had to be convened by the pope; but in the peculiar circumstances of the schism this was clearly impracticable. Both parties would, naturally, demand convocation by their own pope, and insist that he preside over the assembly. As Wyclif realised, neither side could concede this point, therefore no conciliarist solution was possible.[14] It was within this context of strictly defined positions that a variant of conciliarism was invented: the *via concilii particularis*, which sought a solution by holding separate councils of the obediences. But this, too, was incapable of offering any real means of ending the schism. Such separate councils were unlikely to decide against their own candidate for the papacy, as the rival assemblies held at Perpignan and Cividale in 1409 were to demonstrate most effectively.

But these councils could not have been predicted in 1378, nor could the other gatherings at Pisa and Constance. Before these last two could be held, the theories which would justify their being summoned without papal authorisation had first to be formulated and codified, while the aims of conciliarism had also to undergo transformation. For conciliarism to succeed, its form had to be changed dramatically. Indeed, a whole ecclesiastical revolution was required, of a highly specialised type which would not drastically alter the generalised definition of the church, but would lead to a major transformation of its power structure by redefining the repository of ultimate administrative and executive power. This revolution did not occur in the first phase of the schism.

[13] Bzovius, *Annalium ecclesiasticorum*, vol. 15, p. 68.
[14] Loserth, *De potestate pape*, p. 249.

However, although conciliarism was not yet a fully-fledged ecclesiology, nor was it a novel concept in 1378. Its antecedents stretched back to the canonists,[15] although the intellectual impetus towards the rise of a true conciliarist theory was less ancient, deriving from the system developed by Thomas Aquinas. The inherent ambiguities and contradictions of his theories, coupled with an almost unquestioning acceptance of their synthetic validity, were vital for a revival of the age-old problem of sovereignty within a universalist cosmology.[16] The controversies between Pope Boniface VIII and King Philip IV of France, and between Pope John XXII and the would-be emperor Louis of Bavaria, provided the inspiration and justification for considerable political and ecclesiological theorising, in which the ascending interpretation of the derivation of authority acquired increasing definition.[17] Contemporary developments in Italy, and especially the rise of the communes, stimulated further thought in an attempt to find a legal justification for the organisation of a small political entity on populist lines. It was from writers on these issues, notably Marsilius of Padua, William of Ockham, John of Jandun and Bartolus of Sassoferrato, together with the earlier canonists on the corporation theme, that the later conciliarists were to derive (if not misappropriate) much of their theory. But, until the opportunities presented by the schism, the ideas were no more than mere speculation, the populist discussions being academic not only in the sense that the theorists were members of universities. Moreover, there was no subtle transformation from individual theorising to the production of a comprehensive conciliarist thesis: at the outbreak of the schism, there were several major gaps in the construction. In addition, the major differences and conflicts between the earlier theorists all left their mark on their successors, so that when the time came to collate all the ideas in the later

[15] For the history of conciliarism from its canonistic origins, see B. Tierney, *Foundations of the conciliar theory* (Cambridge, 1955). A stimulating survey of the historiography on the subject is in R. Luman, 'A conciliar suggestion', in *The impact of the church upon its culture*, ed. J. C. Brauer, *Essays in Divinity*, vol. 2 (Chicago, 1968), pp. 121–7.

[16] On this, see M. Wilks, *The problem of sovereignty in the later middle ages*, Cambridge studies in medieval life and thought, N.S. vol. 9 (Cambridge, 1963), pp. 134–6.

[17] For conciliarism in this struggle, see Arquillière, 'L'appel au concile', pp. 23–55; Martin, *Origines*, vol. 2, pp. 17–22.

fourteenth century, and thus to produce the supposed 'conciliarist theory', these complexities and others combined to produce not one but several slightly differing theories within the conciliarist movement.[18]

However, although innovatory in fact, the conciliarists of the fourteenth century frequently failed to notice the novelty of their ideas. They saw themselves not as innovators, but as the upholders of the ancient ecclesiastical constitution. This derivative tradition accounts for the continual use of historical precedents in the conciliarist works; it also produced two other variations on the theme of ecclesiastical organisation, both propounded as possible solutions in the early years of the schism. The first was the extremely individualistic scheme adopted by Wyclif, the second the more popular appeal to the long tradition of secular involvement in church matters to impose unity. This last appeal provided a vivid illustration of the contemporary situation: the debates on the schism not only dealt with the legal arguments on the validity of the rival elections, but also stimulated further developments in the ancient conflict between the political and ecclesiastical authorities for control over the church.

Meanwhile, Wyclif's most obvious response to the schism was his blunt rejection of the *via facti*, accompanied by biting attacks on the crusade led by the Bishop of Norwich. In condemning the use of force, Wyclif instead proposed that both popes should resign their temporal lordships to the emperor and revert to the

---

[18] For Bartolism, see W. Ullmann, 'De Bartoli sententia: concilium repraesentat mentem populi', in *Bartolo da Sassoferrato, studi e documenti per il VI centenario*, vol. 2 (Milan, 1962), pp. 705-33, while for the Italian context of Marsilianism, see A. Gewirth, *Marsilius of Padua: the Defender of Peace* (2 vols., New York, 1951-56), vol. 1, pp. 25-30. The conciliarism of Marsilius (for which see ibid., vol. 1, pp. 283-91) provided the impetus for later developments of the theory, influencing several later writers including Dietrich of Niem and Nicholas of Cusa (see P. E. Sigmund, Jr, 'The influence of Marsilius of Padua on XVth-century conciliarism', *Journal of the History of Ideas*, **23** (1962), 392-402). For the relationship between Marsilius and John of Jandun see A. Gewirth, 'John of Jandun and the "Defensor Pacis"', *Speculum*, **23** (1948), 267-72, while for his links with Ockham see Gewirth, *Marsilius*, vol. 1, pp. 288-91; G. de Lagarde, 'Marsile de Padoue et Guillaume d'Ockham', *Revue des sciences religieuses*, **17** (1937), pp. 168-85, 428-54. Ockham's main importance in the development of conciliarism seems to have been to serve as a vehicle for the transmission of ideas from the earlier writers to those who followed him, the latter adopting the theories as they wished: B. Tierney, 'Ockham, the conciliar theory, and the canonists', *Journal of the History of Ideas*, **15** (1954), 40-70, especially pp. 68-70.

apostolic life.[19] For Wyclif this reversion was more important than actually restoring unity: he saw the schism, in so far as it would induce people to return to the simple life, as having a potentially beneficial impact on the church,[20] and (if the English versions of his works can be taken as genuinely his) he saw no objections to the continuation of the dual papacy, provided that the popes lived an ascetic existence.[21]

This immediately raises an issue which was to be crucial throughout the schism; the question of how far the papacy, or a single pope, had to be accepted as a matter of faith. For Wyclif the problem did not exist, neither the papal office nor the individual pope being necessary to his own particular ecclesiology. But he did recognise the difficulty under which others were to labour, of determining to precisely what extent a particular papal election, once its results had been proclaimed, had to be accepted in faith. He fully recognised that where there was a schism, with rival claims to obedience being propounded as matters of faith, such a division would produce an almost irreconcilable split, precisely as occurred with the schism of 1378.[22] Simon de Cramaud was later to point out the basic difficulty, that although the papacy was necessary as an article of faith, allegiance to a specific claimant to the office was not.[23] This precarious distinction was to be the cause of considerable confusion in the debates on the schism. For some writers, for example Matthaeus de Matasellanis, the concentration was to be on the papacy as an institution and the need for an undisputed pope as a matter of faith.[24] For others, such as Cramaud, the difficulties centred on the rival claimants, allowing the schism to be treated merely as an extremely complex case of a disputed succession between two private people, faith becoming involved only in so far as the pamphleteers tended to accept that

---

[19] Buddensieg, *Wyclif's polemical works*, vol. 2, p. 572.

[20] F. D. Matthew, *The English works of Wyclif hitherto unprinted*, Early English Text Society, vol. 74 (London, 1880), p. 463.

[21] T. Arnold, *Select English works of John Wyclif* (3 vols., Oxford, 1869–71), vol. 1, pp. 243–4. The idea of corporate headship of the church also seems to appear in the tracts *De ordine Christiano* and *De potestate pape* (J. Loserth, *Johannis Wyclif Opera minora* (London, 1913), pp. 129–31; Loserth, *De potestate pape*, p. 186). For the development of Wyclif's views on the papacy during the schism, see H. B. Workman, *John Wyclif: a study of the English medieval church* (2 vols., Oxford, 1926), vol. 2, pp. 74–82.   [22] Pollard, *Dialogus*, p. 22.

[23] Balliol College, Oxford, MS 165B, p. 62.   [24] BN, MS Lat. 17184, fol. 241r.

one of the contenders – without being for the moment sure of which – had to be the single legitimate pope.

Despite the distinctive peculiarities of Wyclif's views on the problem of terminating the schism, it is clear that he was not alone in his opinions, particularly in his willingness to allow the schism to continue. In 1381 this was a viewpoint recorded by a poet at Paris,[25] while in the 1390s an anonymous author remarked that this desire to live 'more Grecorum' was typical of the Lollard party in England and of the Fraticelli in Italy.[26] However, the majority of writers rejected any such scheme: their main concern was with the restoration of unity, whereas Wyclif's priorities centred on the removal of the causes of ecclesiastical degeneration, which he interpreted as greed for temporal dominion and possessions.[27]

Wyclif also resembles other writers in his frequent appeals for joint imperial and princely action to eradicate these causes of the schism by removing temporal possessions from ecclesiastical control. However, there was an essential difference in intention. Wyclif wanted the causes of the schism removed, but had no objection to the continuation of the double papacy; whereas the other writers had precisely the opposite intentions – they wanted one or other of the claimants to be removed by the princes, or at least that the princes should initiate the process which would lead to reunification of the church. This did not necessarily imply acceptance or advocacy of the *via facti*; often the appeals to the princes were linked with a call for the implementation of some other method. In the absence of any other authority to which the church could appeal, where there was no generally accepted pope and the cardinals, having caused the schism by their actions, were not trusted to end it, the appeal was to the prince as an alternative earthly head of Christendom to act to restore the integrity of the church. Such appeals revealed a strong sense of

---

25 *Valois*, vol. 1, pp. 390–1.
26 Bayerische Staatsbibliothek, Munich, MS Clm. 7006, fo. 127r. The English versions of Wyclif's works at one point include an analogy to the Greeks (Arnold, *Select English works*, vol. 2, p. 404), and this was also an aspect of Wyclif's doctrine condemned at the Blackfriars Council in 1382 (Workman, *John Wyclif*, vol. 2, p. 416 – although Wyclif denied that his views on this point had been properly understood, ibid., vol. 2, p. 268).
27 Buddensieg, *Wyclif's polemical works*, vol. 2, p. 572.

the constitutional obligations of the monarch within the church, occasionally in a Gallican but more often in a retrospective style. The arguments advanced drew especially on the imperialism of the earlier fourteenth century, and on the conflict between Pope John XXII and Louis of Bavaria; but more antique precedents were also cited quite frequently, especially the involvement of Theodoric in the attempts to settle the schism between Popes Symmachus and Laurentius at the end of the fifth century. Such appeals were, however, unlikely to produce an effective solution at this stage. Although they might pander to the self-importance of the princes, the inherent difficulties – especially the personal incompetence of Wenceslas of Bohemia, and the impossibility of reconciling the Clementist allegiance of those advocating a Gallican course with the Urbanism of the imperialists – meant that the only result of princely action was likely to be a stalemate.

Nevertheless, the appearance of appeals to the princes to assist in the implementation of peaceful methods for ending the schism is amply illustrated by the surviving literature, including the works of the leading proponents of conciliarism at this point, Conrad of Gelnhausen and Henry of Langenstein. The former had at first addressed his *Epistola concordiae* to King Charles V of France, but there also exist copies which were intended for Rupert II of the Palatinate and Wenceslas of Bohemia.[28] The most overt of Langenstein's appeals for secular action is included in his *Epistola . . . exhortatoria imperatoris et aliorum regum et principum ad pacem ecclesie universalis*.[29] This highly rhetorical work contains several emotive statements which, if Langenstein had not already declared his preference for the *via concilii*, might be taken to suggest that he actually favoured the use of force. He disclosed a very highly developed awareness of the latent powers of both empire and papacy (an awareness which also permeated many of his later writings), seeing the two offices as complementary, and possessing sufficient authority to overcome all opposition if they worked in concert.[30] It is, however, difficult to be sure of just what

[28] Bliemetzrieder, *Literarische Polemik*, pp. 85*, 114.

[29] Printed in G. Sommerfeldt, 'Zwei Schismatraktate Heinrichs von Langenstein: Sendschreiben an König Wenzel von 1381 und Schreiben an Bischof Friedrich von Brixen um 1384', *Mitteilungen des Instituts für österreichische Geschichtsforschung*, Ergänzungsband 7 (1907), 443–59.   [30] ibid., pp. 452–3.

De schismate extinguendo

effect Langenstein hoped that this work would have; for although the final call for imperial action to terminate the schism was couched in reasonably pacific terms,[31] the bellicosity which could not be far behind any appeal for secular involvement was controlled only with difficulty.[32]

Similar to Langenstein's letter in tone – and, to some extent, in content – is the work known as the *Tetragonus Aristotelis*, which purports to be a collection of six letters written early in 1382, advocating a general scheme of imperial intervention to resolve the schism and establish Urban VI as the undisputed pope. Both Adalbertus Rankonis de Ericinio and Henry of Langenstein have been suggested as possible authors of the compilation. Although the evidence for ascribing the work to the latter is quite strong, it does not seem to be conclusive. All that can be definitely said on the issue of authorship is that the compilation was almost certainly produced at Prague by someone recently exiled from Paris, and possibly having English connections – although this English association is no more than a mere possibility. The most curious feature of the whole series of letters is that they are forgeries, each one actually being a separate chapter in what is in fact a complete tract. The Universities of Oxford, Prague and Paris are named among the senders and recipients of the letters, the Roman people and Wenceslas of Bohemia also becoming involved as the work progresses.[33]

The most remarkable feature of the letters is the considerable emphasis which they place on the participation of Wenceslas of Bohemia in any attempt to end the schism. He was strongly urged

[31] ibid., p. 459.

[32] ibid., pp. 456–7.

[33] The whole compilation has been most recently edited by F. M. Bartoš, *Tetragonus Aristotelis: konciliaristický projev s počátku velikého církevního rozkolu*, Historický archiv, Česká akademie císaře Františka Josefa pro vědy, slovesnost a umění čísko, vol. 41 (Prague, 1916), pp. 12–42. The uncertainties about the authorship of the work are well reflected in the secondary literature. An Oxonian origin was suggested by T. Lindner ('Über Huttens Schrift, *De schismate extinguendo*', *Theologische Studien und Kritiken*, **46** (1873), 151–61), whose conclusions were accepted by Perroy (*L'Angleterre*, p. 156). The suggestions that the concoction may have been drawn up by Rankonis and Langenstein both derive from Bartoš, who originally argued in favour of the former ('Tetragonus Aristotelis', in *Abhandlungen aus dem Gebiete der mittleren und neueren Geschichte und ihrer Hilfswissenschaften* (Münster, 1925), pp. 233–9), but has more recently championed the candidature of Langenstein ('Das Rätsel des Tetragonus Aristotelis', *Communio viatorum*, **12** (1969), 159–64).

to assert his imperial powers over the church in order to impose a solution to the problem. For the author, this meant establishing Urban VI as uncontested pope through the medium of a general council summoned under imperial auspices. The imperial participation received a twofold justification, both historical and theoretical. The former was based on precedents provided by earlier imperial and royal actions to end schisms,[34] these being used as the basis for an appeal to the theory of imperial patronage over the church,[35] a role which closely corresponded to the tutorial powers over the church which the French were often to ascribe to their monarchs during this period, as Gallicanism developed both in theory and in practice. The theory of imperial patronage was given intellectual support by references to canon law, and to the recently propounded ecclesiological ideas of Marsilius of Padua and John of Jandun.[36]

Force would appear to have been a logical ingredient in this whole programme, but this was never explicitly stated. The author apparently saw a solution being engineered by constitutional change within the church, although his frequent appeals to precedent allowed the innovations to be concealed behind a façade of ancient constitutionalism. Assuming that the cardinals in conclave, although acting as electors, were as such no more than mere representatives of the Roman people,[37] the writer urged this larger group to join with the universities in invoking imperial action.[38] But this was not a completely populist appeal: the 'Roman people' were not correlated with Christendom. Here the *Romana generalitas* seems to have been the particular church at Rome, acting in the election of its bishop on behalf of, but not as representative of, the whole church. As a whole, the appeal was to the upper and lower elements of the church to unite against the cardinals in order to procure the assembly of a general council.[39] The concentration of the attack on the actions of the cardinals was the highlight of contemporary conciliarism, and may indeed have been one of the chief obstacles to the transformation of the theory into one which could have been adopted as an adequate solution to the schism.

[34] Bartoš, *Tetragonus*, pp. 35-9. [35] ibid., p. 39. [36] ibid., p. 41.
[37] ibid., pp. 21, 23, 32. [38] ibid., p. 34. [39] ibid., p. 39.

In the earlier years of the fourteenth century, the role of the cardinals had been focal to the theory of the ecclesiastical constitution, they being represented as the pivotal link between the *plena potestas* of the pope as personification of the *ecclesia*, and the *plena potestas* of the *congregatio fidelium* as its manifestation.[40] As long as the cardinals did not take this role too far, and actually seek to carry out the representative functions which were the logical attributes of this position, their senatorial and increasingly oligarchic position within the Roman church would be unchallenged. But, in 1378, they had acted on the theory, and by their *de facto* deposition of Urban VI had brought their own function into question. This explains why many of the debates of the first phase of the schism concerned themselves with the legality of the cardinals' actions as much as with the validity of the election of Urban VI. It also accounts for the relative unimportance of the cardinals in the early conciliarist schemes, where everything was left to the general council and the princes. This differed greatly from later conciliarism, when the passage of time allowed the cardinals of both colleges to reassert their representative function as intermediaries between pope and *ecclesia*, and reclaim a role in directing the process of altering the constitution of the church.

The extent of the discussion of the *via concilii* within the European academic community at the start of the schism is difficult to determine; it seems that in many places both the universities as corporations and their members as individuals maintained a discreet silence on the subject. Wyclif's anti-conciliar arguments and the involvement of the University of Oxford in the scheme of the Prague letters suggests that there must have been some debate there. The Italian lawyers and theologians must also have stimulated conciliarist theorising at Bologna and elsewhere, although there is little surviving trace of such activity. A letter of Peter Tenorio, Archbishop of Toledo, on the need for a general council [41] suggests that the Spanish universities were aware of the controversy, and Salamanca may have declared itself for a conciliarist solution.[42] It is also probable that members of the University of Lisbon participated in the talks which preceded the

---

[40] See Wilks, *The problem of sovereignty*, pp. 481–7.
[41] Printed in *Thes. Nov. Anec.*, pp. 1099–1120.   [42] Suárez Fernández, *Castilla*, p. 6.

57

Portuguese adoption of the *via concilii*, although the assembly in this instance seems to have been seen as an international political gathering rather than a proper council of the church.[43]

Only for the University of Paris does sufficient evidence survive to allow a proper consideration of the appeal of conciliarism. The reasons for the extensive debate there were many, chiefly deriving from the university's standing as one of the major intellectual centres of Europe, attracting students and masters from all over the continent. It was also politically important within the French kingdom, acting as an adviser to the crown on major matters, and also providing a sizeable proportion of the personnel of government. Internal debate was aided by the existence of a vocal Urbanist minority, while the conciliarist outburst owed much to the long tradition of Marsilian and Ockhamist speculation there, which had made the theoretical relationships between the constituent parts of the church a topic of almost everyday discussion, so that concepts which were elsewhere treated with caution could be openly considered. Thus, in the *Allegationes quorundam magistrorum*, composed even before conciliarism had become a major force within the university, there appeared clear acceptance of the populist interpretation of the ecclesiastical constitution among some academics, who assumed that the whole *congregatio fidelium* would be involved in solving the problem of the schism, even if the details of the scheme to be adopted were as yet uncertain.[44]

The stark chronology of the official Parisian declarations in the debates on allegiance and reunification – for neutrality in January 1379; for Clement VII in May that same year; for the *via concilii generalis* in May 1381; and finally another declaration in support of Clement VII in February 1383 – conceals much of the intensity of the argument. The first declaration shows that the university was contemplating action to end the schism even before its official recognition of Clement VII, while from mid-1379 onwards there is increasing evidence that university opinion was turning towards the adoption of a conciliarist policy.

Much of the surviving literature from Paris which contains

---

[43] Baptista, 'Portugal', pp. 77–8.
[44] For the reference for these, see above, p. 36. The second and fourth headings of the discussion are particularly relevant to this point.

formal proposals for ending the schism at this time was produced by two Germans, both of them theologians: Conrad of Gelnhausen and Henry of Langenstein. During the period from May 1379 to September 1381 they between them wrote four works; Langenstein his *Epistola pacis* in mid-1379 and his *Epistola concilii pacis* (more generally called the *Consilium pacis*) in mid-1381;[45] while Gelnhausen produced his *Epistola brevis* in August 1379 and completed his *Epistola concordiae* in May 1380.[46] The tracts fall into two pairs: the *Epistola pacis* and *Epistola brevis* represent the first datable calls for a conciliarist solution made at Paris, and the strong similarities in ideas expressed in the *Epistola concordiae* and *Consilium pacis* allow them to be treated together.[47] As a whole, these works were to prove the seminal works on conciliarism, their influence continuing through the schism, with the ideas which they contained being frequently borrowed by later writers. Their impact was immediate, provoking something in the nature of a dialogue.[48] Both writers, however, were to be disappointed in their hopes that a conciliarist solution would be adopted: after the death of King Charles V of France in 1380, both of them were to be forced to leave Paris when their opinions conflicted with the political ambitions of Louis of Anjou, and both died before the schism had been terminated.

The motives which produced the *Epistola pacis* and the *Epistola*

---

[45] For editions and commentaries on the *Epistola pacis*, see above, p. 37, n. 93. Chapters 1 and 2 of the *Consilium pacis* are printed in O. Hartwig, *Henricus de Langenstein, dictus de Hassia: Zwei Untersuchungen über das Leben und Schriften Heinrichs von Langenstein* (Marburg, 1857), part 2, pp. 28–31, with the remainder in *Hardt*, vol. 2, pp. 3–60, and Dupin, *Gersonii opera*, vol. 2, pp. 809–40. An epitome is in Scheuffgen, *Beiträge*, pp. 61–75, while an almost complete English translation is in M. Spinka, *Advocates of reform*, Library of Christian classics, vol. 14 (London, 1953), pp. 106–39. On the date, see *Valois*, vol. 1, pp. 356–7. For discussions of the work see ibid., vol. 1, pp. 356–8; Kneer, *Die Entstehung*, pp. 76–86; Bliemetzrieder, *Das Generalkonzil*, pp. 88–98; Luman, 'A conciliar suggestion', pp. 130–42.

[46] The *Epistola brevis* is printed in H. Kaiser, 'Der "Kurze Brief" des Konrad von Gelnhausen', *Historische Vierteljahrschrift*, **3** (1900), 381–6, with the date in the text. The *Epistola concordiae* is in *Thes. Nov. Anec.*, pp. 1200–26, and Bliemetzrieder, *Literarische Polemik*, pp. 111–40 (which gives the date at p. 140). An epitome is in Scheuffgen, *Beiträge*, pp. 77–82. For discussions, see Kneer, *Die Entstehung*, pp. 48–60; Martin, *Origines*, vol. 2, pp. 59–66; Ullmann, *Origins*, pp. 176–81; Bliemetzrieder, *Das Generalkonzil*, pp. 63–76.

[47] For the similarities, see Kneer, *Die Entstehung*, pp. 106–26; Scheuffgen, *Beiträge*, pp. 83–90.

[48] Kneer, *Die Entstehung*, pp. 74–5 and 75 n. 1; Hartwig, *Henricus de Langenstein*, part 1, p. 43 and n. 1; Bliemetzrieder, *Literarische Polemik*, pp. 64*–70*.

brevis were not identical, but their considerations of conciliarism produced virtually identical conclusions. The first work dealt with the possibility of a council only in its final chapters, as something of an appendix to Langenstein's discussion of the validity of the rival elections. Although the author clearly considered that a general council was the best possible method of securing a definitive determination of the issue, with a meeting of church leaders,[49] that this might be the sole effective means of reunification was never as fundamentally assumed as it was in the *Epistola brevis*.[50] Even so, it was Langenstein rather than Gelnhausen who provided the explicit definition of a council, borrowing from William of Ockham to define it as an assembly 'in qua diverse persone gerentes auctoritatem et vicem diversarum partium totius Christianitatis ad tractandum de com[m]uni bono rite convenirent' – a definition later to be used by Gelnhausen as well.[51] It was he who, although not giving any precise indication of what a council was, nevertheless outlined the programme which the meeting should adopt. His scheme, which sought to replace the descending, delegatory system of ecclesiastical authority by a more representative, ascending system, called for provincial or diocesan synods to precede the actual convocation of the general council.[52] That body was to meet under princely protection; but whilst emphasising the role which the secular authorities were to play in reuniting the church (with particular stress on the joint participation of Charles V of France and Wenceslas of Bohemia), the question of the mechanics of the convocation of the council was rather glossed over.[53] Langenstein gave it greater attention, suggesting that the onus for this lay with the rivals themselves in the first instance, arguing that they should issue a joint summons.[54] Both writers agreed on the necessity for the contenders to work together, remarking that a refusal to act by either would be tantamount to an admission of the falsity of his pretensions.[55]

---

[49] *BN*, MS Lat. 14644, fo. 160v, defining the prelates of the church as those 'ad quos spectat determinare auctoritative et obligative in consilio generali'.

[50] Kaiser, 'Der "Kurze Brief"', p. 382.

[51] MS cit., fo. 161r. For Ockham's definition and a comparison with that adopted by Gelnhausen in the *Epistola concordiae*, see Ullmann, *Origins*, p. 181 n. 1.

[52] Kaiser, 'Der "Kurze Brief"', p. 383.

[53] ibid., pp. 383–5.

[54] MS cit., fo. 160v.   [55] Kaiser, 'Der "Kurze Brief"', p. 385; MS cit., fo. 160v.

However, Langenstein did not agree with Gelnhausen's rejection of all other possible solutions to the problem. For the latter, only the *via concilii* could provide the definitive legal judgement on the issue which was required so that the whole church could reach agreement. Gelnhausen felt that other schemes, although they would lead to a *de facto* reunification of the church, would be merely temporary in their effects. Doubts would persist as to their validity, leaving the latent possibility of a revival of the dispute at some future date.[56] Langenstein accepted this view as applied to the *via facti*,[57] but considered that reunion could also be achieved by consultations between representatives of the three main parties (Urbanist, Clementist and neutralist).[58] Here lay the germ of the method which the rival claimants were themselves to advocate at a later stage of the dispute, the *via compromissi*, or way of arbitration and negotiation.

Although Gelnhausen and Langenstein often differed in their views, there was considerable similarity in the ideological bases for their conclusions. Both appealed, for example, to the same legal precept to justify the council: for the first time in the debates, academics cited the maxim that *quod omnes tangit, ab omnibus tractari et approbari debet*.[59] Conrad of Gelnhausen also invoked the Aristotelian concept of *epieikeia*, or equity, again apparently the first academic appeal to that concept in the debates.[60] This was a concept which was to be applied throughout the schism to provide a philosophical justification for actions which, although generally expedient, were equally often blatantly illegal in terms of the received ecclesiastical constitution.

The exposition of conciliarism begun in the *Epistola brevis* and *Epistola pacis* was continued in the *Epistola concordiae* and *Consilium pacis*, of which the former was the more important for

---

[56] Kaiser, 'Der "Kurze Brief" ', p. 385. [57] MS cit., fo. 160v.
[58] ibid., fos 161r–v.
[59] ibid., fo. 161r; Kaiser, 'Der "Kurze Brief" ', p. 383. For the history of this maxim, and its importance, see W. Ullmann, *Medieval papalism: the political theories of the medieval canonists* (London, 1949), pp. 21–4; Y. Congar, 'Quod omnes tangit, ab omnibus tractari et approbari debet', *Revue historique du droit français et étranger*, 4th series, **36** (1958), 210–59; A. Marongiu, 'Q.o.t., principe fondamental de la démocratie et du consentement au XIVᵉ siècle', in *Album Helen Maud Cam*, vol. 2 (Louvain, 1961), pp. 101–15.
[60] Kaiser, 'Der "Kurze Brief" ', p. 386. The concept is not defined, but its basis may be inferred from an earlier reference to natural reason, at p. 383.

the development of the conciliarist ecclesiology. The *Consilium pacis* was too dependent on Gelnhausen's work to add much to the theory, but was of importance as the first work to establish a definite link between church reform and ecclesiastical reunification, allowing the exploitation of a general trend for particular ends.[61] Langenstein's view of the issue differed markedly from that of Wyclif, who considered reform to be a necessity, but saw resolution of the schism as accidental.[62] The call for reform was not, however, new: in contemporary Bohemia members of the University of Prague were leading a reformist movement which, not yet tainted with heresy, incorporated a programme of popular involvement indicative of the general feeling within the church.[63] The *Concilium pacis* adapted this general mood to the provoking circumstances of the schism, calling not merely for reformation, but for re-formation of the divided church, a joint appeal which was frequently to be echoed in succeeding years through to the Council of Constance.

The *Epistola concordiae*, meanwhile, had been produced as a justification of the conciliarist ecclesiology. The background to its production well illustrates the involvement of academics in the discussions of the schism throughout Europe at this early stage of events. The work was intended very much as a counterblast to an anti-conciliarist work produced by Cardinal Petrus Amelius, which had in turn been produced in response to the *Epistola brevis*. Gelnhausen's second work was also meant as a riposte to the arguments of two other Clementist cardinals, Petrus de Barreria and Pierre Flandrin.[64] It was this responsive nature which accounted for the justificatory tone maintained throughout the *Epistola concordiae*, and although the ideas differed little from those of the earlier work, they were expanded and made more explicit.

As with the *Epistola brevis*, the basic premiss was that only a general council was capable of ending the schism, the main concern being to prove the necessity for such an assembly. This was

---

[61] Dupin, *Gersonii opera*, vol. 2, pp. 835–40; *Hardt*, vol. 2, pp. 48–59.
[62] See above, p. 52.
[63] On the Bohemian movement, see H. Kaminsky, *A history of the Hussite revolution* (Berkeley, 1967), pp. 7–23; Leff, *Heresy*, vol. 2, pp. 607–19.
[64] Bliemetzrieder, *Literarische Polemik*, pp. 73*–79*.

clear from the titles of the several chapters. Therefore, although Gelnhausen was occasionally concerned with practicalities, his main preoccupation was with theories; theories which were especially important for establishing the basic ecclesiology of conciliarism by inverting the previous system of papal monarchy in favour of a representative and comprehensive constitutional scheme. To this end the ancient definition of the church as the congregation of all the faithful was invoked, with strong Ockhamist overtones. Pope and cardinals became only a part of the church, not being themselves the church, and their continued existence was not considered necessary for the continued existence of the church itself.[65] Neither pope nor cardinals were to be considered infallible, both being inferior to the unerring universal church represented by the general council.[66] Gelnhausen justified the summoning of such an assembly without papal authorisation by an appeal to necessity, which overrode the law and legitimised actions taken in cases such as the present where there was no definitive legal ban.[67]

The theories propounded in the *Epistola concordiae* temporarily ended the process of defining the theory of conciliarism. The definition was important, but two individuals cannot be considered fully representative of what must have been a much wider movement, at least within the University of Paris. But other conciliarists did exist at Paris, the unnamed authors of ephemeral writings, and the identifiable Guillaume de Salvarvilla. A member of the Norman nation, and one of those who had defected to Urban VI after initially supporting Clement VII, Salvarvilla was (like the Germans) a theologian. It was possibly in April 1381 that he produced his *Determinatio pro concilio generali* [68] – a short work which, in its present form, probably provides only the heads of discussion, the brief notes which were later to be expanded *ex tempore*.

Following Gelnhausen and Langenstein, Salvarvilla argued that only a general council could provide an effective solution to the schism,[69] again appealing to the theory of necessity to justify actions intended to circumscribe the law.[70] The need for a council

---

[65] ibid., pp. 128-9.   [66] ibid., pp. 122-5.   [67] ibid., pp. 130-2.
[68] Printed in Bliemetzrieder, 'Conclusions de Guillaume de Salvarvilla', pp. 53-5.
[69] ibid., p. 53.   [70] ibid., p. 53.

was proved, arguments that the political situation in Europe made such an assembly physically impossible being dismissed as irrelevant. Salvarvilla also denied the possibility that the council might approve the wrong pope, claiming that it would be acting under divine inspiration, and that in any case the claimants could be expected to resign their claims to the council before any decision was taken. Moreover, the council was more likely to arrive at the truth than a war.[71] The problem of presidency was not properly considered, but it seems possible that he accepted that Urban, as first in possession, should preside.[72] Salvarvilla turned instead to justify his contention that the claimants should resign their claims to the council, revealing his belief that residual power within the church lay with that body, and ending with a plea that it should be supported by both prelates and princes. However, he could not resist showing his own prejudices by proclaiming his belief that Urban VI would eventually emerge triumphant.[73]

Just as important as these conciliarist schemes, and possibly more so as indicators of the generality of the concern for an end to the schism, are the more ephemeral works, the poems and pamphlets which circulated at Paris at this time – and which may have been distributed elsewhere, although none has survived. Five examples remain, all from 1381: one small tract, the *Epistola diaboli Leviathan*,[74] and four poems (the *Apologia super generali consilio*, the *Lamentatio ecclesie* and two others).[75] All are anonymous, although the *Epistola* is generally attributed to Pierre d'Ailly,[76] and the suggestion has been advanced that Guillaume de Salvarvilla may be responsible for some of the poems.[77]

---

[71] ibid., p. 54.   [72] ibid., p. 51, although the text itself (p. 54) is non-committal.
[73] ibid., p. 55.
[74] Printed in Tschackert, *Peter von Ailli*, pp. [15]-[21]. An English translation is in I. W. Raymond, 'D'Ailly's "Epistola diaboli Leviathan"', *Church History*, **22** (1953), 185-9, reprinted in C. M. D. Crowder, *Unity, heresy, and reform, 1378-1460: the conciliar response to the great schism*, Documents of medieval history, vol. 3 (London, 1977), pp. 41-5.
[75] The first two are printed in *Valois*, vol. 1, pp. 382-94, a third in Valois, 'Un poème de circonstance', pp. 220-38, and the fourth in P. Meyer and N. Valois, 'Poème en quatrains sur le grand schisme (1381)', *Romania*, **24** (1895), 210-18. See also Bliemetzrieder, *Das Generalkonzil*, pp. 77-83. On the university origins of the group, see Valois, 'Un poème de circonstance', pp. 211-12; Meyer and Valois, 'Poème en quatrains', p. 203.
[76] Raymond, 'D'Ailly's "Epistola"', p. 184, although the attribution doubted by *Valois*, vol. 1, p. 358.
[77] This is suggested by van Asseldonk (*De Neerlanden*, pp. 235-55), but the argument does not strike me as totally convincing.

The *Epistola diaboli Leviathan* dates from the time of the initial conflict between crown and gown over the acceptance of the *via concilii*, a time when the university found its plans obstructed by the concerted opposition of Louis of Anjou and the Clementist prelates. The response to this obstructionism was a highly satirical and vitriolic invective, representative of a *genre* (a letter addressed from a devil to his disciples) which was to be exploited quite frequently by polemicists during the schism. The writer clearly recognised that the Clementists were acting to defend their own interests against a possible Urbanist victory,[78] wilfully hiding behind the defences of human law whilst ignoring the church's overwhelming need and desire for union.[79] Even the French crown was indirectly attacked, as being dominated by Clementists who used their influence to continue the state's adherence to Clement VII and prevent any concrete action to end the schism.[80]

But whether the letter could have achieved anything is doubtful. Its purpose appears almost completely negative, being no more than an emotional outburst with no proper place in the conciliarist debates. This, however, was certainly not the case with the poems. Three of these fit into a definite cycle of debate, which may be dated to the period between March 1381 and the conciliarist declaration issued by the University of Paris on 20 May of that year. The fourth poem does not fit immediately into this group, dating from rather later in the year.[81] There are, however, reasons for supposing that it may have been written by the author of the *Apologia*, and may thus reflect the change in his opinions brought about by the effect of royal reaction to the university's declaration in favour of a general council. Unfortunately, although the poetry illustrates the vitality of contemporary Parisian debate on the schism at a critical period, its practical value is rather limited. The *Lamentatio* can be almost immediately dismissed: its few references to solving the schism are merely plagiarisms from the main conciliarist work, the *Apologia*.[82] The Clementist response to this last also added little, being utterly partisan in favour of the rebellious cardinals. Although the writer

---

[78] Tschackert, *Peter von Ailli*, p. [19].   [79] ibid., pp. [18]–[19].
[80] ibid., p. [18].
[81] *Valois*, vol. 1, pp. 349–56.
[82] *Valois*, vol. 1, p. 394, vv. 101–2; repeated ibid., vol. 1, pp. 383, 385, vv. 7, 24.

invoked princely intervention, with strong overtones of an appeal to the *via facti*, the council was completely rejected.[83]

Of all the poems, the *Apologia* was most vocal in its support for conciliarism, a belief in which underpinned the whole work. The author of this piece (and the writer of the fourth) asserted that rejection of a council by either party implied that the refusers doubted the validity of their own case.[84] Both writers were strongly opposed to the *via facti*;[85] but their attitudes to princely involvement differed, quite possibly as a reflection of the changed circumstances brought about when the French government turned against the *via concilii*. In any case, the author of the *Apologia* pleaded for royal assistance,[86] while the other poet (if it was a different person) rejected princely intervention, arguing that the schism was a purely ecclesiastical matter.[87] Despite this, it is hard to avoid the feeling that he would probably have welcomed royal support for a policy defined by clerics.

The main importance of such poetry derives not from any ideological content it may have, but from the information which it provides on the nature of the debates at Paris. Although there are numerous references to the discussions there between 1378 and 1383, these verses give the first solid indication of the nature and development of the arguments. The main suggestion which they convey is that (despite the earlier tractarian controversies) there may well have been a snowballing of interest from the initial impact made by the *Apologia* in March 1381,[88] the debates increasing through to the formal declaration accepting the *via concilii* on 20 May.[89] The provisional and qualified nature of the official acceptance of conciliarism by the English nation certainly suggests that the developments had been rapid, and that some members of the nation were not yet fully convinced of the validity of that solution, and had not had time to consult their native authorities for advice and instructions. Prior to 1381 the nature of the debate is probably best illustrated by Conrad of Geln-

---

83 See Valois, 'Un poème de circonstance', p. 215.
84 *Valois*, vol. 1, p. 385, v. 24; Meyer and Valois, 'Poème en quatrains', p. 215, v. 47.
85 *Valois*, vol. 1, pp. 383, 385-6, vv. 6-7, 27, 42; Meyer and Valois, 'Poème en quatrains', p. 216, v. 49.
86 *Valois*, vol. 1, p. 388, v. 54.
87 Meyer and Valois, 'Poème en quatrains', p. 214, v. 36.
88 Valois, 'Un poème de circonstance', p. 220, lines 1-8, and *Valois*, vol. 1, p. 382, vv. 47-51, both suggest that the debates had not yet begun.
89 *Ch. Paris.*, no. 1637.

hausen, who had addressed his conciliarist appeals not to the university but to the king. He recognised, as the university would soon have to do so, that the political realities of the situation meant that it would be the crown which would take the truly effective and decisive steps in determining French policy. Indeed, Gelhausen's approaches seem to have had the desired effect, for only shortly before he died Charles V announced his conversion to acceptance of the conciliarist case. Unfortunately, his death in September 1380 meant that there was little possibility of his declaration bearing fruit.

Although the earliest conciliarist debate within the University of Paris is to some extent shrouded in obscurity, there can be no doubting the impact which the eventual conciliarist declaration of May 1381 produced. While in itself rather innocuous, its effects were far-reaching. For the declaration presented nothing less than a blatant challenge to Louis of Anjou, who had only recently taken over the government, and whose whole political future was inextricably involved in an alliance with Clement VII. Anjou's hopes for the Neapolitan crown – the reversion of which after the death of Queen Joanna I had been secured for him by Clement VII – combined with the Avignonese pope's own hopes for a military victory in Italy which would utterly defeat his rival for the papacy to produce a mutual desire for action in the form of the *via facti*. When the Parisian masters decided in favour of conciliarism, Anjou soon reacted to what he can only have considered an act of rebellion, especially when it coincided with the dispute over the rival Clementist and Urbanist chancellors. Jean Rousse, who addressed the prince on the declaration, was arrested and thrown into prison,[90] where he was joined by several other academics.[91] When the rector of the university had the audacity to read out a letter from Urban VI during a congregation, further threats issued forth.[92] Those who had been imprisoned were eventually released only after swearing adherence to Clement VII, and promising never to discuss the *via concilii* – an imposition which was later extended to the whole university.[93]

[90] *Valois*, vol. 1, pp. 341–3.   [91] Meyer and Valois, 'Poème en quatrains', p. 216, v. 54.
[92] *Valois*, vol. 1, pp. 344–5; *Ch. Paris.*, no. 1640. The precise chronology of the events of this period is rather obscure.
[93] Meyer and Valois, 'Poème en quatrains', p. 216, vv. 54–5; *Chron. S. Den.*, vol. 1, p. 88.

Although this blunt treatment was resented, the university was effectively impotent against the duke. The only alternative to submission was flight, and from 1381 to at least 1383 there was a fairly persistent exodus from Paris, the numbers of those leaving probably amounting to several hundred overall. Only some of those who went can be identified, but they included the three main conciliarists, Salvarvilla, Gelnhausen and Langenstein.[94] Many other Germans deserted Paris, while numbered among the French exiles were several of the university officers involved in the affair of the chancellors and the conflict with Louis of Anjou.[95] Several of them later gained promotion from Urban VI, although until their flight most do not seem to have revealed openly Urbanist sympathies.

However, to equate exile with loyalty to Urban VI or belief in conciliarism would be too simplistic – many of those involved probably left Paris for other more personal reasons. The continued difficulties between the university and the mendicant orders may account for the Dominican decision to transfer *en masse* to Prague in 1383,[96] although the choice of university may be significant. Moreover, although the French majority at Paris is likely to have been involved in the conciliarist debates as much as the other nations and faculties, it is significant that generally only those most directly involved in the conflicts can be identified among the exiles. The example afforded by Pierre d'Ailly at this point was probably not atypical of the French reaction to Louis of Anjou's onslaught: he simply retired to Noyon, and did not return to the university until 1383.[97]

As conciliarism itself was not the sole cause of the exodus, as far as the Germans were concerned this movement cannot be considered as a panic-stricken rush to escape from Clementist France. It was very much a lengthy process, both in total and for the individuals involved: Matthias of Janov, for example, arranged his departure from Paris at a very leisurely pace.[98] However, the number of exiles and the pace of the exodus probably increased

[94] *Valois*, vol. 1, pp. 367–8. [95] ibid., vol. 1, p. 367.
[96] Kaminsky, *Hussite revolution*, p. 24.
[97] Salembier, *Pierre d'Ailly*, pp. 62, 66.
[98] E. Valasek, *Das Kirchenverständniss des Prager Magisters Matthias von Janov (1350/55–1393)*, Lateranum, N.S. vol. 37 (Rome, 1971), p. 40.

after the university was forced into submission by Louis of Anjou. It is obvious that conciliarist discussions had occurred within the university long before May 1381 and these, despite their apparently public character, had never been banned. But once the formal decision was taken and the duke realised what it meant, then there came the reaction. To prevent a fifth column developing within the university during his projected absence in Italy, Louis felt that he had to silence both the proponents of conciliarism and the opponents of Clement VII. However, there is no sign of a deliberate policy of expulsion: throughout the schism a small but vocal Romanist party maintained a precarious existence at Paris, and similar groups may have existed at the provincial universities. But Louis of Anjou settled the dispute over conciliarism by brute force. Not for the last time, the course adopted by the University of Paris had led to conflict with the French government; and not for the last time the masters suffered and were effectively defeated, submitting thereafter to a long period of passive obedience and acquiescence in the royal policy.

Chapter 4

A BREATHING SPACE

In contrast with the debates, divisions and conflicts of the opening years of the schism, the second half of the 1380s was a period of comparative peace, almost of anticlimax. The territorial boundaries of the rival obediences were now reasonably firmly defined, and both sides seem to have retreated to within their own frontiers. However, there was, naturally enough, a certain amount of continued skirmishing in the border regions, and neither party was prepared to accept the existence of its rival without question. The Urbanist branch of the Augustinian order continued to nominate lectors at the Clementist universities and *studia*, in preparation for their eventual submission to Urban VI – but cautiously ensured that the nominees were actually given posts at Romanist institutions.[1] The Clementists also occasionally gave vent to outbursts of optimism: an anonymous author in 1394 proudly asserted that the obedience had suffered no reduction in size since the start of the dispute – not even in Portugal.[2]

Within the universities the late 1380s and early 1390s were years of considerably diminished debate. Very few tracts survive from this period, almost the only ones worth mentioning being the surviving fragments of Adalbertus Rankonis de Ericinio's *Tractatus de schismate*, produced within the University of Prague,[3] and Marsilius of Inghen's *Rationes cur Urbano pontifici electo adhaerendum*, written at Heidelberg.[4] Both these works were little more than restatements of the arguments about alle-

[1] E. Ypma, 'Notice sur le "Studium" de Paris au début du schisme d'occident', *Augustiniana*, 18 (1968), 82–99.

[2] *BN*, MS Lat. 1481, fo. 23r.

[3] J. Kadlec, *Leben und Schriften des Prager Magisters Adalbert Rankonis de Ericinio, aus dem Nachlass von Rudolf Holinka und Jan Vilikovský*, Beiträge zur Geschichte der Philosophie und Theologie des Mittelalters, N.F., vol. 4 (Münster, 1971), pp. 50–7, 339–42.

[4] Ritter, *Marsilius von Inghen*, pp. 31–2, 196–204.

giance. The most striking silence throughout this period is that of the French universities. Indeed, all over Europe the apparent entrenchment of the schism seems to have produced a sort of hopeless acceptance of its permanence, an attitude which certainly permeates Matthias of Janov's monumental *Regulae veteris et novi testamenti*, produced at Prague after he had left Paris.[5] In his comments on the schism, Janov remarked that he saw no end to the problem unless the church acted to reform itself.

The academic silence on the schism cannot simply be attributed to wilful indifference. The expansion of universities within Germany diverted several of the major theorists to more practical and immediate administrative problems, Marsilius of Inghen and Henry of Langenstein being among those thus distracted, respectively at the Universities of Heidelberg and Vienna.[6] Other universities faced their own distractions: in England, Cambridge suffered badly during the Peasants' Revolt of 1381, while at Oxford there was a purge of Wycliffites in 1382, and serious rioting between northerners and southerners in 1388.[7] On the continent, Prague suffered from serious disputes between Czechs and Germans in 1384, and internal disputes – especially the dealings over Jean Blanchart's abuse of the chancellorship and a continuing dispute over the Immaculate Conception with members of the mendicant orders – constantly distracted the Parisian masters.[8]

Nevertheless, the schism remained a matter of interest and concern to the universities and their members as individuals. This is

---

[5] V. Kybal and O. Odložilík (eds), *Matěje z Janova, mistra Pařížského, 'Regulae veteris et novi testamenti'*, Sbírka pramenů českého hnutí náboženského, vols. 9–13 (5 vols., Innsbruck and Prague, 1908–26); see also Valasek, *Das Kirchenverständniss*, pp. 157–60; Leff, *Heresy*, vol. 2, p. 615.

[6] Ritter, *Marsilius von Inghen*, pp. 36–9; J. Lang, *Die Christologie bei Heinrich von Langenstein*, Freiburger theologische Studien, vol. 85 (Freiburg-im-Breisgau, 1966), pp. 22–6.

[7] For Cambridge, see C. Oman, *The great revolt of 1381*, 2nd edn (Oxford, 1969), pp. 125–7, 131–2. For Oxford, see J. H. Dahmus, *William Courtenay, Archbishop of Canterbury, 1381–1396* (University Park, Pa., 1966), pp. 84–102, 104–6; J. R. Lumby, *Chronicon Henrici Knighton*, Rolls Series, vol. 92 (2 vols., London, 1889–95), vol. 2, p. 258.

[8] The Prague disturbances are dealt with in V. Chaloupecký, *The Caroline University of Prague: its foundation, character, and development in the fourteenth century* (Prague, 1948), pp. 99–101. For the Parisian disputes, see *Ch. Paris.*, nos. 1504–22, 1557–83; *Bulaeus*, vol. 4, pp. 599–614, 618–34; Salembier, *Pierre d'Ailly*, pp. 67–76; Brady, 'Immaculate Conception', pp. 197–201.

clear from the mass of scattered evidence of varying types, *rotuli* being the most important. A large number of these were constructed by universities of both obediences in the years between 1383 and 1390, the year in which academic activity on the dispute began to revive. The Urbanists took full advantage of their new foundations, of the accession of Boniface IX in 1389, and of the Jubilee proclaimed for 1390, as opportunities to display their loyalty by sending lists of petitions, while on the Clementist side almost every embassy to Avignon seems to have taken a roll of some sort, although large compilations were restricted to a few specific occasions. The Parisian declarations for Clement VII in 1383 and 1387 were fully exploited, as were the successive statements of the Spanish kingdoms.[9] Of these Clementist rolls, two merit especial attention. One is the roll sent by the University of Toulouse in 1387, which reveals a notable reduction in the numbers attending that university from English-held Gascony, presumably as a result of the renewed Anglo-French war.[10] More intriguing than this is a roll (which now appears to be lost) which some members of the University of Bologna sent to Clement VII in 1388.[11] This may have been dispatched by members of the Spanish College to commemorate the recent Aragonese declaration in favour of Clement VII, but it may have another explanation. Given the contemporary activity of French envoys in Italy,

[9] Paris sent rolls almost annually from 1385–89 (Watt, 'University clerks and petitions', pp. 226–7; *Ch. Paris.*, nos. 1496, 1537–41). Angers despatched a *rotulus* in 1384–85 (Fournier, *Statuts*, vol. 3, p. 515), as did Orléans in 1388 (Watt, 'University clerks and petitions', p. 228; Denifle, *Les universités*, pp. 50–1). Members of the University of Salamanca appeared on several rolls sent privately in the later 1380s, while the university constructed its own *rotulus c.* 1388 (J. Goñi Gaztambide, 'Tres rótulos de la universidad de Salamanca de 1381, 1389, y 1393', *Anthologica Annua*, 11 (1963), 290–4; Beltrán de Heredia, *Bulario*, no. 186). Among the Urbanist universities, the new German establishments sent numerous rolls: Heidelberg in 1387 and 1389 (E. Winkelmann, *Urkundenbuch der Universität Heidelberg* (2 vols., Heidelberg, 1886), vol. 2, nos. 33, 46); Cologne in 1389–90 (H. Keussen, *Die Rotuli der Kölner Universität*, Mitteilungen aus dem Stadtarchiv von Köln, vol. 7, part 20 (Cologne, 1891), pp. 2–3); while the masters of Vienna discussed a roll in 1386, and sent one in 1389–90 (P. Uiblein, *Acta facultatis artium universitatis Vindobonensis, 1384–1416*, Publikationen des Instituts für österreichische Geschichtsforschung, 6 Reihe: Quellen zur Geschichte der Universität Wien, vol. 2 (Graz, 1968), pp. 10–11, 41–6, 48, 51–3). The University of Cambridge also prepared a roll which it intended to send to Boniface IX in 1390 (E. F. Jacob, *Essays in the conciliar epoch*, 3rd edn, Manchester, 1963, p. 229).

[10] C. E. Smith, *The University of Toulouse in the middle ages* (Milwaukee, 1958), pp. 149, 209.   [11] *Chron. S. Den.*, vol. 1, pp. 516–19; *Valois*, vol. 2, p. 148.

seeking defections from Urban VI, and the fact that 1388 saw a Bolognese revolt against that pope, it is possible that this stray *rotulus* represents a serious attempt by the University of Bologna to transfer its allegiance.[12] It appears that an oath of allegiance to Urban VI was being imposed within the university in 1388; but as only one instance appears to be recorded, whether this imposition was in any sense general is uncertain.[13]

Apart from the *rotuli*, concrete evidence of personal allegiances is also provided by occasional corporate declarations and individual flights. When John II of Aragon declared for Avignon, Matthew de Clementis escaped to the newly-founded Urbanist university at Heidelberg.[14] Jean de Montson, his theories on the Immaculate Conception discredited at Paris, and the pursuit of him having extended to Avignon, transferred his allegiance to Urban VI, and thereafter appears as an energetic supporter of the Roman line.[15] There had also been unexplained defections among the Clementists at Toulouse.[16] Those Englishmen who were attending the University of Avignon in 1378, and who had there subscribed a roll which was delivered to Clement VII in Italy, may also have changed their minds, although the precise interpretation of the evidence is uncertain. Both John de Wyke and Thomas Southam appeared on this *rotulus*, and yet both continued their ecclesiastical careers in England without interruption, so had presumably remained loyal to Urban VI.[17] The career of John Acton, a Dominican and graduate of Oxford, progressed less smoothly, receiving a major interruption when he was forced to leave England, quite possibly because his Clementist proselytising had aroused the wrath of the king.[18] During the pontificate of Benedict XIII, Acton was to gain considerable notoriety as one of the chief defenders of the legitimacy of the Avignonese succession. At Bologna, the Spanish College continued to send petitions for

---

12 *Valois*, vol. 2, pp. 147–50.
13 *Chartularium studii Bononiensis* (13 vols., Bologna, 1909–40), vol. 4, p. 161.
14 See above, p. 31, n. 57.
15 For his case, see above, n. 8.
16 *Valois*, vol. 1, p. 306.
17 The *rotulus* is in Denifle, *Les universités*, pp. 83–5, the English petitions being abstracted in Bliss, *Petitions*, vol. 1, p. 544. For Southam and Wyke see A. B. Emden, *A biographical register of the University of Oxford to 1500* (3 vols., Oxford, 1957–59), vol. 3, pp. 1733, 2109.
18 *Bulaeus*, vol. 5, p. 40.

benefices to Avignon,[19] while at Paris only the Scots and some inhabitants of the Burgundian lands appeared as representatives of the English nation on *rotuli* sent to Clement VII.[20] There is also the remote possibility that a small Clementist group lingered on at the University of Lisbon.[21]

But individuals and small minorities could not do much about the overall problem of the schism, although they could occasionally reveal the impact which the ecclesiastical division was making on the universities and their members. Thus, Jean Blanchart complained that the schism had led to his impoverishment by reducing the number of benefices which he held.[22] The split also caused administrative problems within the universities. The most important of these was the serious decline of the German nation at the University of Orléans. By 1384 the situation there was so bad that the nation had been forced to pawn its seal.[23] The exodus of the Germans to Prague (where their increased numbers may account for growing rivalry between the nations), and the subsequent expansion of universities within the Holy Roman Empire, had now made it unnecessary for Germans to leave their homeland in order to study. Even the University of Paris may have been affected by this situation, if the *lacuna* in the *Acta* of the English nation there between 1383 and 1392 is of any significance.[24]

In addition to these difficulties, the ghosts of the Parisian conflict between the rival Urbanist and Clementist chancellors still lingered. The Urbanists continued to dispute the validity of degrees conferred by the 'antipapal' chancellor, although the position regarding their own admission to degrees was clarified by Pope Boniface IX in the early years of his pontificate.[25] The pope's action may have been in response to events at the University of Heidelberg in 1386–87, where the masters had refused to recognise the qualifications of Parisian graduates who wished to enroll

[19] Beltrán de Heredia, *Bulario*, no. 197.
[20] *Ch. Paris.*, vol. 3, pp. 462–3. This situation was repeated with the roll sent in 1403 (ibid., vol. 4, pp. 109–10). For an assessment of the fraction of the English nation represented on these Parisian rolls, see Verger, 'Le recrutement géographique', p. 868.
[21] Moreira de Sá, *Chartularium*, no. 412.   [22] *Bulaeus*, vol. 4, p. 606.
[23] Fournier, *Statuts*, vol. 1, pp. 145, 152.
[24] *Auct. Ch.*, vol. 1, pp. 660–1 and 660 n. 1.   [25] *Ch. Paris.*, no. 1672.

at the new university, but who had received their degrees from the Clementist chancellor.[26]

Amongst these administrative wranglings there was little sign of any developments in the intellectual approach to the problem of the schism and the need for ecclesiastical reunification. The first signs of a revival of university interest in these problems do not really appear until 1390–91, with the development of a debate at Paris on the academics' right to consider the issues. This may, however, have been the second such attempt to revitalise the discussions. Bulaeus suggests that in 1387 the Parisian masters had made approaches to both Charles VI and Clement VII, in an attempt to make some progress.[27] The pope may have responded favourably to these advances: in 1389 he was a willing partner in attempts made by John of Gaunt to revive European political discussions of the issues.[28] The French king, however, was less encouraging, and it may well be that his rejection of the masters' approaches provided the background for another formal Parisian declaration of support for the Avignonese pope.[29] The university's precise proposals are not recorded, but there is a possibility that they may be echoed in two passages of Philippe de Mézières' *Songe du vieil pèlerin*, a work completed in 1387–89. Although it may be that the writer was merely recalling the arguments advanced at Paris during the debates of 1379–82, the mechanics of the general council proposed in the *Songe* are not incompatible with Bulaeus' suggestion that the *via cessionis* was among the Parisian proposals of 1387. As an alternative, to be adopted if conciliarism failed, de Mézières argued for a version of the *via facti*, which was virtually a French formulation of the scheme put forward by Henry of Langenstein in his *Epistola exhortatoria*.[30]

Apart from this brief and obscure spasm of activity, the debates on the schism within the universities appear to have stagnated

[26] A. Thorbeke, *Die älteste Zeit der Universität Heidelberg, 1386–1449* (Heidelberg, 1886), pp. 29–30; Winkelmann, *Urkunderbuch*, vol. 2, nos. 34–5; *Ch. Paris.*, nos. 1656–8.

[27] *Bulaeus*, vol. 4, p. 618.

[28] J. J. N. Palmer, *England, France, and Christendom, 1377–99* (London, 1972), p. 191.

[29] *Ch. Paris.*, no. 1655; *Bulaeus*, vol. 4, p. 618; *Valois*, vol. 2, p. 394.

[30] Philippe de Mézières [ed. G. W. Coopland], *Le songe du vieil pèlerin* (2 vols., Cambridge, 1969), vol. 2, pp. 293–6, 439–40.

until 1390, when there was renewed agitation for the restoration of academic freedom of discussion at Paris. Precisely why this should have revived then is uncertain. It may have been in reaction to the peace negotiations between England and France in 1389, and John of Gaunt's project for an international conference on the schism. There is, however, no evidence of direct French involvement in this latter scheme.[31] The precise chronology of the revival of interest at Paris is somewhat uncertain, although the sequence of events seems clear. Following a large congregation of masters the university sent a delegation to address the king. Its leader – possibly Gilles des Champs[32] – delivered a forceful speech, emphasising the need for an end to the schism, and reminding the king and the princes of their obligations to work towards union.[33] The exhortation did not, however, have the desired effect: the university had misjudged its timing. With the ending of the Anglo-French war Charles VI and his relatives were increasingly attracted by Italian adventures – principally Louis II of Anjou's inherited Neapolitan aspirations and Louis of Orléans' hopes of carving a 'kingdom of Adria' out of the papal states. These projects were all seen as part of yet another French programme to solve the schism by the *via facti,* Clement VII being taken to Italy with the French conquerors and imposed on Rome as the sole pope. The shadows of this policy were to influence French governmental action on the schism for the next few years, until the whole plan collapsed in 1391.[34] The steps taken by the university to revive its debates coincided with the first stages of this policy, and the reaction of the French government was suitably blunt. The approaches were rejected, Charles VI threatening the masters with his displeasure, and imposing silence on them.[35] This renewed royal ban on debates was supported by the lawyers,[36] a situation which provides the *terminus post quem* for the first major surviving Parisian tract on the schism for almost a decade. This is the *quaestio* on the theme *Utrum Parisiensis*

31 Palmer, *England,* pp. 191–2.
32 *Valois,* vol. 2, pp. 396–7.
33 ibid.
34 Palmer, *England,* pp. 192–3; J. J. N. Palmer, 'English foreign policy, 1388–1399', in *The reign of Richard II: essays in honour of May McKisack,* ed. F. R. H. du Boulay and C. M. Barron (London, 1971), pp. 87–100.
35 *Valois,* vol. 2, p. 397; *Chron. S. Den.,* vol. 1, pp. 694–5.   36 *Valois,* vol. 2, p. 397.

universitas ad prosequendum unionem ecclesiae ad semper et pro semper obligatur.[37] Although the work is anonymous it may be attributable to either Gilles des Champs or Jean Gerson.[38] Given the timing of its appearance, the work presumably contains many of the arguments earlier outlined to the king by the university's delegates, even if the aim differed slightly from that occasion.

While obviously in a tradition derived from the earlier conciliarist writers, this tract was little concerned with conciliarism itself. The main concern was to justify the ecclesiastical position of the universities, especially that of Paris, firmly establishing both their position in the church's order of precedence and their right to debate theological issues. The author asserted the institutionalisation of the academics' role within the church, claiming that the doctors had been established and empowered by the church as a whole to advise the prelates on ecclesiastical issues.[39] The basic premiss of the whole discussion rested on the intolerability of schism and the obligation of all to work for reunion.[40] Throughout, the latent importance of Parisian involvement in the debate was assumed, while doctoral negligence was viciously attacked.[41] The author – arguing from a standpoint which revealed his immense pride in being a member of the university[42] – claimed that rejection of the university's claim to participate in the debates was an error in faith.[43] For him the university simply had to debate the issue, because of its privileged position within the church, the negligence of the prelates and the university's national position as an adviser to the crown.[44]

The writer also gave some consideration to the methods of attaining union (favouring conciliarism and rejecting arbitration[45]) before turning to what was for him a more pressing matter: the question of the royal ban on debates and the support which this had received from the lawyers. These matters had been mentioned at the start of the tract among the reasons for there being no debate whatsoever,[46] but both claims were abruptly

---

[37] *Glorieux*, no. 253a; *Ch. Paris.*, no. 1663; *Valois*, vol. 2, p. 397; Bliemetzrieder, *Das Generalkonzil*, pp. 115–17.

[38] *Ch. Paris.*, vol. 3, p. 595.

[39] *Glorieux*, vol. 6, pp. 7, 9, 16.

[40] ibid., vol. 6, p. 5.

[41] ibid., vol. 6, p. 11.

[42] ibid., vol. 6, pp. 15–16.

[43] ibid., vol. 6, p. 16.

[44] ibid., vol. 6, pp. 16–17.

[45] ibid., vol. 6, pp. 6, 10–11.

[46] ibid., vol. 6, p. 2.

rejected. The lawyers were accused of error, almost of heresy, and were at one point actually labelled schismatics.[47] The rejection of royal authority followed naturally from the author's definition of the ecclesiological status of the university: if their position within the church placed the universities under a positive obligation to debate the schism, then to deny both the position and the obligation must be an error.

Although there is no sign that this tract had any immediate effect, its author (if he was not Gerson) was not the only academic urging the king to take action. For Jean Gerson preached his sermon *Adorabunt* before the king on 6 January 1391, possibly after the renewed ban on university activity,[48] and again called for liberty of discussion and royal action to end the schism.[49] But it was not until June 1392, when he delivered his sermon *Accipietis*, that Gerson made his first valid practical contribution to the debates, calling for an end to Anglo-French hostilities and joint action by Charles VI and Richard II to achieve ecclesiastical reunion.[50]

By the time Gerson came to preach this sermon, the Parisian movement to regain freedom of discussion had gained considerable momentum. Robert du Quesnoy seems to have first become involved in the issues of the schism in 1392,[51] and it was possibly about this time that Johannes de Moravia (later elected proctor of the English nation to work for reunion[52]) began his own public preaching on the subject.[53] There are also indications that the debates were beginning to percolate down from the masters to the students. Both Pierre de Plaoul and Jean Gerson included references to the schism in their lectures in 1393,[54] but the impact which their pronouncements had on their listeners is uncertain, and the net result may have been merely to compound confusion.[55]

---

[47] ibid., vol. 6, pp. 19–20.
[48] *Glorieux*, no. 342. See also *Valois*, vol. 3, pp. 395–6; J. B. Morrall, *Gerson and the great schism* (Manchester, 1960), pp. 30–3.
[49] *Glorieux*, vol. 7/2, pp. 530–4.
[50] *Glorieux*, no. 340. See also Morrall, *Gerson*, pp. 33–4.
[51] *BN*, MS Lat. 1480A2, p. 254.
[52] *Auct. Ch.*, vol. 1, pp. 687, 689–91.
[53] At least, such is suggested by Simon de Cramaud: *BN*, MS Lat. 1475, fo. 36v.
[54] P. Glorieux, 'L'année universitaire 1392–1393 à la Sorbonne à travers les notes d'un étudiant', *Revue des sciences religieuses*, **19** (1939), 444–5.   [55] ibid., p. 441.

Nevertheless, once begun, the movement for academic involvement in the European debates on the schism could hardly be
stopped. During the years in which the discussions mushroomed –
the years between the deaths of Urban VI in 1389 and of Clement
VII in 1394 – the academic community of Europe, under the
leadership of the University of Paris, at last showed signs of
becoming a constructive and cohesive force in the progress towards
the reunification of the church.

In France, the collapse of the policy centred on the Italian
ventures had permitted a steady expansion of discussion of the
schism, but this still required a more dramatic impetus to allow
further effective development. This impetus was provided in
1392–3 by the mission sent to Charles VI by Boniface IX as part
of his own programme for seeking an end to the schism.[56] This
mission proved to be the dynamic for the complete overthrow of
the royal ban on discussion within the university, and the scope
of the debates rapidly increased. Believing the Romanist ambassadors to have encountered difficulties and indeed imprisonment
at Avignon, the University of Paris appealed to the king on their
behalf.[57] It was presumably on this occasion that Charles VI
proclaimed his desire for reunion.[58] The masters responded to
this pronouncement, and to the reception of the Roman envoys,
with public celebrations in January 1393.[59] Although there are
difficulties about the precise dating, it may have been on the
occasion of this meeting between the king and the university
representatives that Gilles des Champs presented a series of
five conclusions on the schism. These included advocacy of
the *via cessionis*, combined with the hint of possible withdrawal of obedience from the rival popes in order to force its
implementation.[60]

More precise indications of the nature of the debates at Paris
at the time of the visit by Boniface IX's envoys may be gained

---

[56] For the pope's letter, see *Chron. S. Den.*, vol. 2, pp. 48–53.

[57] ibid., vol. 2, pp. 54–5; *Valois*, vol. 2, p. 400.

[58] This may be inferred from the claim for expenses made by the royal messenger to
Avignon, *Valois*, vol. 2, p. 400 n. 5.

[59] *Chron. S. Den.*, vol. 2, pp. 56–7; *Ch. Paris.*, no. 1665. On the whole episode, see
Glorieux, 'L'année universitaire', pp. 478–81; *Valois*, vol. 2, pp. 398–403.

[60] *Ch. Paris.*, no. 1666; *Valois*, vol. 2, p. 404; Bliemetzrieder, *Das Generalkonzil*,
p. 118.

from the extant section of Jean Gerson's disputation for his mastership in theology, his tract *De jurisdictione spirituali*.[61] Although this work is of intrinsic importance as a declaration of Gerson's personal attitudes on the schism at what was very much the start of his public career,[62] its main importance derives from the circumstances of its appearance. For the disputation was delivered under the presidency of the chancellor of the university himself, Pierre d'Ailly, in December 1392. Its subject matter – the validity or otherwise of the resignation of spiritual authority – and the involvement of the chancellor together highlighted the university's determination to speak out on the schism, regardless of the attitude which might be adopted by the crown.

The disputation itself dealt with the three issues which required settlement before any effective solution could be applied to the schism: 'an spectat ad fidem quod sit unum caput in Ecclesia Dei; . . . an scandalizati et qui non tenant partem veram faciant hoc ex pura malitia; . . . an verisimilis sit via melior et sanctior quam per resignationem aut oblationem ad resignandum'.[63] The wording of the last of these points reveals an obvious bias in favour of the *via cessionis*, which continues throughout the tract. The possibilities of the *via facti* and conciliarism were discussed, but turned down,[64] and although Gerson did consider anti-cessionist arguments, his responses were somewhat superficial. Even so, the scope of the discussion at so early a stage in the revived debates within the university reveals that there must have been a good deal of thought given to the alternative solutions, and is a striking tribute to the masters' refusal to accept any royally imposed ignorance. Moreover, although the ideas expounded in the *De jurisdictione spirituali* were still rather primitive in form, the work contained hints of possible future developments. Gerson's statements that the pope and the cardinals were obliged to resign if so required, coupled with an implicit attack on those who refused to act to end the schism as being *ipso facto* perpetrators of heresy,[65] are especially significant. For

61 *Glorieux*, no. 87. See also Morrall, *Gerson*, pp. 24–8; G. H. M. Posthumus Meyjes, *Jean Gerson: zijn Kerkpolitiek en Ecclesiologie* (The Hague, 1963), pp. 23–9.
62 Posthumus Meyjes, *Jean Gerson*, p. 28.
63 *Glorieux*, vol. 3, p. 3.
64 ibid., vol. 3, pp. 6–7. 65 ibid., vol. 3, p. 7.

these are the first signs of an argument which rapidly assumed prime importance in tracts produced in the search for an end to the division, equating persistent schism with heresy in order to provide the formal justification for the deposition of both claimants, precisely as was to happen at the Council of Pisa in 1409.

The reception of the Roman embassy at Paris produced an immediate reaction at Avignon. Clement VII sent his own advocates to counter the effect of the Roman agents,[66] and also sought to strengthen his party within the university. Jean Goulain, a master of theology, was commissioned as one of his chief defenders, arguing in favour of the *via facti* and the forced expulsion of Boniface IX from Rome. In June 1393, Cardinal Pedro de Luna was also sent to Paris to support Clement's cause. Both advocates received a hostile reception: Goulain was excluded from the proceedings of the university for a while, and the cardinal was subjected to an address by Guillaume Barrault which restated the earlier propositions of des Champs. Possibly these admonitions had the desired effect, as Goulain's exclusion proved to be merely temporary, while Pedro de Luna – if he had needed to be convinced – made a public declaration of his acceptance of the *via cessionis*.[67]

But not all Clementist opposition to the university's activities was to be dealt with so easily. During 1393–94 the Archbishop of Narbonne led a concerted attempt to obstruct any revival of royal activity on the schism,[68] while Clement VII himself sought to intervene by attempting to draw some of the university leaders (notably d'Ailly and des Champs) to Avignon. His plan failed when the individuals concerned refused to leave Paris.[69] In the midst of these activities, others were also trying to influence the university, as in the case of Bernard Alemand, who sent a copy of his own tract on the schism to the masters for their consideration.[70]

For the reviving interest in the schism which became apparent

[66] *Ch. Paris.*, no. 1664.
[67] *Ch. Paris.*, nos. 1667, 1669–70, 1673; *Chron. S. Den.*, vol. 2, pp. 58–61; *Valois*, vol. 2, pp. 419–25; *Auct. Ch.*, vol. 1, pp. 680–1; and also Ehrle, *Alpartils Chronica*, p. 411. [68] *Valois*, vol. 2, pp. 425–6.
[69] ibid., vol. 2, p. 421. [70] ibid., vol. 2, p. 406; *Ch. Paris.*, no. 1671.

in 1393–94 was not a matter which affected the University of Paris alone. After 1381 the masters realised that, although the university might discuss the issues, it was the crown which controlled practicalities. Consequently, although there was still no decision on what policy should be urged on the king, the academics acknowledged that he would need to be convinced both of the need for action and of the importance of the role which he should allot to the university in advising him on the matter. This concern found poetic expression in Jean Petit's *Complainte de l'église*,[71] composed between April 1393 and January 1394.[72] Bewailing the degeneration which the schism had produced within the church, Petit reminded the king of his duty towards that body,[73] and summarised the means which the university was ready to place at his disposal in order to remedy the schism.[74] The poem was not merely intended for King Charles VI: it also called for action by the royal dukes and foreign rulers.[75]

Meanwhile, the university's preparations for action moved inexorably on. January 1394 witnessed a kind of referendum among the academics, who were invited to submit comments on a list of nine questions dealing with the schism.[76] Many of the matters raised had already been dealt with in *Utrum Parisiensis universitas*, but the most biting questions – and those which were undoubtedly intended to attract the most attention – had no connection with the earlier work. These requested a judgement on

---

[71] *BN*, MS Fr. 12470, fos 1r–5r. See *Valois*, vol. 2, pp. 408–10; Coville, *Petit*, pp. 29–36.

[72] Coville, *Petit*, pp. 30–2; *Valois*, vol. 2, p. 408 n. 2. [73] MS cit., fos 2v–3r.

[74] ibid., fo. 3r:

> Ta fille l'universite
>
> Moult de voies se trouvera
> Selon raison et equite
> Par quoy ce fait se finera
> Et comme l'on doit proceder
>
> Par conseil ou par arbitrage
> Ou par l'un a l'autre ceder
> Ou a un tiers preudomme et saige;
> Elle est prete de desployer
>
> Le tresor de saincte escripture
> Pour dieu veuilles toy emploier . . .

[75] ibid., fo. 3v.

[76] *Ch. Paris.*, no. 1677; Salembier, *Pierre d'Ailly*, pp. 96–7. For a suggestion of an earlier date, see Bliemetzrieder, *Das Generalkonzil*, p. 118.

the utility and expediency of the three possible solutions of resignation, a council, or arbitration, and also a statement of the extent
to which compulsion might be used to induce acceptance of any
of them.[77] The schedules were collected – possibly as many as ten
thousand – between 28 January and 25 February 1394.[78] Such
activity would have been pointless if the crown still intended to
prevent the university making any progress in its debates, but this
obstacle had been removed following a meeting between the king
and university representatives in January 1394.[79] Indeed, the crown
seems to have experienced a revival in its own concern about the
schism, and nominated its own representatives to combine with
the university in considering the problems.[80]

Having celebrated its release from its fetters, the university soon
turned to the business of deciding a policy and persuading the
king to endorse it. On 26 February a congregation of some four
hundred masters discussed how they should advise the king.[81]
Guillaume Barrault was again deputed to address him,[82] while
the task began of preparing an abstract of the schedules presented
in response to the questionnaire. This summary contained all the
main arguments for each of the three ways,[83] but it soon became
clear that the freedom of discussion granted in January would be
retained only with difficulty. A barrier again descended between
the crown and the university, due in part to the reinforcement of
the Clementist party at court by the arrival of the Archbishop of
Narbonne [84] and in part to the assumption of the government by
the Clementist Dukes of Berry and Orléans in the absence of
Philip of Burgundy.[85] Despite corporate protests by the university [86] and individual complaints such as that offered by Gerson
in his sermon *Pax vobis*,[87] there was little that could be done.
But the university did not retreat: while the masters continued

---

[77] *Ch. Paris.*, no. 1677: the eighth and ninth questions.
[78] ibid., no. 1678, and references.
[79] ibid., no. 1674; Bliemetzrieder, *Das Generalkonzil*, p. 119; *Valois*, vol. 2, pp. 406–7;
    Chron. S. Den., vol. 2, pp. 94–9.
[80] *Ch. Paris.*, no. 1676.
[81] ibid., no. 1679.
[82] ibid., vol. 3, p. 610; *Valois*, vol. 2, p. 412.
[83] *Ch. Paris.*, no. 1680.
[84] ibid., no. 1681.
[85] *Valois*, vol. 2, pp. 413–5.
[86] *Ch. Paris.*, no. 1682.
[87] *Glorieux*, no. 366. See also *Valois*, vol. 2, pp. 412–13; Posthumus Meyjes, *Jean
    Gerson*, p. 31.

their attempts to restore contact with the king, work was progressing on the production of the first public statement by the university on the schism for some years, in the form of a letter intended for presentation to the monarch.[88]

This letter, approved in a general congregation held on 6 June 1394, represents the crystallisation of many of the arguments and ideas advanced within the university in the preceding three years. It bemoaned the state of both church and kingdom, complaining that the king was controlled by evil counsellors who wished only to destroy the good name of the university and bring about the utter ruination of the church.[89] It contained a constant demand that the king listen to the advice of the university and work for union, with a general tirade against those who had abused the church for their own purposes in order to achieve wealth and social advancement through simony and other offences.

But the letter's main concern was with the three ways which the masters considered best for bringing about the reunion of the church. The first to be dealt with was the *via cessionis.* Although this was defined, the masters seem to have been unsure of what should happen after the resignations had been effected, and left the question of the subsequent papal election undecided – the academics were uncertain whether this should be performed by the cardinals surviving from the pontificate of Gregory XI alone, or by the union of both existing colleges.[90] However, the masters were convinced that cession was probably the best of the three ways: it was the least troublesome and would be generally acceptable, whilst also removing most of the barriers of partisanship which obstructed reunion by other means. For double resignation managed to avoid a decision on the validity of each of the original elections of 1378 by effectively annulling both. The reputations of the rivals would also be enhanced by allowing them to retire honourably.[91]

Of the other two possible methods of reunification which were discussed, that of arbitration or a particular council [92] was recog-

---

[88] Printed in *Chron. S. Den.*, vol. 2, pp. 136–83; *Bulaeus*, vol. 4, pp. 687–96; also incompletely in *Ch. Paris.*, no. 1683, and *Raynaldus, ann.* 1394, no. 3.

[89] *Chron. S. Den.*, vol. 2, pp. 166–73.

[90] ibid., vol. 2, pp. 142–7.

[91] ibid., vol. 2, pp. 144–7.

[92] ibid., vol. 2, pp. 146–51.

nised as possessing certain advantages, not least that the claimant who rejected it would automatically render his case suspect.[93] Moreover, this method did not impinge on the theory of papal immunity from judgement: the final outcome would not be a judgement between popes but a determination of right in a straightforward case of disputed succession.[94] One justification for this view might have been that the judgement would only be delivered against the antipope, but it seems possible in any case that the academics did not really care if the papal immunity was impugned, for they argued that the pope ought to be subject to the authority of the whole church. The papal claim to immunity was treated as something essentially false, being based on human rather than divine law.[95]

The case for a general council [96] was advanced less forcefully; but then many of the arguments had already been put forward in support of the other methods. It was again noted that intransigent schism was equivalent to heresy, and with no solution in sight the present division might well become as perpetual as that of the Greeks.[97] A council was therefore considered necessary not merely to deal with the question of faith, but also to fulfill the ecclesiastical obligations of brotherly chastisement when faced with the urgent need to judge the rival claims by some means or other. Unfortunately, however, the responses to the anti-conciliar arguments advanced – a charge that any council was bound to be biassed, and the difficulty of arranging the legitimate convocation of such an assembly – were rather vague.[98] However, hidden among the verbiage of this consideration of conciliarism there was a striking indication of academic views regarding the procedure of such a gathering, with a revolutionary suggestion that the role of the universities in working to end the schism should be institutionalised by granting them their own independent representation at any future council.[99]

Whatever the tone of its contents, the letter was not intended to be delivered to Charles VI as any form of ultimatum. Although the Parisian masters considered their position sufficiently secure

[93] ibid., vol. 2, pp. 146–7. [94] ibid., vol. 2, pp. 148–9.
[95] ibid., vol. 2, pp. 148–51.
[96] ibid., vol. 2, pp. 150–61. [97] ibid., vol. 2, pp. 152–3.
[98] ibid., vol. 2, pp. 158–61. [99] ibid., vol. 2, pp. 150–1.

to declare that if either claimant rejected all three ways without offering an effective alternative he should be treated as a schismatic heretic (for anyone who continued the division within the church was obviously in the wrong),[100] such an attitude could not be adopted towards the King of France. Regardless of its private views, the university dared not act openly against the crown. The king was therefore to be presented with a series of options, but he alone was to decide on the actual policy to be adopted.

But composition of a letter to the king proved rather less difficult than actually delivering it. And Charles VI could not unilaterally reunite the church; that required a general movement among the whole Latin obedience. During June and July 1394 the masters of Paris encountered considerable difficulties in their attempts to present their case to the king, but at the same time there are indications that they were beginning to formulate their own form of 'foreign policy', and were establishing their own contacts with other interested parties.

Relations between the university and the French government had worsened steadily during the months that the letter was being prepared. The continued factionalism among Charles VI's relatives, together with the obstructionist tactics of the envoys of Clement VII, meant that the masters' approaches were constantly rebuffed, often with threats. Moreover, the university's concern to end the schism may well have become something of a political embarrassment to the French, the original encouragement of the process by the king having been closely associated with foreign policy and the contemporary Anglo-French peace negotiations. These, with all that depended on their outcome, were thrown into uncertainty by the revolt which broke out in Gascony in mid-1394, against Richard II's alienation of the duchy of Aquitaine from the English crown to John of Gaunt.[101] Only with difficulty did the University of Paris eventually succeed in securing an audience with the king, on 30 July. Guillaume Barrault again spoke for the corporation, presenting its ideas and attacking both the rival popes.[102] His oration met with no immediate response: the university would have to wait for the king's reply.

[100] ibid., vol. 2, pp. 160-3.   [101] Palmer, *England*, pp. 195-6.
[102] *Chron. S. Den.*, vol. 2, pp. 132-5; *Ch. Paris.*, no. 1686; *Valois*, vol. 2, pp. 415-17.

Meanwhile, once the letter to the king had been completed, the academics seem to have embarked on a policy deliberately intended to broaden the scope of their activities, and had begun to establish contacts with other institutions and individuals. At the same time it began preparations for a general manifesto on the schism, the production of which had been foreshadowed in the letter to Charles VI.[103] However, the rapid developments of the next few months and the fundamental alteration in the situation brought about by the death of Clement VII probably meant that this formal compilation of Parisian views was never completed.

Nevertheless, this abortive move to produce a manifesto is not the sole indication of a growing concern for contacts with other bodies. It seems quite possible that the university treated the letter of 6 June as a circular, while there is also evidence of direct communication with Clement VII and other interested parties. Clearly, the contacts with Avignon were seen as complementing the university's approaches to the king. In a letter of 17 July 1394 the masters attempted to persuade the pope to accept the validity of the three ways, summarising the arguments set out in their letter to Charles VI – a copy of which he had already forwarded to Avignon. In addition the academics protested against the unfriendly activities of the Cardinal of Narbonne, and warned the pope of the dangers which threatened the church because of the continued division.[104] The cardinals at Avignon were contacted in similar terms, and were apparently won over.[105] Clement's reaction was less favourable,[106] so that the university sought to pacify him by preparing another letter which, however, was never sent, the need for it being overtaken by events.[107] Shortly after receiving the letter of 17 July Clement VII had fallen ill and taken to his bed. On 16 September 1394, he died.

In addition to their contacts with Avignon, the Parisian masters also engaged in correspondence with the King of Aragon and the Urbanist Cardinal of Alençon, both contacts being continued

103 *Ch. Paris.*, no. 1684.
104 ibid., no. 1690; *Bulaeus*, vol. 4, pp. 699–700; *Valois*, vol. 2, pp. 425–6.
105 *Bulaeus*, vol. 4, pp. 700–1; *Valois*, vol. 2, p. 426; *Ch. Paris.*, vol. 3, p. 633.
106 *Valois*, vol. 2, p. 426; *Chron. S. Den.*, vol. 2, pp. 184–7.
107 *Bulaeus*, vol. 4, pp. 701–3; *Valois*, vol. 2, pp. 426–7; *Ch. Paris.*, no. 1693.

during the pontificate of Clement's successor, Benedict XIII.[108]
Among the universities, both Cologne and Vienna seem to have
been informed of developments at Paris. However, although these
university contacts are of extreme importance in the present case,
they are poorly documented. Thus, there exists but one letter
(dated 5 July 1394) from the University of Cologne to that of
Paris, while the known correspondence in the opposite direction
is limited to the reply to that letter, sent at an unknown date.[109]
Nevertheless, even this meagre evidence is of importance, providing the first real sign of corporate activity by the masters of
Cologne on the schism. Their involvement in the debates was to
become increasingly important as the schism progressed. From
Vienna, there is no sign of official university contact with Paris,
but Henry of Langenstein was certainly in correspondence with
Pierre d'Ailly in 1394, praising the Parisian concern for union,
and urging the masters to proceed from their general consideration of the methods for attaining reunion of the church to the
adoption of a specific policy.[110]

Langenstein's letter to d'Ailly was not his first involvement in
this particular phase of the schism. Although, since 1386, his
attentions had mainly been concentrated on ensuring the stability
of the revived university at Vienna, once that had been achieved
his literary activities recommenced. After 1393 he published a
succession of works on the schism, among them his own poetic
plea for action, the *Carmen pro pace*.[111] Although an important
work, its significance is reduced when compared to the almost
contemporary letter addressed to Rupert III of the Palatinate.[112]
In this, Langenstein revealed a major change of emphasis in his
thinking, turning away from his previous appeals for joint Franco-
Imperial activity to a call for action by the German princes as a

---

[108] *Valois*, vol. 2, p. 418; *Ch. Paris.*, nos. 1689, 1692; *Bulaeus*, vol. 4, pp. 705–9.

[109] See R. N. Swanson, 'The university of Cologne and the great schism', *Journal of Ecclesiastical History*, 28 (1977), 4.

[110] *Ch. Paris.*, no. 1695; Salembier, *Pierre d'Ailly*, pp. 95–6; Bliemetzrieder, *Das Generalkonzil*, pp. 131–3.

[111] The first sixty-seven lines are printed in Kneer, *Die Entstehung*, pp. 127–9; the remainder in H. von der Hardt, *Ineditum carmen antiquum Henrici de Hassia . . . pro pace . . . scriptum Viennae a. 1392* (Helmstadt, 1715).

[112] Printed in G. Sommerfeldt, 'Die Stellung Rupprechts III von der Pfalz zur deutschen Publizistik bis zum Jahre 1400', *Zeitschrift für die Geschichte des Oberrheins*, N.F. 22 (1907), 301–11. The date is discussed ibid., pp. 295–8.

whole, a programme in which Rupert was to have a leading part.[113] As the basis of his argument, Langenstein worked from the precedent of the schism between Innocent II and Anacletus II in the twelfth century, the analogy being so extended that it is difficult to avoid the conclusion that Langenstein wished to claim for himself the role of a second St Bernard. Not for the last time, the growing force of German nationalism put in an appearance, emphasising – by reference to the decay of the French universities and the rise of those within the empire [114] – the increasing international tensions which were beginning to add their own complications to the issue.

There is a strong contrast between the vagueness of parts of this letter to Rupert and the acceptance of the positive aspect of the Parisian programme expressed in Langenstein's letter to d'Ailly. But the future of these inter-university contacts was very uncertain. The letter to Pierre d'Ailly may not have reached Paris until late August 1394; by that time the university there had already received the royal reply to the letter of 6 June. The response, given on 10 August, had not been gratifying, amounting rather to a complete rejection of the Parisian programme, again banning debates, and ordering the cessation of all correspondence on the schism both within and without the realm.[115] The masters of Paris reacted forcefully. Already disgruntled by the way in which they had been treated, for them the royal reply was the last straw. The university suspended its activities, and refused to cooperate with the government.[116]

This situation prevailed until the death of Clement VII, which changed everything. The cardinals had already accepted the validity of cession, but elsewhere there were doubts. The correspondence with the Cardinal of Alençon and the Universities of Vienna and Cologne nevertheless held out hopes that the Urbanist obedience might be willing to join Paris in acting to end the schism, while the support of the King of Aragon was an indication of agreement from the Clementists. For the moment, however, there was little that could be done. All now depended on the activities of the cardinals themselves, at Avignon.

[113] ibid., pp. 309–11.   [114] ibid., pp. 310–11.
[115] *Chron. S. Den.*, vol. 2, pp. 182–5; *Valois*, vol. 2, pp. 417–18.
[116] *Chron. S. Den.*, vol. 2, pp. 184–5; *Valois*, vol. 2, p. 418.

Chapter 5

DE SUBTRACTIONE OBEDIENTIE I

The death of Clement VII in September 1394 presented those of the Avignonese obedience who were concerned to end the schism with an opportunity which they could not afford to miss. Unfortunately, however, it proved impossible to achieve any really coordinated effort. At Paris, the masters joined with the crown to urge the cardinals to defer the election of a new pope.[1] At the same time the academics asked the king to summon a national council, reopen his negotiations with Boniface IX and restore to the university its freedom to discuss the schism, all of which formed part of a coherent programme for reunification of the church which was to be led by the French king. Charles VI granted all their requests, the masters reciprocating by recommencing their academic activities.[2]

But the pleas to the cardinals to defer an election were ignored, and Pedro de Luna emerged from the conclave as Pope Benedict XIII. However, he had taken an oath, both as cardinal (with the other members of the college) and as pope, to work for reunion by all possible means, including resignation if necessary.[3] This oath and its effects were to be much debated in coming years. In the meantime, fearing possible Parisian hostility to his election, the new pope sent a conciliatory letter to the masters,[4] but his fears of their disapproval proved groundless. In a letter of 23 October 1394 the university welcomed his election, praised his

[1] *Bulaeus*, vol. 4, pp. 710–13; *Chron. S. Den.*, vol. 2, pp. 192–7.
[2] *Bulaeus*, vol. 4, pp. 709–10; *Chron. S. Den.*, vol. 2, pp. 192–3.
[3] On the conclave, see *Valois*, vol. 3, pp. 11–16; M. Souchon, *Die Papstwahlen in der Zeit des grossen Schismas* (2 vols., Brunswick, 1898), vol. 1, pp. 211–31 (with the conclave oath printed at pp. 296–300). This was not the first attempt made by the cardinals to control the aftermath of a papal election by means of an electoral capitulation, nor was it to be the last. In 1352 the cardinals had devised the first such agreement at the conclave which elected Innocent VI, although it proved unenforceable (Ullmann, *Short History*, pp. 230, 289–90).
[4] *Bulaeus*, vol. 4, pp. 723–4.

reputation, and urged him to implement the *via cessionis* as soon as possible.[5] Although the masters expressed their willingness to obey the pope's orders in the search for reunion,[6] they also recognised the attractions of power, and duly warned the pope against them.[7] Benedict replied by attempting to allay these fears, but how far he was successful is uncertain.

Following the doubts of the interregnum and the ready recognition of the new pope, the University of Paris followed its normal course and petitioned for benefices. This petitioning, however, was of a more private nature than normal; no great *rotulus* was prepared.[8] The other Clementist universities showed no such reluctance to send official rolls.[9] But the Parisian desire for union was unabated. It was probably only shortly after the election of Benedict XIII that an anonymous jurist within the university produced the *Conclusio universitatis juribus*,[10] a work which strongly advocated the *via cessionis* and subtraction of obedience. That such action should be taken against both claimants was declared in the opening section of the work, being justified on the grounds that refusal to act (in particular, rejection of the proposals advanced by the University of Paris) was tantamount to schism and heresy.[11] Not even Benedict XIII was free from accusation: having succeeded Clement VII, he had also inherited his liabilities.[12] The arguments in favour of withdrawal of obedience were continued even during the supposed replies thereto, with the writer claiming that subtraction of revenues was the only effective method of coercing the rivals back on to the road to union,[13] and arguing that such withdrawal should last until the

---

[5] ibid., vol. 4, pp. 713–15; *Chron. S. Den.*, vol. 2, pp. 206–19.

[6] *Chron. S. Den.*, vol. 2, pp. 214–17.

[7] ibid., vol. 2, pp. 208–11.

[8] *Ch. Paris.*, nos. 1714–18; Bliss, *Petitions*, vol. 1, pp. 580–5, 587–8, 592–3.

[9] For the rolls from the French universities, see Denifle, *Les universités*, pp. 79–80; Fournier, *Statuts*, nos. 233, 409, 728, 1450, 1891, 1912. For the Avignonese roll, ibid., nos. 1270–1, and for that from Perpignan, ibid., no. 1488. A roll from the University of Lérida is in Griera Gaja, *Miscelánea*, vol. 1, pp. 414–61. The existence of a *rotulus* from the University of Salamanca may be inferred from the large number of papal grants made at this time: Beltrán de Heredia, *Bulario*, nos. 223–6, 237–8, 244–51, 253, 255, 257–8, 260, 262–3, 265–79, 281–6 (although some of these may refer to an earlier roll sent in 1393; ibid., no. 220).

[10] *BN*, MS Lat. 1481, fos 123r–132r.

[11] ibid., fos 123v–124r.   [12] ibid., fo. 125v.

[13] ibid., fo. 130r: 'non videtur maior Inductio ad unionem quam bonorum subtractio

91

whole church had decided on the validity of the rival claims.[14] However, when it came to considering the mechanics of putting his programme into effect, the author became rather vague: although he apparently wanted a general council to appeal to the popes to work for union, he soon became entangled in the legal objections to such action, falling back on the old argument of necessity to allow eventual action by the secular power.[15] His waverings continued as the tract progressed: he wished the princes and prelates to enforce the withdrawal of obedience (which was to affect the cardinals as well as their popes, in the hope that the pope next elected would be worthy of the office), but he failed to produce a formula for the continued administration of the church in such circumstances, leaving it to the princes, prelates and university to devise their own method.[16] His only contribution was a vociferous exhortation to the rivals to act to end the schism, or face the consequences.[17]

Meanwhile, the renewed freedom of correspondence granted to the university in September 1394 was bearing fruit, in renewed contacts with John II of Aragon and the Cardinal of Alençon,[18] as well as correspondence with others at Rome.[19] The *Acta* of the English nation suggest hopes of further expansion of these contacts: on 13 November 1394 it was agreed to register copies of all letters between Paris and other universities on the schism, the first sign of any idea of concerted academic activity.[20]

Another strand of the university's policy, the national council of the French church, eventually opened on 3 February 1395.[21]

. . . [et] bona subtracta reddenda non sunt, quibus utilius necessaria subtraherentur, ut coactj redirent ad unitatem a qua recesserant'.

[14] ibid., fo. 131r: 'nullus horum contendencium ad obedienciam subtractam vel subtrahendam est restituendus, donec universalem ecclesiam Informaverit super Iure suo papatus'.

[15] ibid., fol. 131v: 'videtur quod hec monitio solum fieri debeat per concilium universale tanquam per Iudicem competentem . . . [sed] possunt . . . monerj per prelatos ecclesie et doctores sacra theologie et Iuris primo loco . . . et in casu timoris aut metus reprobandissimorum, fiat hoc monitio per temporales principes mandato prelatorum, studiorum, et ceterorum virorum ecclesiasticorum precedente'.

[16] ibid., fos 131v–132r.   [17] ibid., fo. 132r.

[18] On the Alençon correspondence see *Thes. Nov. Anec.*, p. 1135; *Bulaeus*, vol. 4, pp. 725-7, 785. For the Aragonese contacts, *Bulaeus*, vol. 4, pp. 719-22, 728. See also *Valois*, vol. 3, p. 38 (especially nn. 4–5).

[19] *Valois*, vol. 3, p. 38; *Bulaeus*, vol. 4, pp. 727-8.   [20] *Auct. Ch.*, vol. 1, p. 696.

[21] On the council see *Valois*, vol. 3, pp. 33-7; Salembier, *Pierre d'Ailly*, pp. 109-11; *Bulaeus*, vol. 4, pp. 729, 732-9.

The universities were well represented in this assembly.[22] The Parisian attitude, while still advocating the three ways of abdication, council and arbitration, was obviously beginning to concentrate on a drive for acceptance of the *via cessionis*, which had been advocated by Pierre d'Ailly in a sermon preached on 1 February.[23] Nevertheless, there was real debate at the council, where Pierre d'Ailly (despite his sermon) appeared as a defender of Benedict XIII against his opponents.[24] The latter included Gilles des Champs, Pierre le Roy and Simon de Cramaud, all of whose schedules favoured the *via cessionis*.[25] Despite the debate the final statement – drawn up by Cramaud – was an unequivocal acceptance of the policy of abdication, with hints of royal action against the rivals if they proved recalcitrant.[26] The disappearance of most of the ballots presented at the conclusion of the discussions makes it impossible to assess just how far this statement was an accurate reflection of the feelings of the assembly. Nevertheless, with this formal decision by the French kingdom (but not, as yet, the University of Paris) in favour of the *via cessionis*, with no alternative thereto, there opens one of the most critical phases of the schism. France had adopted a strict policy, binding its proponents as much as its opponents, and leaving neither much room for manoeuvre. A clash of institutions now became almost inevitable: the Benedictine papacy against the French monarchy.

The history of the University of Paris in all this is rather confused; with the increasing employment of university members on government business it is often impossible to differentiate between royal and university attitudes or envoys. This first becomes clear with the joint embassy sent to Benedict XIII in spring 1395.[27] Although there were two distinct groups of envoys, both of them contained individuals of high academic standing. The university emissaries took with them a letter – dated 14 April – which urged the pope to accept one of the three ways outlined in the letter

[22] A full list of participants is in *Chron. S. Den.*, vol. 2, pp. 220–3.
[23] ibid., vol. 2, pp. 224–5.
[24] Ehrle, *Alpartils Chronica*, pp. 470–4.
[25] The schedules of des Champs, le Roy and Cramaud are in *ASV*, Arm LIV. 21, fos 55r–59r, 61r–v (see Ehrle, *Alpartils Chronica*, pp. 468–9 – his references being to the old foliation of the MS).
[26] *Chron. S. Den.*, vol. 2, pp. 226–45.
[27] For this see *Valois*, vol. 3, pp. 44–67; Coville, *Petit*, pp. 36–43; *Chron. S. Den.*, vol. 2, pp. 248–323.

addressed to Charles VI in June 1394, although the choice of method to be adopted was left to the pope.[28] But the university's representatives were virtually excluded from the negotiations, encountering frequent opposition not only from the papal creatures but also from the royal dukes on the embassy, who resented the independent stand which the university was taking in its policy on the schism.[29] Even when confronted, Benedict proved evasive on the issue of resignation, although most of the cardinals gave it their approval.[30] The pope, however, offered to refer the matter to the clerks of the University of Avignon, 'whom he considered the wisest in the world'.[31] He presumably expected that his own proximity and the large Spanish contingent within that university would lead to a blunt rejection of cession.

Impeded by the pope, the negotiations unavoidably collapsed in early July. For the University of Paris the only result had been a head-on clash with one of Benedict's most fervent supporters, the exiled Englishman, John Acton. His propositions against the *via cessionis* and its advocates caused a great outcry at Paris.[32] But perhaps more damaging and painful to the university was another work by him addressed to Benedict XIII, containing perhaps the most virulent of all attacks on the Parisian academics.[33] In this tract the status of Benedict XIII was strongly defended, while the *via cessionis* was condemned as illegal, a bad precedent, and in any case an incomplete solution, since it would leave the opposition unconvinced of their errors, thereby allowing them to die in that state to the consequent detriment of their souls.[34] The whole Parisian letter to Charles VI of June 1394 was condemned as false, scandalous and erroneous in faith;[35] the policy of the Parisians, those 'importunos, clamosos, et scandalosos pseudo magistros et doctores',[36] was subjected to a steady onslaught, in which Acton lambasted their arrogance, and to all intents and purposes charged them with heresy.[37] Paris soon

[28] The date appears in a copy in *BN*, MS N.A. Lat. 1793, fos 71r–77r.
[29] *Chron. S. Den.*, vol. 2, pp. 312–15.   [30] ibid., vol. 2, pp. 314–15.
[31] ibid., vol. 2, pp. 279–80.
[32] For the propositions see *Valois*, vol. 3, p. 55; *Raynaldus*, *ann.* 1395, nos. 12–13.
[33] Bibliothèque municipale, Grenoble, MS 117, fos 74r–77v.
[34] ibid., fos 74r–76v.
[35] ibid., fo. 76v.
[36] ibid., fo. 76r.   [37] ibid., fos 76v–77r.

responded to this attack, quite possibly because Acton's works were proving inspirational for other opponents of the university's policy. Certainly, one anonymous writer incorporated Acton's most vehement accusations into his own tract *verbatim* and then, to compound the effect, proceeded to add his own series of insults.[38] The overall Parisian reaction to Acton's diatribes is perhaps most succinctly reflected in the comments of the transcriber of one of the works in a Grenoble manuscript, who appended the remark that the tract was 'stolide et male fundata'.[39]

It was in the context of the failed French mission to Benedict XIII that the University of Paris prepared one of the most important documents of the schism, the general epistle of 25 August 1395, sometimes known as *Quoniam fideles*.[40] The dissemination of this letter throughout Europe inaugurated a new phase of the schism, and stimulated much of the theorising which occurred in the next few years. The letter which the university envoys had taken with them to Avignon in April was now recast, with dramatic effect: from being a pacificatory appeal to the pope to accept the way of abdication in preference to – but not to the exclusion of – other suggested solutions, the letter was now transformed into a clarion call to the rest of Christendom to press for implementation of the *via cessionis* with no alternative. In contrast with the moderation of the previous letter, all other methods for ending the schism were to be totally rejected,[41] and

---

[38] *ASV*, Arm. LIV. 36, fos 99–107, especially 103r, 106v.

[39] Grenoble, MS cit., fo. 77v.

[40] This is most fully treated in Jacob, *Essays*, pp. 61–2, but a proper edition is urgently needed. Despite a tradition which has somehow developed that the letter exists in only one MS, this is very far from being the case. The following references are to *BN*, MS Lat. 14643, fos 49r–52r, which gives the original letter and (as marginalia) the alterations later made.

[41] Thus, in the first version, the university had declared: 'non alias [vias] dampnare aut alio quovismodo improbare voluntas sit' (fo. 49r), but this was totally changed. The most important alteration in the letter was made at fo. 49v. In the original version, the appropriate passage read: 'nec existimet aliquis nobis in animo esse, per hac verba dampnare vias alias quas dudum approbavimus: non illas repudiamus aut dampnamus; sed tamen eis annexa sunt plurima pericula erroris aut fallacie seu scandalli demonstra[m]us, a quibus ista tuta est et libera; quare eam precellere iure ceteris dicimus, quidem et semper alius censuimus et in prefata eciam epistola de tribus viis edita expressimus'. In the revised version, all mention of the previous letter (that sent to Charles VI in June 1394) was expunged in order to produce a more definite and harsher statement: 'Aliis utique viis ab ista quam plurima erroris, fallacie, aut scandali pericula sunt annexa, a quibus ista tuta est et libera, quare eam precellere iure ceteris dicimus'.

the earlier concern not to offend the pope disappeared entirely.[42] With this declaration the University of Paris adopted a policy as rigid as that decreed for the rest of the realm in February, and embarked on a programme of agitation to ensure its implementation. So energetic was the university in its dealings with the French government on this issue, that at one stage an opponent commented that 'in hijs que concernunt statum ecclesie, rex francie et legales magis debent credere studio paryssiensis quam summo pontifici'.[43] On the other hand, the university may perhaps have been rather too anxious about putting its policy into effect; so much so that its insistent advocacy could prove counterproductive. As an anonymous commentator on one of the frequent councils of the French church remarked, the main effect of repeated university interruptions of the council's discussions in order to present its case was to disillusion the prelates and cause many of them to desert the proceedings before they came to any conclusion.[44] Finally, and not least, the rigidity of the policy adopted by the university may also have had deleterious internal repercussions, causing considerable dissension and disturbance because of the need to prevent and quash any expressions of individual opposition to the *via cessionis* among members of the university.

These side effects of the declaration were not, however, to become obvious for some time. The immediate result of the decision to issue the letter of 25 August 1395 was a further approach to the king at the end of the month, when the revised proposals on cession were put forward in the context of a highly Gallican programme for their implementation. The king was urged to summon another council to discuss the barriers to reunion presented by continued papal control over provisions to benefices and

---

[42] Thus, the mollifying phrases of the final statement – including the plea that 'si quid fortasse durius aut asperius insonuit, id ardentissimo zelo domus dei, quj nostras mentes comedit, et non irreverencie aut de persona vestra sinistre suspicionj, ascribatis' (MS cit., fo. 52r) – were replaced by a general appeal to Christendom to adopt the *via cessionis* and no other.

[43] Biblioteca Apostolica Vaticana, MS Barb. Lat. 872, fo. 88v.

[44] *ASV.*, Arm. LIV. 22, fo. 57v: 'multum displicuit eis [i.e. the prelates] inportunam requisicio universitatis, quia cottidie veniebant ad interrumpendam consilia prelatorum, et omni die faciebant unam arengam et quasi cum minis et clamoribus petebant super facto ipsorum providere, intantum quod aliqui prelati tedio affecti [fuerunt], quod ante finita consilia recesserunt'.

continued papal taxation, both of which allowed Benedict to build up and maintain his anti-cessionist party; to establish contacts with other powers of both obediences to induce them to adopt the *via cessionis*; to then hold a council to discuss further steps towards union; and finally to extend royal protection to the advocates of cession and take action against its detractors – the university here giving way to its sense of grievance against John Acton with a specific plea that he be kept incarcerated until he had apologised for his insults to the university and the French government.[45] The end of August also saw a second 'referendum' within the University of Paris, the questions under discussion[46] being the basis of considerable pamphleteering throughout France, probably because Benedict XIII forwarded copies of them to his supporters at other universities for their consideration.[47]

At Paris itself, Jean Gerson expressed his views on these questions in his tract, *De substractione obedientiae*,[48] appearing as a moderating influence in his attempts to silence demands for any immediate withdrawal of obedience from Benedict XIII. He condemned the revolutionary nature of the attack on papal power, particularly objecting to the use of a plebiscite to determine matters affecting the church, as such a method reduced the faculty of theology to minority status.[49] Gerson instead asserted the faculty's right to pre-eminence in any doctrinal discussions, arguing that the university should accept its decisions in such matters.[50] The unilateral nature of the Parisian action was also attacked as divisive, since it would reduce the chances of cooperation between universities of opposing obediences,[51] and threatened to make the differences between the obediences even more rigid. Less stridently, Gerson also sniped at the *via cessionis* itself, suggesting that even if Benedict did resign there was no guarantee that Boniface IX would follow his example.

The defence of Benedict XIII was continued by another Parisian master, Stephanus de Labarella, in a methodical tract which may

---

45 *Valois*, vol. 3, pp. 74–5; *Thes. Nov. Anec.*, pp. 1135–6.
46 *Raynaldus, ann.* 1395, no. 9; *Bulaeus*, vol. 4, fos 753r–754r.
47 On the pamphleteering see *Valois*, vol. 3, pp. 72–4, with the transmission of the questions being suggested at 72 n. 3.
48 *Glorieux*, no. 254.
49 ibid., vol. 6, p. 23.
50 ibid.   51 ibid., vol. 6, p. 22.

not have been his sole contribution to these debates.[52] His hostility to the *via cessionis* was apparent from his consideration of whether it could be justified:[53] it was bluntly attacked as unauthorised, unproductive, unnecessary, indecisive and ineffective. The arguments behind the attack were frequently illuminating, particularly when Labarella condemned cession as unproductive. Here he pointed out a major flaw in the cessionists' arguments; for although mutual abdication would remove the rivals it would not solve the problem of reunification of the church, as the cardinals of the rival obediences would still be considered schismatic heretics, a situation thus arising in which the church would be left with no machinery to carry out another papal election.[54] The availability of other possible methods of solving the problem was constantly referred to by Labarella who, to judge from his treatment of Benedict's own suggestion of the *via compromissi*[55] and the vaguer *via juris*,[56] would probably have preferred one of them. Certainly, either of them would obviate all future difficulties by providing the necessary determination between the parties which was what Labarella wanted.[57] Cession, however, was nothing but an accumulation of disadvantages: if Benedict accepted it he would merely be admitting the weakness of his own case;[58] any forced resignation would be invalid and would merely lead to further complications since any supposed 'successor' to Benedict would in reality be nothing more than an additional antipope;[59] while, if they persisted in their demands for resignation, the French would be admitting that they had been deceived throughout the schism.[60]

Labarella's antipathy to the *via cessionis* naturally extended to the electoral capitulation of 1394.[61] This, apart from being nonbinding almost by definition, was condemned as 'fraudulenter et cautelose . . . in mente concepta, et non secundum jus'.[62] The oath

---

[52] Grenoble, MS cit., fos 98r–103r: the reference to other works appears at fo. 101r.
[53] ibid., fos 98r–99r.
[54] ibid., fo. 98v: 'ante Renunciationem alius eligi non potest, post vero Renunciationem eciam, quia pretenduntur omnes Cardinales scismatici et heretici, igitur eligere non poterunt papam'.
[55] ibid., fos 100r–v.
[56] ibid., fos 100v–101r.
[57] ibid., fo. 101r.
[58] ibid., fo. 99r.
[59] ibid., fos 99v–100r.
[60] ibid., fo. 100r.
[61] ibid., fos 101r–102v.
[62] ibid., fo. 101v.

was contrary to the liberties of the church, and would have disastrous consequences not only by allowing the princes to interfere in ecclesiastical matters but also by encouraging rather than removing schism. Moreover, even if the electoral capitulation was generally binding, the pope was nevertheless in no sense obliged to resign, since the conditions implicit in the arrangement had not yet been fulfilled – and in all probability could not be.[63] Finally, Labarella indulged in an attack on the Avignonese cardinals for the ease with which they changed their minds, transferring their loyalties from the pope to the French princes as soon as the latter had reached Avignon. So hasty had been the conversion that the cardinals could no longer be considered trustworthy as witnesses on the issue.[64]

Although the University of Paris was at the centre of the debates provoked by the referendum, its members were not the only academics to respond to the questionnaire. Commentaries produced at Toulouse mark the inception of a long and bitter conflict between the two universities on the schism, in which Paris opposed Benedict while the Toulouse academics provided some of his staunchest supporters. The most prolific author at this stage seems to have been Sancho Mulier,[65] although the Parisian questions were also discussed by Aymeric Natalis, whose tract consistently favoured Benedict XIII.[66]

Against Natalis' determined defence of Benedict, Mulier's attitude towards the *via cessionis* seems less certain. In the longer of his two works, dealing with only two of the Parisian questions, he certainly appeared as a defender of the Avignon pope against the Parisian onslaught. On the issue of cession itself, Mulier argued that the pope should not thus sin to end the schism,[67] since he could not abdicate without the consent of the church. The recent Paris council, and indeed the Gallican church as a whole, were incapable of giving the necessary authority;[68] but Mulier was less certain as to whether a call for resignation made by the cardinals could be considered sufficient, and preferred to leave

[63] ibid., fo. 102r.
[64] ibid., fos 102v–103r.
[65] Works by him are ibid., fos 20r–25v, and in *ASV.*, Arm. LIV. 22, fos 70r–72v.
[66] *ASV.*, Arm. LIV. 20, fos 184v–191v; Grenoble, MS cit., fos 14r–19r.
[67] Grenoble, MS cit., fos 20r–21r.   [68] ibid., fo. 21r.

that issue in doubt.[69] Yet Mulier does not seem to have objected
to the principle of abdication; his objections were to the form in
which it was being proposed by the Parisians, 'id est, alijs Regibus
et principibus et Regnis et prelatis nescientibus et inconsultis'.[70]
This was a situation which could only give rise to scandal throughout the Avignonese obedience.[71] The attack on the formulation
extended to the wording of the demand for abdication itself,
which was condemned as 'multipliciter deffectuosa in modo'[72] –
the signal for a rather semantic dissection of the demand to prove
its falsehood and invalidity.[73] As the request had been drawn up
in the University of Paris, Mulier did not fail to seize the opportunity thus presented to engage in a direct attack on that university's attempts to monopolise the discussions, seeking to deflate
the self-importance of the Parisian academics by asserting the
rights of others to be consulted and to debate the issues: Paris
was not the sole repository of knowledge.[74]

Having thus shown that cession was not advisable in the existing situation, Mulier then proceeded to demolish other aspects of
the attack on Benedict XIII. He argued that, even if Benedict was
obliged to abdicate (another indication that Mulier had not totally
rejected cession) he could not be threatened with the penalties of
heresy. He dealt at length with the distinction between schism
and heresy to prove his point: although Benedict might be
threatened with the penalties of schism, the implementation of
the *via cessionis* was not an article of faith and therefore failure
to abdicate could not be treated as heresy.[75] Mulier also dealt with
the issue of whether the Avignonese pope, considering the amount
of time which had been spent on the search for a solution to the
schism and the amount of advice which he had been offered, could
possibly excuse himself on the grounds of ignorance.[76] Having
put the arguments which were the basis of the attack, Mulier

[69] ibid., fos 21r–v.   [70] ibid., fo. 21v.
[71] ibid., fos 21v–22r.   [72] ibid., fo. 22r.
[73] ibid., fos 22r–23r.
[74] ibid., fo. 22r: 'dato quod omnes parisienses sunt sapientes, tamen non omnes
sapientes sunt parisienses, igitur plures alij; quia et de alijs Regnis et studijs sunt
interrogandj super questione qua queritur per quam viam decet unirj ecclesiam'.
[75] ibid., fos 23r–24v.
[76] ibid., fo. 24v: 'utrum, attento spacio temporis et requestis sibi factis et plena
deliberatis . . . ac deliberacione super . . . hijs habita, papa possit excusarj per
ignoranciam'.

skillfully inverted the whole debate to Benedict's advantage. Ignorance would have to be pleaded in a matter of faith, which meant the declaration of who was legal pope (for the existence of a pope was an article of faith) rather than the acceptance of a method of terminating the schism. There could be no ignorance pleaded concerning the readily available facts of the elections of 1378, which made it quite clear that the Roman line were intrusive antipopes and those of the Avignonese succession were the legitimate pontiffs.[77]

Despite this flash of loyalty to Benedict XIII, it seems clear that Mulier's attack on the Parisian proposals was directed chiefly against the method by which they had been formulated. The ill-conceived nature of the attacks on the pope was a point to which he returned in his second consideration of the subject. Again, he distinguished between schism and heresy, and attacked any view that Benedict could be compelled to resign. In particular, he pointed to the inconsistency of the argument that Benedict, by refusing to resign, was a schismatic heretic, therefore no longer pope, and therefore could be forced to abdicate. Just what was he to resign? If he had already ceased to be pope, how could he resign a papacy which he did not have? 'Nullus debet renunciare rei in qua nullum ius habet'. All would be well if Benedict's detractors were merely concerning themselves with the papal title and insignia, the accidents of the papacy, but they were actually talking in terms of a legal right which, according to the terms of their attack, simply did not exist in the first place.[78]

Despite his attacks on forced cession, it nevertheless seems clear from the later development of this short tract that Mulier felt that abdication would probably be the best way to end the schism. However, he recognised the complexities of the situation, and declared the flexibility of his own views with the statement that his tract was not being published in any determinative manner, but merely to provide fuller information on the issues involved.[79]

In contrast with Mulier's fairly moderate stand the views of Simon de Columb, a Spaniard and a master of the University of

[77] ibid., fos 25r–v.
[78] *ASV.*, Arm. LIV. 22, fos 70r–71r, especially fo. 70v.
[79] ibid., fos 71v–72r.

Avignon,[80] were nothing short of hostile to the *via cessionis*. If his three short tracts,[81] which were apparently intended for Benedict's perusal,[82] were truly representative of the opinions prevalent within the university at Avignon then there can be no surprise that Benedict had wished the masters there to pronounce judgement on the Parisian programme before delivering his own decision on abdication. The whole combination was framed as a series of answers to three sets of questions: those contained in the Parisian questionnaire; Columb's own 'questiones tacite correspondentes questionibus Parisiensibus';[83] and four others dealing with cession. Taken together the replies amounted to a strong affirmation of Benedict's cause, denying the need for or validity of cession and attacking any suggestions that the pope should be removed.

It was the Parisian questions which related directly to cession which were the subject of Columb's first consideration. His chief concern was with the conclave pact, which he generally proved to be invalid and non-binding. In doing so he attacked the view that Benedict had been elected as some sort of temporary pope, taking the analogy to matrimony to declare that 'nec deus nec mundus sponsum ecclesie temporalem seu maritum accepit'.[84] He also emphasised the change in Pedro de Luna's status on his elevation to the papacy, arguing that the oath taken as a cardinal could not be held to be binding on him as pope, since he could not oblige himself as cardinal to resign a status which he did not yet possess.[85] This forward-looking aspect of the electoral capitulation was again referred to in the discussion of the general role of the cardinals, denying them any powers to determine when the pope should be obliged to resign.[86] There is a somewhat ironic side to this argument, with both Johannes de Legnano and Baldus de Ubaldis appearing among the authorities cited in defence of the Avignonese pope.[87] Benedict's reaffirmation of the electoral pact

---

[80] He appears on *rotuli* sent to Benedict XIII in 1394 and 1403: Fournier, *Statuts*, vol. 2, p. 342; Denifle, *Les universités*, p. 86.

[81] Grenoble, MS cit., fos 30r–35v, 36r–40r, 40v–42r. Although distinct units, these works do form something of an entity.

[82] The third tract was addressed 'sanctitati vestre' by 'Devota creatura vestra' (ibid., fo. 40v).

[83] ibid., fo. 36v.

[84] ibid., fo. 31v, this point being again considered at fos 32v–33v.

[85] ibid., fos 31v–32v.

[86] ibid., fos 34r–v.

[87] ibid., fo. 34v.

after his elevation was so interpreted to justify the pope's present stance: he had simply confirmed the legal force of the oath taken during the conclave, and that had been non-existent. Benedict had merely announced that he would follow the spirit (but not the letter) of the agreement, and had made no specific mention of any part to be played in the proceedings by the cardinals. He was therefore free to explore other methods of reunification, in his own time.[88]

However, although Columb had been defending Benedict, the fairly quiet tone of his arguments thus far manages to give the impression that he would have accepted the validity of the *via cessionis* as a last resort. A hint that this was not the case appeared right at the end of the discussion, with the assertion that forced cession was quite out of the question, arguing instead that Christendom should gather round and defend Benedict against the incursions of the intruder.[89] The hostility to the *via cessionis* thus hinted at became more obvious in the second of the three works, which was concerned to defend Benedict's rights and authority in considering ways of ending the schism, other than by abdication. The advocates of cession were at one stage likened to the mob which had howled for Christ's crucifixion,[90] while Benedict was strenuously defended against charges that his search for alternative solutions to the schism was merely a delaying tactic which thus rendered him liable to accusations of heresy.[91] Columb strongly asserted Benedict's authority, arguing that others ought to submit to his decision on the issue,[92] going so far as to urge that the pope's opponents be proceeded against if they remained obdurate.[93]

The antipathy to cession reappeared in Columb's third tract, he proving to his own satisfaction that 'cessio est quedam libidinosa prostitucio Intellectus humanj, et sic nec conveniens nec expediens animarum salutj'.[94] He even declared that 'per cessionem a veritate receditur';[95] for thereby the essentially legal aspect of the

---

[88] ibid., fos 34v–35v.

[89] ibid., fos 35v–36r, his views being best summarised in his remark: 'Debet ergo papa defendj in papatu, et omnis christianj mundi sibj assurgere et deffendere debent contra intrusum Ius non habentem' (fo. 35v).

[90] ibid., fo. 38v.   [91] ibid., fos 38v–39r.

[92] ibid., fos 37v–38v.   [93] ibid., fos 39v–40r.

[94] ibid., fo. 40v.   [95] ibid., fo. 41r.

problem would be blurred. But Columb also had a practical case to argue: that cession would not abolish the rival obediences which might, even after a double abdication, continue to elect their own popes.[96] Conciliarism was also attacked – as it had been in the second tract.[97] For Columb the issue demanded a legal settlement so that whoever was rightfully pope would retain the papacy while his rival would abdicate.[98] As far as he was concerned, this would not require much determination, Columb making his loyalties quite clear with the suggestion that the Roman claimant should resign and submit to Benedict.[99]

While these debates continued, the consequences of the outright acceptance of cession threatened the University of Paris itself. Benedict XIII sought to establish his own party there, which may account for the promotion of Pierre d'Ailly to the bishopric of Le Puy in mid-1395, his position as chancellor being taken by Jean Gerson.[100] D'Ailly was treated with reserve by the university for a while as a result of this, to the extent of being barred from university discussions, particularly those on the reunification of the church.[101] Johannes de Moravia, despite his earlier activities, was also chary about cession and was consequently harried by its supporters.[102] The pope, however, approved of his loyalty, and in 1396 attempted (unsuccessfully) to install him as professor of theology at Toulouse.[103] The extent of the pope's activities may be reflected in an anonymous complaint made in 1398 against the energy – and success – with which Benedict had sought to suborn the academics of his obedience, particularly those of Paris and

---

[96] ibid., fos 42r–v.

[97] ibid., fo. 37v.

[98] ibid., fo. 41v, demanding 'inquisicionem veritatis . . . ut . . . qui verus est cathedram teneat, et intrusus cedat'.

[99] ibid., fo. 42v: 'non video ergo tucrus Remedium, quam quid sequaces intrusi gratijs, muneribus, et favoribus ad partem nostram iusticie trahantur, et in hoc laboretur, vel quod saltim instrusus cum consilio et assensu suorum anticardinalium ad partem nostram, si fierj potest, trahantur, et quod intrusus cedat domino nostro saltim de facto cum Ius non habet, et super hoc interponantur plures labores. Et ista via videtur michi sanctior, expediencior, et conveniencior salutj animarum post inquisicionem veritatis, quam nullus fidelium ut credo dubitet, saltim de parte nostra, esse apud dominum Benedictum papam unicum nostrum'.

[100] *Ch. Paris.*, no. 1719, *Glorieux*, vol. 2, pp. 5–6; Salembier, *Pierre d'Ailly*, p. 114.

[101] *Auct. Ch.*, vol. 1, pp. 708–9; *Valois*, vol. 3, pp. 70–1.

[102] *Auct. Ch.*, vol. 1, pp. 712–13.

[103] A. Thomas, 'Lettres closes de Charles VI et de Charles VII addressées à l'université de Toulouse', *Annales du Midi*, **27–8** (1915–16), 179–82.

Toulouse.[104] There is no reason to dispute this statement, as several members of the University of Paris are known to have fallen under suspicion; [105] while towards the end of 1395 there was a veritable explosion of anger when some members of the faculty of law attempted to send a secret *rotulus* to Avignon,[106] an event which probably accounts for the formal banning of *rotuli* by the university in February 1396.[107]

Benedict XIII meanwhile continued his preparations for a proper counter-attack. Intending to belittle Paris he permitted the establishment of a faculty of theology at Salamanca; [108] and also instituted legal proceedings in the *curia* to deprive individual Parisian academics of their benefices. The university was thus forced onto the defensive, and retaliated in March 1396 with an impassioned appeal against Benedict to the 'next unique, true, orthodox, peaceful, and universal pope'.[109] This was followed by a flurry of papal annulments and renewed university appeals through to 1397.[110] Both sides had thus formally declared their positions. Benedict based his stand on extreme papalism, which is best revealed in his constitution banning any appeals against a pope.[111] The Parisian attitude was more ambiguous: the appeal documents were intended as much as instruments of propaganda as anything else, so that apart from the brief section containing the appeal itself, they provided the opportunities for verbose attacks on the proposed alternatives to the *via cessionis* and for bombastic exercises in self-glorification.

While the Parisian masters were engaged in this conflict with the pope at Avignon, their ideas were being rapidly disseminated throughout Europe. As part of the programme advanced in 1395, King Charles VI had been urged to join with the university in a series of foreign missions, many such embassies being sent in the next few years. But although the schism was to be the prime con-

---

104 F. Ehrle, 'Neue Materialen zur Geschichte Peters von Luna (Benedicts XIII)', *Archiv für Literatur- und Kirchengeschichte des Mittelalters*, **6** (1892), 264.

105 *Auct. Ch.*, vol. 1, pp. 707–8; *Valois*, vol. 3, p. 71.

106 *Ch. Paris.*, no. 1733; *Auct. Ch.*, vol. 1, pp. 715–16; *Bulaeus*, vol. 4, fos 752r–v.

107 *Bulaeus*, vol. 4, fo. 755r; *Ch. Paris.*, no. 1727; *Valois*, vol. 3, pp. 100–1.

108 V. Beltrán de Heredia, *Cartulario de la universidad de Salamanca (1218–1600)*, vol. 1, Acta Salmanticensia, vol. 17 (Salamanca, 1970), pp. 227–8.

109 *Bulaeus*, vol. 4, pp. 819–20.

110 ibid., vol. 4, pp. 801–26; *Valois*, vol. 3, pp. 87, 141–2.

111 *Bulaeus*, vol. 4, pp. 820–1.

sideration of these missions, it was to be by no means their sole concern: the embassy sent to Spain in 1396 was also exploited by the University of Paris to continue its earlier pursuit of Jean de Montson.[112] The degree of success encountered by the missions naturally varied: Wenceslas of Bohemia, for example, refused to grant an audience to the university ambassadors.[113] However, in October 1395 the Archbishop of Cologne, in response to a mission sent there, wrote to the university and urged it to continue its work to end the schism.[114] Later, when John of Bavaria declared neutrality for his prince-bishopric of Liège in 1398, he made specific mention of the work of the French king and the masters of Paris towards the reunification of the church.[115] But not all went so straightforwardly all the time. The nature of the negotiations and the issues at stake sometimes meant that the University of Paris was confronted by its opponents with some rather unpleasant home-truths. Thus, the envoys sent by Pope Boniface IX to the Reichstag held at Frankfurt in 1397 were instructed to denigrate the activities of the Parisians by referring to the discord which had troubled the university at the outbreak of the schism, and to the exodus which had occurred there in the early 1380s.[116]

Important as the relations between the University of Paris and the various crowned and mitred heads of Europe might be, it is not they which demand most attention at this point. The chief concern must be with the spread of Parisian ideas throughout Europe, and the reaction within the universities to this dissemination, particularly as the impact of the general letter of August 1395 was maintained by the issue of a further circular letter addressed to the universities in March 1396.[117] Unfortunately, the general paucity of evidence frequently obscures the situation. Thus, letters to the Universities of Padua and Bologna dated 12 September 1395, which appear to be covering letters for copies of *Quoniam fideles*, provide what appear to be the only signs of

---

[112] J. Vieillard and R. Avezou, 'Lettres originales de Charles VI conservées aux archives de la couronne d'Aragon à Barcelone', *Bibliothèque de l'Ecole des chartes*, 97 (1936), 329 n. 2.

[113] *Chron. S. Den.*, vol. 2, pp. 418–19.

[114] *Bulaeus*, vol. 4, fos 751v–752r.

[115] ibid., vol. 4, p. 869.

[116] Biblioteca Apostolica Vaticana, MS Pal. Lat. 701, fos 408v–409r. I owe this reference to Dr Margaret Harvey.   [117] *Bulaeus*, vol. 4, pp. 773–4.

contacts with the Italian universities.[118] There is no direct evidence for contacts with the University of Cologne, but it is inconceivable that, after the correspondence of mid-1394 and the Parisian mission actually sent to Cologne in autumn 1395, the masters can have been unaware of what was happening. There is also little sign of Spanish involvement in the debates, although the frequent Franco-Spanish diplomatic contacts presumably fostered some inter-academic communication. However, the Salamancan masters may have been involved in the debates which were held there in July and August 1397, and their ideas may underlie a letter sent by the King of Castile to Martin of Aragon in September of that year.[119] This letter rejected almost all the methods of reunification so far suggested, arguing rather that the popes should be left to settle the issue themselves.[120]

More concrete evidence survives for Parisian contacts with the University of Vienna, which had received a copy of *Quoniam fideles* in September 1395.[121] However, reaction was delayed until April 1396, by which time the second letter had been received, and an additional Parisian mission had arrived at the city with further proposals on cession.[122] These proposals were discussed by the Viennese faculty of arts on 30 April,[123] and on the following day, after having announced its support for the *via cessionis*, the university agreed to send a delegation to discuss the matter with the dukes.[124] The dukes' reply (as reported to the university on 5 May) was also favourable to the Parisian standpoint.[125]

But although the Viennese masters had announced their acceptance of cession in principle, they did not wish to desert Boniface IX. The faculty of arts declared that it had no intention of prejudicing the rights of the Roman claimant,[126] a stand which virtually ensured that nothing practical would result from the

---

[118] The letter to the University of Padua is in Biblioteca Nazionale, Naples, MS Vienn. latino 57 (olim 3160), fos 156r–v; that to Bologna appears in *ASV.*, Arm. LIV. 36, fos 125r–v. Only the first gives the year.

[119] Suárez Fernández, *Castilla*, pp. 37–8, 213–23.

[120] ibid., pp. 222–3.

[121] F. J. P. Bliemetzrieder, 'Antwort der Universität in Wien an diejenige zu Paris, 12 Mai 1396, wegen der Zession der beiden Päpste', *Studien und Mitteilungen aus dem Benedictiner- und dem Cistercienser-Orden*, **24** (1903), 101.

[122] ibid., p. 101.

[123] Uiblein, *Acta*, pp. 131–2.

[124] ibid., pp. 132–3.

[125] ibid., p. 133.

[126] ibid.

negotiations. Nevertheless, the Viennese did prepare a formal response to the propositions of the Parisian envoys, on 12 May 1396.[127] This was only intended to be taken as a preliminary statement: it was expected that a detailed response would be sent once the views of the dukes and Boniface IX were definitely known.[128] In the meantime, the university restated its acceptance of the *via cessionis*.[129] The dukes, however, changed their minds about the issue (possibly after having received news of an unfavourable papal response to the cession proposals). The masters accordingly had to change their opinions and the formal detailed reply to the Parisian embassy appears never to have been prepared.

But this was not the only Viennese consideration of the schism in this period. Henry of Langenstein continued his writing on the issue until his death in 1397. His most important contribution to the debates at this stage was the *Epistola de cathedra Petri*, completed in 1395–96.[130] In this work he outlined four possible methods of ending the schism: a judicial commission to determine the validity of the rival papal claims; joint resignation by the claimants, to be followed by an election performed only by those cardinals surviving from the pontificate of Gregory XI; judgement by a general council; or, finally, abdication by the rivals and another election performed by a small group of delegates (not cardinals) who were to be nominated by the claimants prior to their resignations.[131] Although encouraging princely participation in this work for union, Langenstein specifically rejected the *via facti*, along with certain other methods which he considered ineffective.[132] His preference was for cession, a choice which marks a distinct alteration from his views of the early 1380s. The conciliarism which he had then advocated, with its aim of deciding which of the then rivals was the legitimate pope, he now recognised as being anachronistic: whereas it might have been a feasible remedy when the schism was itself a novelty it could not be applied in 1395.[133]

All these continental contacts were, however, peripheral to what was to prove the main French (and therefore Parisian) concern at

127 Bliemetzrieder, 'Antwort', pp. 102–5.   128 ibid., p. 105.
129 ibid., p. 104.
130 Kneer, *Die Entstehung*, pp. 100–4, 134–45.   131 ibid., pp. 135–7.
132 ibid., pp. 142–4.   133 ibid., pp. 138–9.

this point in the schism, which was for Anglo-French cooperation to implement a solution. This was already being discussed in negotiations held in May 1395,[134] but there seems to have been no attempt made to contact the English universities at this stage. Nevertheless, it seems quite clear that debates on the schism were being held at Oxford at least, quite possibly under the influence of these Anglo-French diplomatic contacts. Nicholas of Fakenham produced two *questiones* in the summer or early autumn of 1395, in one of which he listed a number of possible remedies for the schism, while the other discussed princely involvement in the preliminaries for a general council.[135] Further evidence suggests that by about the same time the University of Oxford was already divided into two main camps, with the majority advocating a conciliarist solution to the schism while a sizeable minority argued for the *via cessionis*, possibly backed up by some form of coercion.[136] It was in such circumstances that the University of Paris sent an embassy to England bearing the general epistle of August 25, the envoys being charged with the task of converting both Richard II and the Oxford masters to an acceptance of cession. The envoys never reached Oxford, almost certainly because the king was aware of the opinions of the masters there and wished to save the French from a decidedly hostile reception.[137]

Although there had been these preliminary debates at Oxford, it is difficult to decide whether these had any formal character, and they certainly had not led to the formulation of any definitive pronouncement by the university. The truly formal debates followed the receipt of the Parisian letter (which, unlike the envoys, had not been detained in London) in November 1395, being initiated by Nicholas of Fakenham's *Determinatio de schismate*.[138] This work was deliberately provocative, summarising the earlier debates and presenting the contrasting views on

134 Perroy, *L'Angleterre*, pp. 364-5.
135 M. Harvey, 'Two "Questiones" on the great schism by Nicholas Fakenham, O.F.M.', *Archivum Franciscanum Historicum*, 70 (1977), 97-127, especially pp. 108-27.
136 Bayerische Staatsbibliothek, Munich, MS Clm. 7006, fos 126r-127r.
137 *Chron. S. Den.*, vol. 2, pp. 326-7; *Valois*, vol. 3, p. 76.
138 Printed in F. J. P. Bliemetzrieder, 'Traktat des Minoritenprovinzials von England Fr. Nikolaus de Fakenham (1395) über das grosse abendländische Schisma', *Archivum Franciscanum Historicum*, 1 (1908), 577-600, 2 (1909), 79-91.

the schism without offering any definite conclusions.[139] The tract is occasionally idiosyncratic, while an implied assertion of Richard II's rights to the French throne did not bode well for the projected Anglo-French cooperation.[140] But this negative aspect was partially compensated for by expressions of academic internationalism, justifying cooperation between England and France on the grounds that those countries possessed the three greatest universities in existence.[141]

In discussing the schism itself, Fakenham first considered the possibilities for the immediate restoration of unity within the church. His instinctive response was negative – immediate reunion would be possible only by joint resignation, which Benedict XIII had already rejected, and coercion would be permissible only if heresy was involved.[142] Besides, union would be unattainable until the anticardinals had been dealt with, which was not yet possible.[143] However, the need for a settlement was obvious: canonically there could be only one pope. Fakenham therefore suggested that reunion should be attempted either by cession, engineered in either particular or general councils (of which he considered the former more expedient), or by the deduction of the obscured truth, effectively the *via compromissi*, by bringing the opposing claimants and their cardinals together to sort out the issue between themselves.[144] However, neither of these was really the best way to end the dispute, which would be by invocation of the secular power to depose Benedict and allow Boniface to reign unopposed.[145]

Only after all this was the central issue of the tract arrived at, a detailed discussion of the *via cessionis*, the arguments against it in this instance having a distinctly Romanist bias.[146] The deadlock produced by the equal weight of the arguments could, Fakenham asserted, be broken by the application of the doctrine of expediency based on *epieikeia*. Although accepting that deposition of a pope was theoretically possible only in cases of heresy, he asserted that the application of *epieikeia* obliged both claimants

139 ibid., vol. 2, p. 91.
141 ibid., vol. 2, p. 87.
142 ibid., vol. 1, pp. 583-4.
144 ibid., vol. 1, pp. 593-4.
145 ibid., vol. 1, p. 594.

140 ibid., vol. 2, p. 86.

143 ibid., vol. 1, p. 584.

146 ibid., vol. 1, pp. 595-600, vol. 2, pp. 79-80.

to resign, and allowed the use of any necessary force to achieve that end.[147]

Even after this justification of forced resignation, the practical difficulties of its implementation remained. In dealing with these, Fakenham was rather vague. However, he did hint at the possibility that the pope's confessor, becoming his temporary superior in the confessional, could instruct him to resign.[148] He also suggested a practical application of *epieikeia* derived from his interpretation of the deposition of Pope John XII. On that occasion a charge of causing grave scandal had provided sufficient justification for the actions taken against the pope, *epieikeia* there giving legitimisation on the grounds of necessity and expediency.[149]

Yet what if the popes refused to resign and particular councils proved impotent against them? In such circumstances Fakenham suggested recourse to a general council.[150] The summons to such an assembly could be issued jointly by the rivals, although neither of them was to act as president of the gathering. The summons could also be issued by their prelates, while if the ecclesiastics failed to act the power of assembly was to pass to the secular princes.[151] Although this stage of the argument was justified by the invocation of imperial precedents, Fakenham made it clear that the leadership of this secular activity was to be assumed jointly by Richard II and Charles VI.[152]

In opposition to this activity, it could still be argued that papal involvement remained a necessity to legitimise the council,[153] but to this opinion Fakenham yet again offered his universal panacea of *epieikeia*. Necessity circumvented the law, which became irrelevant in such novel circumstances.[154] Fakenham had almost identified the concept of *epieikeia* for what it now actually was: an argument of expediency based on the view that the ends justified the means, no matter how illegal they were in terms of the accepted ecclesiastical constitution.

Despite Fakenham's often emotional language, epitomised by the violent attack on the Avignonese cardinals with which he

---

147 ibid., vol. 2, pp. 80–5.
149 ibid., vol. 2, p. 84.
151 ibid., vol. 2, p. 86.
153 ibid., vol. 2, p. 87.

148 ibid., vol. 2, p. 82.
150 ibid., vol. 2, pp. 85–6.
152 ibid., vol. 2, pp. 86–7.
154 ibid., vol. 2, pp. 87–8.

ended his tract,[155] the work's impact is difficult to assess. The writer was, after all, merely repeating the arguments of others, and the strongly Romanist sympathies which he revealed were probably shared by many contemporary Englishmen. They were certainly shared by Nicholas Radcliffe, a monk of St Albans and graduate of Oxford. His *Questio de schismate*, although probably not written at the university, may well reflect English academic opinion in its determination to remain loyal to Boniface IX and to resist the Parisian proposals on cession (unless, that is, their application was restricted to the resignation of Benedict XIII alone).[156]

Moreover, the University of Oxford adopted a strongly Romanist standpoint in its letter to Richard II of 17 March 1396, which marks the culmination of the debates following the receipt of the Parisian letter.[157] Its opening call was for the abdication of Benedict XIII, so that the division caused by the cardinals' rebellion against Urban VI in 1378 might be healed under his successor. While accepting double abdication as a theoretical solution, Oxford rejected the Parisian proposals as practically impossible. Each college of cardinals might elect its own successor to the abdicated pontiffs; and even if both groups united it would be impossible to find a place where they could hold a totally free and universally acceptable election.[158]

Moreover, cession was not an easy solution. Recent Parisian experience with Benedict XIII had admirably reflected its difficulties.[159] The logical consequence of abdication by the pope should be resignation by the cardinals, which would cause problems over the subsequent election of a new pope – unless that was to be left, as formerly, to the Roman clergy.[160] Oxford argued that rather than allow that to happen it would be better for the antipope – Benedict XIII – to resign in favour of Boniface.[161]

---

[155] ibid., vol. 2, pp. 88–91.
[156] Jacob, *Essays*, pp. 65–9; British Library, London, MS Royal 6.D.x, fos 277v–282v.
[157] *Bulaeus*, vol. 4, pp. 776–85; G. Ouy, 'Gerson et l'Angleterre: à propos d'un texte polémique retrouvé du chancelier de Paris contre l'université d'Oxford, 1396', in *Humanism in France at the end of the middle ages and in the early renaissance*, ed. A. H. T. Levi (Manchester, 1970), pp. 56–73.
[158] Ouy, 'Gerson', pp. 58–9.
[159] ibid., p. 60.
[160] ibid., p. 61.   [161] ibid., p. 61.

Continuing its attack, Oxford argued that cession was, in addition, neither safe nor perfect, as there was no guarantee that re-union would necessarily follow.[162] The university, unable to conceal its Romanist sympathies, had already expressed its attitudes towards the problem at the beginning of the letter, arguing that those in the wrong – the Benedictines – should be persuaded to recognise their errors and submit.[163] To this end, and although still considering that the unilateral resignation of Benedict and his cardinals was the best and quickest way of terminating the schism,[164] Oxford argued for the convocation of a general council as the most expedient method of reuniting the church. Apart from all else, it was the only method thoroughly compatible with the existing ecclesiastical constitution, and requiring no innovations: all arguments against it were therefore rejected.[165]

So total and tactless a rejection of the Parisian proposals naturally produced a storm at that university. Reaction is perhaps best exemplified in a series of glosses on the Oxford response produced by Jean Gerson in mid-1396, which gave full expression to the shock and disappointment which the reply produced, almost a sense of incredulity at the totality of Oxford's rejection of the *via cessionis*.[166] In contrast with the outraged responses, however, Pierre d'Ailly at least adopted a more realistic attitude, recognising the Oxford statement for what it truly was: a declaration that other countries would not allow their policy on the schism to be dictated to them either by Charles VI or by the masters of Paris.[167] The University of Paris had achieved its aim of stimulating discussions on the termination of the schism throughout Europe; the masters could not complain if occasionally they met with rebuffs. Besides, the problems encountered abroad were to be nothing in comparison with the difficulties which were to be faced when seeking to persuade the rest of France to carry out the policy which the university had taken such pains to formulate.

[162] ibid., pp. 62-8.
[164] ibid., p. 68.
[166] ibid., pp. 73-9; *Glorieux*, no. 533.
[163] ibid., pp. 61-2.
[165] ibid., pp. 69-72.
[167] Ehrle, *Alpartils Chronica*, pp. 476-7, 480.

Chapter 6

DE SUBTRACTIONE OBEDIENTIE II

The rejection by the University of Oxford of the Parisian proposals regarding the *via cessionis* had been received at a critical stage of the debates within France itself. Preparations had been in hand since April 1396 for the second national council of the French church, although the assembly did not actually begin until August.[1] The official Parisian line, revealed by Pierre Plaoul in his speech of 29 August, had by then hardened into a demand for total subtraction of obedience from Benedict XIII.[2] But the Parisians were divided, with Pierre d'Ailly appearing as a supporter of a council of the obedience.[3] The conflict with the University of Toulouse appeared again during the proceedings of the council, with Sancho Mulier and Pierre Ravat appearing among Benedict's defenders against the attacks of the Parisians.[4]

The outcome of this council was a reaffirmation of the policy of subtraction of obedience, although its implementation was to be delayed until Benedict had been given another chance to accept the *via cessionis*.[5] The Parisian masters were naturally disappointed at this result, but the university's policy was encountering considerable national and international opposition: even Castile issued a formal rejection of cession early in 1397.[6] There was also dissension within the university itself, those involved including Jean Gerson. His tract, *De schismate, vel de papatu contendentibus* incorporated a spirited rejection of most of the university's proposals in favour of Benedict's own suggestion of

---

[1] On this council, see *Valois*, vol. 3, pp. 88, 104-7; Ehrle, 'Neue Materialen', pp. 193-224, with a presence list at pp. 211-16 giving the university representatives at p. 213. A separate list of members of the University of Paris who were present appears at pp. 219-20.

[2] Ehrle, 'Neue Materialen', p. 221.

[3] Ehrle, *Alpartils Chronica*, pp. 476-80.

[4] Ehrle, 'Neue Materialen', pp. 220-2.

[5] *Valois*, vol. 3, p. 107.

[6] *Chron. S. Den.*, vol. 2, pp. 524-5.

the *via discussionis*.[7] But the proponents of cession and subtraction were unrelenting: in February 1397 Jean Courtecuisse harangued the king and called for the immediate withdrawal of financial support from Benedict XIII in order to procure his abdication.[8] This speech had no immediate result, although later in the year the crown did attempt (apparently ineffectively) to limit the papal power of provision to benefices.[9]

Meanwhile, although the precise situation is admittedly obscure, tension seems to have been increasing among the Parisian academics, as the discord within the university became more obvious. During the course of its debates, the corporation sought to impose an oath on its members obliging them to work for the implementation of the joint policy of cession and subtraction. This brought a rapid royal reaction: an ordinance of 12 September banned all discussion of cession within France, prohibited pamphleteering and ordered that all anti-cessionist documents should be surrendered and gathered in.[10] Although this partially satisfied the university's programme it was something of a Pyrrhic victory, for the masters' freedom of action was again restricted.

The nature of the developing power struggle within the University of Paris is by no means clear. Statements made later suggest considerable conflict, but of the debates themselves only scattered tracts remain. Among these can probably be included one by the lawyer Petrus de Muris [11] which, although adding little of originality to the discussions of withdrawal of obedience, did reassert the claims of the academics to participate in the attempts to persuade the rivals to come to terms before the further stages of the process were carried out.[12] The most striking aspect of this work, however, was its strong reaffirmation of conciliarism as a practical solution to the problem, urging that the assembly be summoned by the secular princes – specifically, by Charles VI of

---

7 *Glorieux*, no. 255; Posthumus Meyjes, *Jean Gerson*, pp. 51–3.

8 *Chron. S. Den.*, vol. 2, pp. 526–7; A. Coville, 'Recherches sur Jean Courtecuisse et ses oeuvres oratoires', *Bibliothèque de l'Ecole des chartes*, 65 (1904), 475, 498–9.

9 *Valois*, vol. 3, pp. 145–6.

10 ibid., vol. 3, pp. 144–5.

11 Öffentliche Bibliothek der Universität Basel, MS A.V.15, fos 157r–162r. For other MSS see *Valois*, vol. 3, p. 138 n. 4.

12 MS cit., fo. 159r: 'monendi sunt per fideles catolicos principes et prelatos, ac sacre teologie et utriusque Iuris doctores et magistros In quibus consistit Ius publicum'.

France and Wenceslas of Bohemia acting together – with the consent of the cardinals.[13] So assured was the author of the feasibility of this programme that he even went so far as to suggest possible locations for the council, naming Asti, Vienne and Lyons, any of which would be acceptable because they were all under the joint jurisdictions of the empire and members of the House of Valois.[14] Although there were to be attempts to achieve united action by the French and the empire, culminating in 1398 in a meeting between Charles VI and Wenceslas at Rheims, in view of France's determination to force through the policy of subtraction and resignation it is hardly surprising that de Muris's conciliarist suggestions seem to have fallen on deaf ears.

However, his claims for an academic role in the discussions of the schism were not to be so lightly dismissed. They were recognised in another work dating from about this time, an anonymous tract which, although possibly not written by a university member, nevertheless acknowledged Parisian influence on policy.[15] The author urged the masters to take action, but at the same time argued against withdrawal of obedience from Benedict XIII.[16] Instead he advocated two alternatives: either resignation by both the rivals, or else that the colleges of cardinals should wait until both popes had died and then unite for a joint election.[17] In the meantime, taking account of the university's determination not to send *rotuli* to Benedict, the writer suggested that the academics should send their petitions for benefices to the crown.[18]

The anti-subtractionist tone of these tracts received its most elaborate exposition in a work addressed by Raoul d'Oulmont to Charles VI early in 1397,[19] almost precisely at the same time as Jean Courtecuisse was making his demands for immediate withdrawal of obedience. The work was a virtual reiteration of the arguments against subtraction which Oulmont had apparently presented at the council held at Paris in 1396. Its opening statements asserted papal supremacy and plenitude of power, view-

---

13 ibid., fo. 161v.   14 ibid., fo. 162r.
15 *BN*, MS Lat. 1481, fos 135r–150r.
16 ibid., fo. 149v.
17 ibid.
18 ibid., fo. 150r.
19 For MSS see *Valois*, vol. 3, p. 139 n. 4. The citations which follow are to Balliol College, Oxford, MS 165B, pp. 217–40.

points which pervaded the whole tract.[20] The writer's partisanship was immediately obvious, with his statements that the election
of Urban VI 'nulla fuit ipso iure, et notorie nulla', whereas that
of Clement VII 'bona fuit et valida'.[21] Moreover, whatever doubts
there may have been about the validity of the rival elections of
1378 had all been dispelled by 1394. The election of Boniface IX
was attacked as invalid, he having been elevated to the papacy
only by those who had been promoted to the cardinalate by
Urban VI (and who were, therefore, anticardinals as far as Oulmont was concerned).[22] In contrast with this, the election of
Benedict XIII could not be challenged. He had been elected not
only by the cardinals created by Clement VII, but also by all
those who survived from the pontificate of Gregory XI, whose
successor he therefore became.[23] Benedict XIII could thus effectively ignore events after March 1378 as a mere interregnum
between the death of Gregory XI and his own election, a dramatic
alteration in the definition of the legitimacy of the Avignon
papacy which was to sustain both Benedict and his cause right
through to 1429. Having by these arguments decided the issue of
legitimacy, Oulmont then called for princely intervention in order
to defeat Boniface IX and establish Benedict as pope at Rome,
a plea based – as was much of the tract – on historical precedents.[24]
Oulmont could also proceed to challenge the *via cessionis*, declaring that, as Benedict was so obviously the legitimate pope, 'non
est licitum nec expedit dominum benedictum renitentem compellere ad viam cessionis, seu ad cessionem papatus intruso bonifacio
offerendum, nec etiam ad cedendum si intrusus cedere vellet'.[25]
Any such forced resignation would be invalid by definition.[26]

Oulmont's opposition to abdication and subtraction was firmly
based on his ecclesiology of papal supremacy. His views of the

20 ibid., p. 218.
21 ibid., pp. 220–1.
22 ibid., pp. 221–2.
23 ibid., p. 222: 'Eleccio dominj benedicti xiii in papam fuit et est sancta et valida,
ponito eciam quod eleccio Clementis vij nulla fuisset. Patet, quia sede vaccante per
mortem Clementis, vel saltem gregorij xj, fuit a veris cardinalibus concorditer electus;
et eleccio bonifacij intrusi non potuit impedire. Patet . . . quia cardinales creati per
Innocentem vj, per urbanum v, et gregorium xj, de quibus non est dubium quin
veri sunt cardinales, in ipsum consenserunt'.
24 ibid., pp. 222–4.
25 ibid., p. 224.   26 ibid., p. 225.

relationship between the pope and the church were strict, denying that the laity had any authority to interfere in ecclesiastical matters without invitation.[27] He also challenged several of the implications of cession: to be effective it necessitated double abdication, but Boniface would probably not resign even if Benedict did, a situation which meant that the schismatic adherents of the Roman pope would not have had judgement delivered against them, and nor would their counter-accusations have been refuted.[28] For Oulmont the withdrawal of obedience was no less than the ecclesiastical equivalent of patricide and *lèse majesté*, liable to bring its perpetrators into perpetual disrepute.[29] He also dealt at length with the idea of papal immunity from judgement, pointing out that a trial would be legal only if Benedict was a heretic, which was not the case. He had not rejected resignation unreasonably as he had offered other ways which had not yet been attempted, while still more existed (including a general council). Nor could he be considered a heretic when he truly believed himself to be the legal pope.[30]

Oulmont then proceeded to deliver a biting attack on the practical aspects of the French policy, beginning with a fundamental questioning of French authority in the matter. Abdication would certainly be an acceptable solution to the schism if the pope agreed with it, but he alone could decide which was the best way to end the difficulty. That power was not held by the princes – Oulmont having already sufficiently demonstrated that their authority was inferior to that of the pope – and nor could it be assumed by a council summoned without papal authorisation (presumably a reference to the recent Parisian proceedings) which could not claim to represent the whole church.[31] The consequences of any subtraction of obedience were also considered, drawing attention

[27] ibid., pp. 225-9.   [28] ibid., p. 226.
[29] ibid., pp. 228-9.
[30] ibid., pp. 229-31.
[31] ibid., p. 232: 'si dicatur quod via cessionis est electa, et contra illam non licet arguere, ut alij dicunt, Respondo dupliciter. Primo, quod verum est tanquam brevior et perfectior, ut pluribus videtur, si papa placeret. Secundo potest dici: a quibus est electa? Pluribus forsan videtur, quod a non habentibus potestatem, quia nec per papam nec per concilium autoritate ipsius congregatum; et saltim ad hoc debuisset congregari concilium tenencium partem suam, et auctoritate ipsius, aliter non valeret nec deberet dici concilium sed conciliabulum seu conventiculum vel monopolium prohibitum'.

to the threat of governmental instability posed by the automatic excommunication of the king which would follow such blatant disregard for the power of the keys,[32] not to mention the threat of a further schism within France between the king and those of his subjects who were more willing to obey the pope than the crown.[33] Such difficulties might also percolate through the French church, causing the people to withdraw allegiance from their bishops, and thus threatening the church's discipline, if not its very existence.[34]

Such dangers could not be over-stressed, particularly as any weakening among the Benedictine obedience would be regarded with relish by their opponents.[35] Oulmont further attacked the proposals to deprive the pope of his financial prerogatives over the French church, which would thus deny him the means of providing for the church's needs.[36] The international implications of any unilateral action were also pointed out, as they would probably be counter-productive. Such action should not be taken when there had only recently been Anglo-French negotiations seeking to resolve the problem.[37] Finally, the writer noted that the universities would be adversely affected by any withdrawal of obedience from the pope, for if the prelates thereby gained control of promotions to benefices they would provide for their own familiars in preference to graduates, causing financial difficulties and hardship for students.[38]

It was to counter arguments such as these – including those offered on the one hand by the University of Oxford, and on the other by the Benedictine cardinal Martin de Salva – that Simon de Cramaud had slightly earlier completed the first version of his *magnum opus*, the lengthy treatise *De subtractione obedientie*.[39] Although considerably amended in later versions, which continued to be produced until subtraction was effected in 1398, the underlying ideas of this work showed little alteration apart from

---

[32] ibid., p. 232.   [33] ibid., p. 233.   [34] ibid., p. 233.
[35] ibid., p. 233.   [36] ibid., pp. 234-7.
[37] ibid., p. 238.   [38] ibid., p. 239.
[39] I have to thank Professor H. Kaminsky, of Florida International University, for kindly allowing me the use of a copy of the typescript of a draft of his forthcoming edition of this tract. In the following notes, the quotations appear as in the typescript, but the references have (as far as possible) been brought into line with a copy of the tract in Balliol College MS 165B, pp. 1-99.

their increasing hostility to the popes as the climax of 1398 drew nearer.

Propagandistic in purpose, the work contained little justification for the *via cessionis* itself which, like subtraction, was simply assumed to be valid.[40] Partial withdrawal of obedience to preserve the Gallican liberties received scant attention, although Cramaud openly hinted at a Gallican rebellion in the suggestion that although the Roman church was the mother of the other churches, it was not their ruler.[41] Conciliarism was treated rather more seriously. The tract had a considerable impact throughout Europe, even after its main aims in France had been achieved in 1398, but it is in many ways a disconcerting work. Cramaud felt no compunction about twisting his authorities where necessary; and there is occasionally something rather nastily evasive about his arguments, such as his justification for the rejection of allegiance after so many years, a justification which raises more doubts than it settles.[42] In the circumstances of the tract's purpose, Cramaud's occasional statements of loyalty to Benedict XIII also ring rather hollow.[43]

To be effective in arguing his case, Cramaud adopted a defensive stance against the anti-subtractionist arguments, which were basically those later collected by Raoul d'Oulmont. But the tract

[40] MS cit., pp. 4–5: 'via cessionis seu renunciacions amborum contendencium de papatu, cum certis precedentibus revocacionibus processum et confirmacionibus promocionum, et statim in forma iuris sequente eleccione futuri unici et indubitati pastoris . . . est ad delendum penitus scisma et uniendum ecclesiam melior et brevior, et in omnibus, stante casu sicut est, conveniencior'.

[41] ibid., pp. 48–51.

[42] Thus, he claimed (ibid., pp. 36–7): 'Multa per pacienciam tolerantur que, cum veniunt in discussionem per quam melius videtur veritas, minime tolerantur . . . Sic quod licet tenuerim quod est dictum, tamen si nunc materia discussa, videam in materia incertitudinem respectu tocius ecclesie talem, que non potest bene venire in lucem, et scandalum nephandissimum in tota christianitate ortum propter duas elecciones, licet michi dicere quod proprie locum habet . . . Et si cum bona consciencia obedivi meo usque nunc, quando video illa de quibus est dictum, possum sibi obediencia substrahere'. This naturally provokes the question of why it had taken so long for Cramaud to realise that there was a dispute about the facts of the case, a weakness in the argument which he recognised, and to which he gave a feeble reply in later versions of the tract. There was also the problem of trying to reconcile this obvious claim for the rights of the individual conscience with his later assertion that a royal declaration on allegiance ought to be obeyed regardless of personal feelings (below, n. 66); but this difficulty he seems totally to have ignored.

[43] Indications of pseudo-Benedictine loyalty are peppered through the tract; e.g. MS cit., pp. 36, 97.

also revealed anti-subtractionist activity not mentioned in Oulmont's work. Thus, Cramaud referred to another possible solution
to the schism which was apparently being canvassed within the
University of Paris, that both popes should reign unchallenged
until one died, the survivor being recognised as sole pontiff.[44]
This scheme Cramaud rejected out of hand.[45] He also mentioned
accusations which were being levelled against Charles VI, that if
he abandoned Benedict XIII he would be inviting charges that he
desired a puppet pope, in that he was willing to proceed against a
foreigner, but had not acted against his cousin Clement VII.[46]
That such suggestions were being made at about this time is clear
from the statements prepared by Pierre d'Ailly for the Parisian
councils of 1395 and 1396.[47] Moreover, as the Urbanists had made
reference to Charles V's family loyalties to reinforce their accusations against him as instigator of the schism (accusations which
appeared most forcefully in the *Tetragonus Aristotelis* compilation of 1382), it was perhaps only logical that the need to disprove
such allegations should be exploited by the Benedictines in their
attempts to justify Charles VI in not taking action to end the
division.

The longest section of the *De subtractione obedientie* dealt with
the issue of withdrawal of obedience itself. Cramaud offered a
series of suppositions to justify rebellion against the pope,[48] incorporating a good deal of discussion on the legal need for any
retraction of obedience.[49] He argued that both rivals, by their
refusal to abdicate, had become schismatics and heretics[50] – an
accusation which increased in intensity in successive revisions of
the work. For Cramaud, subtraction of obedience would serve a
functional purpose, removing the greed which was the fundamental cause of the schism, and thereby preparing the way for
eventual reunion.[51] In his attitudes towards this *libido dominandi*
Cramaud reveals a superficial similarity with the analysis of the
issues earlier presented by Wyclif. But, in contrast with Wyclif,

44 ibid., p. 14.
45 ibid., p. 14.
46 ibid., p. 20.
47 Ehrle, *Alpartils Chronica*, pp. 472–3, 477.
48 MS cit., pp. 24–5, 37–8.
49 ibid., pp. 24–41.
50 ibid., pp. 41–6.
51 ibid., p. 54: 'obediencia substracta, cessabit affectus et libido dominandi, et inducen-
tur ita ad cessionem et pacem et unionem ecclesie, etc.'

Cramaud was convinced of the need for there to be a pope as a matter of faith, although he had to justify the use of the secular power to terminate the schism.[52] He had, therefore, to transfer his arguments from the purely ecclesiastical sphere of church versus papacy in order to find some legitimate method in accordance with the ecclesiastical constitution whereby a royally enforced withdrawal of obedience could be justified. This he achieved by incorporating the royal office within the ecclesiastical hierarchy: kings were prelates within the church, obliged to maintain its internal peace.[53] Not only ought they to act, they were empowered to do so, and had to fulfil their duties by using that power under penalty of mortal sin.[54] Amongst the options open to them was action by the withdrawal of allegiance.[55]

But it was necessary for Cramaud to advance from generalities to specifics, to justify the policy of subtraction in this particular instance. The basic issue was one of judgement of disputed facts, but in the circumstances there was no-one competent to determine the issue and therefore subtraction of obedience in order to force abdication was the only possible course.[56] Cramaud presumably had this situation in mind when he later remarked that although the use of force would generally invalidate an election in this case it would not negate a forced resignation.[57] As had happened in previous works on the schism, the canonistic justification based on necessity was here invoked.[58] However, had there been a com-

---

[52] Cf. his remark (ibid., p. 62): 'licet non sit ex fide dicere, Iste est papa et iste non est papa, tamen ex fide est quod unum debemus habere'.

[53] ibid., pp. 55-7.

[54] ibid., pp. 28-33: 'supponitur quod ad sedacionem huius scismatis et pacem ecclesie totis viribus procurandum, reges sunt astricti sub pena peccati mortalis . . . et de iure canonico et divino habent potestatem ambos concertantes compellere ad viam pacis; ergo si non faciant, mortaliter peccant . . . Et adhuc hodie possunt iudicare, quando ecclesiastica potestas deficit . . . Ex quibus infero correlarie quod reges eciam non requisiti debent totis viribus ad pacem ecclesie laborare, alias non excusantur a peccato . . . ergo . . . debent reges et tenentur diligenter inquirere, quid in isto vix solubili dubio sit agendum'.

[55] ibid., p. 33: 'Hiis . . . premissis . . . reges non possunt sine offensa dei scisma tolerare; ergo possunt et debent ambobus concertantibus, viam pacis eis consulte et digeste oblatam non acceptantibus, obedienciam substrahere'.

[56] ibid., pp. 35-6: 'Nec est qui super hoc iudicet . . . nec concilium nec cardinales . . . Et minus compromissarii'.

[57] ibid., pp. 90-1: 'Ex quibus clare concluditur quod licet eleccio que non est facta libere sed per impressionem vel compulsionem non valeat, cessio tamen istorum duorum concertancium facta per compulsionem et potencium regum erit iusta et canonica'. [58] ibid., p. 95.

petent judge available to determine the issue of fact, Cramaud may well have opted for some form of conciliarism, and there are hints of this in his attempts to produce a conciliarist justification for the French adoption of the policy of subtraction. At one point he produced a somewhat specious interpretation of the events which had culminated in the joint Anglo-French-Castilian approval of the *via cessionis* in 1396, transforming the Parisian assembly of 1395 and the subsequent political and diplomatic manoeuvrings into something which he claimed was the equivalent of a general council of the church.[59]

A more sober treatment of conciliarism appeared in the final section of the treatise, where it received a logical refutation. The facts of the case were by now too complex to allow for anything so simple as a straightforward decision between the two claimants.[60] The disparate size of the opposing parties meant that the Romanists would be able to overwhelm their opponents (Cramaud here presaging complaints which were actually to be made at the Council of Constance about the potential numerical preponderance of the Italian episcopate in any general council).[61] Moreover, he declared that the outcome of any council at this stage would be quite unpalatable, making one party retrospectively schismatic and producing innumerable complications, including the invalidation of all ordinations and appointments received from the adjudged antipope and his adherents. Cramaud here revealed the growing dilemma which faced those in the church who sought to end the schism but were already quite fully committed simply because of their ecclesiastical careers when he declared that he and others would not accept any decision which adversely affected their own hold over their benefices.[62]

Similar reasoning was applied to justify the rejection of the *via compromissi*,[63] while the *via facti* was merely condemned and discarded as 'omino dampnabilis'.[64] Naturally, Cramaud advocated cession and subtraction, presenting a reasonably detailed pro-

[59] ibid., pp. 58–9.
[60] ibid., pp. 78–84.
[61] ibid., pp. 81, 83.
[62] ibid., p. 84: 'Ego testificor de me ipso, quod . . . si sentencia concilii veniret contra Benedictum, ego recalcitrarem quantum in me esset; et iuste secundum me . . . Et ita credo quod faciant alii'.
[63] ibid., p. 85. [64] ibid., p. 85.

gramme for their implementation derived from his own summary of the conclusions of the council held at Paris in 1395.[65] He also declared that the policy adopted by the crown should be obeyed by everyone, even if the action proposed offended their individual consciences.[66]

Overall, the *De subtractione obedientie* was one of the most important tracts produced during the schism, but its continued circulation even after withdrawal of obedience had been decreed in France indicated that much still remained to be done. This was perhaps the whole point of the work itself, with its emphasis on the practical aspects of the situation. Although the theory had to be justified to some extent, a practical programme already existed in the decisions of the 1395 assembly. This was intended to cover all the contingencies preparatory to the drastic step of a double papal resignation; it was a scheme for settling the differences between the opposing sides so that the new, unique, pontiff could commence his reign in peace without inheriting the internecine strife of the schism. Unfortunately, as a programme it was hopelessly premature.

In any case, there is a strong possibility that this scheme was not truly representative of Parisian opinion. Despite the restrictions on debate, discussions had continued, with further calls for a full and proper consideration of the issues.[67] There were signs of continued internal opposition to subtraction, as in the case of Henry Poelman d'Arnhem's obstinate adherence to Benedict XIII during his period of office as rector of the English nation – a loyalty which eventually led to his deprivation.[68] Meanwhile a national climax was steadily approaching, with preparations during the early months of 1398 for a further council of the French church which was to give the definitive statement of the policy to be adopted in dealing with Benedict XIII. The French were not the only people preparing for this assembly: the pope

[65] ibid., p. 77.
[66] ibid., p. 89: 'reges non habent considerare consciencias singulorum, sed solum quod bona intencione et ad finem pacis procedant. Et subiecti in hoc debent ipsis omnes obedire, et si habent remorsum consciencia, illi qui habent debent ipsum deponere vel talem conscienciam captivare, et obedire regibus . . . Et si vellent sequi suam conscienciam erroneam, nichilominus reges compellent eos suis ordinacionibus obedire'.
[67] *Auct. Ch.*, vol. 1, pp. 759–60. [68] ibid., vol. 1, pp. 765–8; *Valois*, vol. 3, p. 141 n. 1.

himself had been taking steps in an attempt to safeguard his position, and had sent the Cardinal of Pamplona to Paris to obstruct any moves to implement the *via cessionis*.[69] The result of the cardinal's activities was some rather acrimonious correspondence which fully reflects Benedict's appreciation of the threat to his position which was posed by the impending Gallican assembly.[70]

That meeting itself opened on 14 May 1398, and continued until August.[71] The debates were formalised but intense, the speakers on both sides including the staunchest adherents of their respective policies. Eventually, after a last-minute intervention by the University of Paris, the party advocating subtraction of obedience from Benedict XIII proved triumphant. But although the council of 1398 represents the climax of the French debates on the withdrawal of obedience, the importance of the assembly as it affected university members was not restricted to the straightforward proceedings of the gathering. At least in relation to the University of Paris, the council was the full embodiment of the concept of 'university' in its widest sense, as a corporate body comprising all the graduates of a particular institution. As such, the council allowed for debates between regent and non-regent masters of the university, between residents and non-residents, and thus revealed the tensions which could develop within the overall definition as differing interests came into play. For the provincial universities, the smallness of their delegations and other reasons meant that the situation was less complex than it was for the Parisians.

The evidence available for the assembly falls into three basic categories: the external deliberations of the University of Paris, as it tried desperately to impose its hard-line policy on the meeting; the attitudes expressed in speeches during the council; and most important of all, the personal interpretations of the situation revealed in the secret schedules presented at the termination of

---

[69] *Chron. S. Den.*, vol. 2, pp. 572–3; Ehrle, 'Neue Materialen', pp. 247–8.
[70] Ehrle, 'Neue Materialen', pp. 248–53; *Chron. S. Den.*, vol. 2, pp. 572–9.
[71] On this council, see *Valois*, vol. 3, pp. 150–87; Martin, *Origines*, vol. 1, pp. 275–87; Ehrle, 'Neue Materialen', pp. 271–87; Posthumus Meyjes, *Jean Gerson*, pp. 56–61; Salembier, *Pierre d'Ailly*, pp. 162–6; H. Bourgeois du Chastenet, *Nouvelle histoire du concile de Constance* (Paris, 1718), pp. 3–84 (this, and all succeeding references, is to the section of *preuves*).

the debates. The first category is the least important, the university as a corporation apparently taking little action until towards the end of the meeting. This inactivity may have been due to internal discord: the exact size of the subtractionist party is uncertain, but at one stage Pierre Ravat (although admittedly not himself a member of the University of Paris) declared his belief that subtraction was supported by barely a third of the Parisian masters [72] – a view which received some support from a statement made by the Archbishop of Tours, who suggested that the subtractionists had rather bludgeoned their policy through the university.[73]

Apart from the speeches of its representatives at the council, the university apparently remained silent until 11 June, when a memorandum addressed to the king again urged a policy of cession and subtraction, demanding the immediate implementation of both. This was enlarged on at an audience held on 14 June.[74] This public declaration influenced several of the ballots presented at the council,[75] but not sufficiently to give a clear-cut victory. The subtractionist party was therefore obliged to increase its numbers artificially by drafting in additional academics to bolster its final tally.[76]

As important as the opinions of the university in its effect on the debates, and in all probability more influential, was the proximity of the king. There was obvious royal control over the speeches against Benedict, perhaps involving collusion between the crown and the university speakers: both Gilles des Champs and Pierre le Roy referred in advance to a speech to be made by Pierre Plaoul,[77] although this may simply indicate their presence at the university congregation at which this last speech had been approved. A speech by des Champs also suggests that the members of the royal administration who were also masters of the University of Paris gave priority to their royal duties over their personal

---

[72] Bourgeois du Chastenet, *Constance*, p. 12.
[73] Archives Nationales, Paris, J.518, fo. 438r.
[74] Bourgeois du Chastenet, *Constance*, pp. 77–9; *Valois*, vol. 3, p. 162.
[75] H. Kaminsky, 'The politics of France's subtraction of obedience from Pope Benedict XIII, 27 July 1398', *Proceedings of the American Philosophical Society*, **115** (1971), 377 n. 55.
[76] ibid., p. 377.
[77] Bourgeois du Chastenet, *Constance*, pp. 41, 61.

views of the situation.[78] Even the supporters of Benedict XIII had
to remember the royal presence, and their speeches were therefore
defensive in tone. Typical of these was Pierre Ravat's second
oration which, whilst denying royal authority within the church,
added a caveat considerably reducing the impact of his remarks.[79]
The final section of that speech also revealed Ravat's awareness
of crown influence on the politics of the schism, incorporating a
direct appeal to Charles VI not to abandon the traditions of his
dynasty and, by supporting withdrawal of obedience, become a
party to schism.[80]

Although present officially in his capacity as Bishop of Macon,
Pierre Ravat can be considered throughout this assembly as being
in reality an unofficial representative of the University of Toulouse. That university also had three official representatives, Vital
de Castelmoron, Sancho Mulier and Jean de la Coste. All, apart
from the first, appeared at the council as vigorous defenders of
Benedict XIII.[81] Ravat was the main advocate, however, constantly questioning and attacking the validity of subtraction.
Many of his arguments, as was also the case with Jean de la
Coste's rather pedantic speech, were little more than recapitulations of those earlier advanced by Raoul d'Oulmont. Sancho
Mulier was more original, providing a penetrating analysis of the
subtractionists' case – which he compared to the *via facti* – and
arguing that if force was rejected against an antipope, then the
invocation of it against a legitimate pope was even more repre-
hensible.[82] For Mulier, subtraction of obedience would work
against rather than for the *via cessionis*, making its proponents'
position quite untenable.[83] Partial withdrawal of obedience he considered to be merely a contradiction in terms.[84] Moreover, whatever its motivations, subtraction would be worse than never having
recognised a true pope: the Romans might be pagans because they
wanted Pedro de Luna to renounce what they considered mere
pretensions, but the French would be heretics for demanding the
expulsion of a true pope.[85]

[78] Kaminsky, 'Politics', p. 374.   [79] Bourgeois du Chastenet, *Constance*, p. 54.
[80] ibid., pp. 55-6.
[81] Ravat's speeches are ibid., pp. 5-13, 49-56; that of Mulier (throughout misnamed
    Petrus Emilarius) is ibid., pp. 13-16; that of de la Coste at pp. 17-20.
[82] ibid., p. 13.   [83] ibid., pp. 13-14.
[84] ibid., p. 14.   [85] ibid., p. 15.

There was obviously a growing division within France, a division of which the continuing conflict between the Universities of Paris and Toulouse was clearly symptomatic. The root of this division was revealed by Ravat in his second speech. For the advocates of withdrawal, it was Benedict himself who was the cause of the whole problem; for their opponents it was the Romanists who were alone to blame.[86] For Benedict's defenders, attacks on the pope were seen as retrospective attacks on Clement VII and an admission that France had been misled on the schism since its inception.[87] The difference was also emphasised by contrasting attitudes to royal involvement in the dispute. For Benedict's supporters, led by Ravat, the royal right to interfere did not exist, unless such intervention was first requested by the church.[88]

Ravat's attacks on subtraction served very much as a stimulus for the supporters of the Gallican policy. His harsh treatment of the *De subtractione obedientie* forced Simon de Cramaud to adopt a defensive attitude in his speeches, but he nevertheless developed his ideas on the purposes of both partial and total withdrawal, and on conciliarism.[89] Pierre le Roy's speech was more practical, defending subtraction by appealing to the ancient liberties of the Gallican church,[90] and justifying royal intervention on the grounds that both rivals had sought French assistance to end the schism.[91] Gilles des Champs went even further in his defence of royal action, making an extraordinarily all-embracing statement giving the king *carte blanche* to intervene to end the dispute even if the church did not invite him to do so.[92] He defended Charles VI's support of Clement VII [93] and called for a council of the obedience which, being effectively general, had sufficient authority to ordain subtraction.[94]

Of all the subtractionist speeches, that made by Pierre Plaoul was the only one which was officially representative of the views of the University of Paris. In his consideration of the issues he asserted the dispensability of the individual pope, and argued in

---

[86] ibid., p. 52.

[87] ibid., p. 51.

[88] ibid., p. 54.

[89] His speech is ibid., pp. 20–8; see especially p. 26.

[90] His speeches are ibid., pp. 29–36, 56–63.

[91] ibid., pp. 62–3.

[92] ibid., pp. 39–40, his speech being at pp. 37–49.

[93] ibid., p. 44.

[94] ibid., p. 43.

favour of both partial and total subtraction of obedience.[95] Like the other defenders of those policies he was forced to reply to Ravat, and to deny that there had been great opposition to subtraction within the university: instead he claimed that it had received unanimous approval when debated in congregation.[96] But the opposition's barbs seem to have struck home, for Plaoul's speech also included a reference to the Albigensian Crusade which can only be interpreted as a strong hint to the king that Toulouse's anti-subtractionist activities should be curtailed.[97]

However, it was only after the discussions that real decisions could be taken, and these depended on the ballots offered at the end of the proceedings.[98] Not surprisingly, the University of Toulouse led the attack on subtraction, condemning French action thus far.[99] But their case was not totally negative: the university's representatives called for consultations with Benedict XIII about abdication, and also about the possibilities of summoning a council of the obedience. This, they argued, would not be a waste of time, as such a council would be necessary to declare the withdrawal of obedience.[100] Similar arguments were applied to a council of both obediences, that it would be better to have one immediately rather than wait.

The clash between the Universities of Paris and Toulouse rather overshadows the activities of the other universities at this assembly, although they appear in any case to have been minimal. However, in declaring the results of the ballot, Arnauld de Corbie specifically mentioned the provincial universities as having supported subtraction – with the exception of Toulouse, which was pointedly not mentioned.[101] The individual schedules themselves reflect this provincial acceptance of the policy of withdrawal. The Angers representative made his support conditional on the policy being carried out with the assent of a majority of the cardinals,

---

[95] ibid., pp. 63–74.   [96] ibid., p. 64.

[97] ibid., p. 67.

[98] The originals of these are preserved in Archives Nationales, Paris, J.517, a contemporary copy being in J.518, fos 360v–490v (to which all the following notes refer). A much later transcript is in *BN*, MS Lat. 1480A2, pp. 183–667.

[99] Archives Nationales, J.518, fo. 362v.

[100] ibid., fo. 363v: 'cum eciam post substractionem haberet necesse convocari Consilium . . . breviori modo fieret nunc quam substractionem facta, quia cum necesse habemus ad illud devenire, totum tempus intermedium perdimus'.

[101] Bourgeois du Chastenet, *Constance*, pp. 81–2.

although whether his ballot properly reflected the university's opinion is unclear, as he admitted to not having consulted other members on the issue.[102] Montpellier's official envoys seem to have been Johannes Gordon and Pierre Cottin,[103] with a certain Jean Aquillon appearing on behalf of an unidentifiable group of doctors.[104] All accepted subtraction, as did the envoys from Orléans,[105] although later reaction by that university suggests that its representatives may have exceeded their commission in so doing.[106] The programme which they suggested was quite detailed, seeking action by both obediences and (with or without the consent of the cardinals) a rapid reunification of the church.[107]

But, ultimately, it was the Parisian masters who dominated the proceedings and whose votes are the most informative. Not everyone could be bulldozed into accepting the university's policy, as the Archbishop of Tours revealed in his long anti-subtractionist statement.[108] Although generally non-committal, he attacked the university arguments, listing the difficulties which would follow from the withdrawal of obedience – including an emphasis on the resulting divisions within the European academic community [109] – and pointing out that the programme might actually be counter-productive and merely encourage the Romans in their stand.[110]

---

[102] MS cit., fo. 362r.   [103] ibid., fo. 362r.

[104] ibid., fos 364r–v.

[105] ibid., fo. 361v, their presence being confirmed by a later document in *BN*, MS Lat. 1479, fo. 37r.

[106] *BN*, MS Lat. 1479, fo. 37r.

[107] Archives Nationales, J.518, fo. 361r: 'quia dicta substractione sic facta periculosissimum esset sic diu persistere, videtur nobis necessarium esse quod illi de alia obediencia celeriter requirantur quod ipsi etiam subtrahent totalem obedienciam suo; et in casu quo sic facient, necesse erit quod ambe partes obediencie per representacionem cum collegiis Cardinalium utriusque obediencie, vel saltim Collegia Cardinalium utriusque obediencie, in uno loco conveniant; quod si Collegia Cardinalium convenire non vellent, quod ambe obediencie per representacionem conveniant ad providendum de unico vicario ihesu Christi. Quod si alia obediencia ad predicta convenire non velit, tunc convenit obediencia nostra per representacionem una cum Cardinalibus obediencia nostra ad providendum ulterius nobis, etc.; vel eciam sine Cardinalibus si (quod absit) convenire non vellent'.

[108] His response, which appears to be the actual ballot, is ibid., fos 435v–436r. This was supported by a lengthy additional statement opposing subtraction, ibid., fos 436r–439r.

[109] ibid., fo. 436v: 'scisma particulare erit inter universitates istius obediencie inter se et earundem ex una parte cum aliis universitatibus alterius obediencie'.

[110] ibid., fos 436v–437r: 'Si dicatur quod iam universitas deliberavit et petivit a Rege substractionem, respondent aliquj quod intencio sane deliberacionem fuit sicut

Of the other individual ballots, that prepared by Simon de Cramaud was predictably subtractionist, being little more than a précis of his *De subtractione obedientie*. Force and arbitration were rejected, double cession advocated.[111] He also urged consultations between the cardinals and representatives of the various kingdoms in order to elect a new pope and either force the rivals to resign or else punish them as schismatics.[112] Gilles des Champs offered a more precise programme, whereby if Benedict had not resigned after obedience had been withdrawn for a year, a council of the obedience was to proceed against him as a schismatic. Any counter-action was to be prevented by the simple expedient of arresting the pope. The king should also control events by blocking exits from the kingdom and censoring letters. Negotiations should be opened with the Roman obedience to persuade it to adopt a similar programme. This would be followed by a meeting of proctors of both obediences to begin preparations for union, which would be achieved by a confrontation of both popes at Genoa.[113]

Other schedules revealed similar idiosyncracies. Jean Courtecuisse, whilst seeking subtraction and negotiations between the obediences, still argued that the Avignon obedience should recognise no other pope while Benedict lived.[114] Jean Petit also accepted cession and subtraction, but some sense of urgency pervades his vote, which called on the Paris meeting to reach some definite conclusion, otherwise he feared that the schism would not be resolved during his lifetime.[115]

However, not all Parisian graduates accepted withdrawal of obedience without qualification. Thus Henry de Vienne, Abbot of S. Pharaon at Meaux,[116] accepted the validity of a policy of resignation but rejected unilateral subtraction by France. This would

reperietur si libere permittatur loqui, quod equo pede et simili cursu removeretur obediencia ab utroque contendencium, quia aliter remocio ista non prodesset ad unionem habendam, sed pocius scisma confirmavit quia nostra pars fieret debilior et conculcatior et ita alii videntes hoc numquam vellent similiter deprimere suum, sperantes quod tandem pars nostra se ipsum impugnans deficeret et sua de die in diem fortificaretur'.

111 ibid., fos 364v–366r.
112 ibid., fo. 366r.
113 ibid., fos 390v–391r.
114 For his vote see Coville, 'Recherches', pp. 488–9.
115 His conclusions are printed in Coville, *Petit*, p. 45.   116 MS cit., fos 400v–402r.

merely be ineffective – Benedict would not resign while he retained support somewhere, even if only in Aragon.[117] He therefore
suggested a programme of diplomatic activity, although the
Romans (as the originators of the schism) were specifically to be
excluded from these arrangements.[118] The University of Paris
should also extend its contacts with other universities [119] so that
both obediences could work together to achieve a universal total
subtraction.[120]

The differences apparent in these few individual statements
were characteristic of the whole series of schedules, the nuances
making it clear that the apparent and stated unity of the University of Paris was quite deceptive. Although almost all believed
that they were following the dictates of the university ('a quo', as
the Dean of Rouen remarked, 'nec volo, nec debeo recedere'),[121]
individual phrasing reveals the lack of any real consensus. The
differing attitudes towards Benedict XIII himself admirably
reflected these dissensions: Pierre le Duc, Abbot of St Victor lez
Paris, accepted that Benedict was the legitimate pope, but nevertheless argued that he ought to resign,[122] whereas Roland Ranier
doubted the claims of both rivals.[123] Concern about the vagueness
of the situation might underlie statements such as that of Isam-
bard Martel that subtraction was a charitable act which would
benefit Benedict's soul if it did force him to resign.[124] However,
probably nearer to the general opinion was the demand for subtraction to prevent France from becoming tainted by the pope's
crimes.[125] The generalised attack on the pope continued throughout the subtractionist ballots, Benedict being likened to a second
Pilate,[126] and identified as a disturber of the church who deserved
to be accused of schism [127] and even heresy.[128] Occasionally it was
even suggested that he was acting in collusion with Boniface IX
to obstruct union.[129]

All this was, however, peripheral to the main concern with
cession and subtraction. Here again the Parisian ballots reveal

[117] ibid., fos 401r-v.
[118] ibid., fos 401v-402r.
[119] ibid., fo. 402r.
[120] ibid., fo. 402r.
[121] ibid., fo. 435r.
[122] ibid., fos 397r-v.
[123] ibid., fo. 384v.
[124] ibid., fo. 380r.
[125] ibid., fo. 435r.
[126] Guillaume du Jardin, ibid., fo. 368v.
[127] Roland Ranier, ibid., fo. 384v.
[128] Guillaume du Jardin, ibid., fo. 369r.
[129] ibid., fo. 367v.

great differences of opinion. Although there was general agreement on the Gallican proposals for the withdrawal of revenues,[130]
there was uncertainty as to just how total the eventual subtraction
of obedience should be. Pierre le Roy wished for it to be complete,
but was prepared to accept a partial withdrawal.[131] For Nicholas
de Beauvais, however, partial subtraction could be no more than
the first step, leading to complete withdrawal if Benedict's subsequent actions – including any form of counter-action – revealed
him as a pertinacious schismatic.[132] The fear of a possible harsh
papal reaction to any French action is clear from the schedule
prepared by Jean Bourrillet, who demanded that the subtraction
be total and immediate so that Benedict would be unable to
deliver any effective counter-attack.[133]

But the real differences of opinion among the graduates were
revealed elsewhere, in their views on the aims and duration of
the subtraction. Most academics seem to have treated the withdrawal of obedience as an end in itself, hardly considering the
next stage; but when they did express their opinions on this point,
the views of the university members contrasted greatly. Pierre le
Duc certainly seems to have seen subtraction as an end in itself,
presumably expecting that princely action (if sufficiently widespread) would act as the force to produce resignation.[134] The
Bishop of Soissons called for immediate withdrawal from both
claimants and action to secure a third election.[135] Pierre Fleurie
combined princely duty with a third election in a scheme whereby
Charles VI would withdraw obedience, take action to depose the
rivals and then arrange a joint conclave of the cardinals of both
obediences to elect a new pope and punish the former rivals as
schismatics.[136] Gilles de la Place saw Benedict, rather than the
schism, as the object of the attack – which indeed he was for
some people – and therefore urged that the subtraction be maintained until he was removed from the papacy by death or deposition, and union at last achieved.[137] Ursin de Tallerande, with a
similar outlook, sought withdrawal until Benedict voluntarily

---

[130] e.g. ibid., fos 366v, 370v–371r, 427r.   [131] ibid., fo. 427v.
[132] ibid., fo. 389v.
[133] ibid., fo. 386v.
[134] ibid., fo. 397v.   [135] ibid., fo. 412v.
[136] ibid., fos 369v–370v.   [137] ibid., fo. 388r.

accepted cession.[138] Others who (like Gilles de Justefaz and Pierre Godard) saw the schism as the chief issue uncompromisingly demanded subtraction until union had been achieved, by whatever means.[139] Tallerande's scheme was specifically rejected by some of these, Nicholas d'Estries echoing Jean Petit in declaring that any offer of resignation made by Benedict would be mere dissembling, designed to disrupt the activities of the Parisian assembly rather than bring about the reunification of the church.[140]

Although all of these differences in attitudes are significant as far as they relate to the state of the University of Paris, when the time came to collate the ballots they were all sufficiently minor to be glossed over. Accordingly, it was declared that 'subtraction' had the support of the majority at the council, and in due course subtraction was decreed, on 28 July 1398.[141] The break with Avignon was intended to be total, and would be formalised by royal authority, thus effectively creating a schism within the Avignonese obedience. An ecclesiastical system was imposed which was to be as nationalistic in effect as any Wycliffite or Hussite could desire, although with the distinction that the subtraction thus ordained was never intended to be permanent. But precisely how long it would last still remained a matter of conjecture.

---

138 ibid., fo. 433v.
139 ibid., fos 388v, 390r.
140 ibid., fo. 377v. See also the opinion of Eustace de Rieu, ibid., fo. 418r.
141 *Chron. S. Den.*, vol. 2, pp. 598–644; *Valois*, vol. 3, pp. 183–7.

Chapter 7

DE RESTITUTIONE OBEDIENTIE

Despite the aspirations held by the French as they sought to implement their policy of subtraction of obedience from Benedict XIII, once that policy was put into effect its failure soon became obvious. Only part of the Avignonese followed the French lead in withdrawing support from the pope,[1] while even military action in Avignon itself failed to reduce Benedict to submission. The only result was a stalemate.[2] The French themselves did not greet subtraction with wholehearted enthusiasm, the opposition to it centring on Toulouse, where Charles VI had to instruct his officials to enforce compliance with the withdrawal decrees.[3] Meanwhile, the Roman obedience was making its own views on the situation known in response to constant French diplomatic pressure, embassies and letters having been sent throughout Europe.[4] French attention seems to have focussed on England where, after he had received a mission from Charles VI in August 1398, in which the envoys included Jean Courtecuisse,[5] King Richard II turned to the Universities of Oxford and Cambridge for advice, which was duly offered early in 1399.

The statement by the masters of Cambridge reiterated many of the opinions which had characterised the Oxonian letter of 1396, supporting Boniface IX, attacking his opponents, and rejecting

---

[1] The Castilians subtracted obedience from Benedict XIII in December 1398 (*Raynaldus, ann.* 1398, nos. 25–6). The cardinals and the city of Avignon had rebelled in September (*Valois*, vol. 3, pp. 192–3, 195–6). For the unevenness of the rejection of Benedict, see ibid., vol. 3, pp. 283, 286–9.

[2] On the struggle for Avignon, see *Valois*, vol. 3, pp. 197–205.

[3] E. Roschach, *Ville de Toulouse: inventaire des archives communales antérieures à 1790: I, Série AA* (Toulouse, 1891), pp. 102–3.

[4] See *Valois*, vol. 3, pp. 283–6, 289–90, 295–6; Weizsäcker, *Reichstagsakten*, vol. 3, pp. 181–2.

[5] W. Ullmann, 'The University of Cambridge and the great schism', *Journal of Theological Studies*, N.S. **9** (1958), 55–6; Perroy, *L'Angleterre*, pp. 384–6 (with the instructions of the envoys at pp. 416–18); *Valois*, vol. 3, pp. 291–3.

many of the Parisian arguments as inapplicable.[6] The university declared that, after Charles VI and his subjects had subtracted their obedience from Benedict XIII, their best course would be to submit to Boniface IX as their legitimate pope – although any argument that the English should withdraw from Boniface was strongly repudiated,[7] on grounds very similar to those earlier advanced at Paris by Raoul d'Oulmont to justify continued adherence to the pope of Avignon. The Cambridge masters also proposed two other possible solutions, versions of the *via cessionis* and the *via concilii*. The first envisaged the resignation of Benedict XIII, to be followed in due course by that of Boniface after he had made the necessary arrangements for the succeeding election.[8] The second scheme required Boniface to summon a general council of the whole church – the Greeks being represented as well as the Latins – to carry through a programme of wholesale reunification and reformation. This plan would obviously have been unacceptable to the Benedictines: if they attended the council, they would necessarily be denying their own claims for their pope. But Cambridge argued that, if the Benedictines were absent, the council should nevertheless proceed to determine the validity of the elections of 1378 (in such circumstances, a foregone conclusion) and declare which of the claimants should resign.[9]

Many of the ideas proposed by the Cambridge masters reappeared in the statement of the University of Oxford, issued on 5 February 1399.[10] However, there were major differences. As in its declaration of 1396, Oxford accepted the theoretical validity of the *via cessionis*, but recognised that, for practical purposes, it could not be implemented. The university therefore again proposed a council, but on this occasion, although remaining generally loyal to Boniface IX and the accepted ecclesiastical constitution, was prepared to consider somewhat unorthodox methods of assembling such a body, a change of attitudes which may reflect recent French influence.[11]

---

[6] Printed in Ullmann, 'Cambridge', pp. 68–75. [7] ibid., pp. 57–60, 72–3.
[8] ibid., pp. 60, 73. [9] ibid., pp. 60–1, 73–4.
[10] Printed in M. Harvey, 'The letter of Oxford University on the schism, 5 February 1399', *Annuarium Historiae Conciliorum*, 6 (1974), 123–33.
[11] On the letter, see M. Harvey, 'The letters of the University of Oxford on with-

The continuing loyalty of the Romanist obedience to its popes was also revealed in contemporary statements emanating from the University of Cologne. The first of these, a fragment of a letter arguing against a declaration of neutrality, which the masters sent to a meeting of the electoral princes *c.* 1399, probably reflects the corporate opinion of the university. A more individual statement appears in a series of glosses appended to the tract *Ad ostendendum clare* (itself a reworking of the final section of Simon de Cramaud's *De subtractione obedientie*) which were completed in 1400.[12] In neither instance was there any indication of a mellowing of attitudes, or any reduction in loyalty to the Roman pope. Both works utterly rejected any subtraction of obedience which, in the glosses, was at one point bluntly equated with the *via facti*.[13] These glosses, with their emphasis on conciliarism as the most effective method of achieving the reunification of the church, point to the growing acceptance of that viewpoint at Cologne, in common with the rest of the Romanist obedience. With their strong antipathy to the French, and insistence on imperial authority, the glosses also illustrate the continuing influence of nationalism in the discussions of the schism.

Immediate Parisian reaction to these Bonifacian statements is not clear, but Simon de Cramaud's letter to the Archbishop of Canterbury, written *c.* 1400,[14] may well represent a response to the English declarations. Cramaud justified withdrawal of obedience as a constructive rather than destructive step;[15] he rejected the claims of both rivals, and argued that obedience to either was a mortal sin, even going so far as to urge rejection of attempts by the monarchs to intervene in the issue of deciding allegiances in order to impose their own viewpoint.[16] The argument that the Benedictines should submit to Boniface prior to any judgement of the issues was denounced as simplistic and naive;[17] Cramaud instead urged corporate activity by the princes in cooperation with the church.[18] He vigorously denied any suggestion that the French

drawal of obedience from Pope Boniface IX', *Studies in Church History*, **11** (1975), 187–98.

12 Swanson, 'Cologne', pp. 5–9.
13 ibid., p. 8 n. 1.
14 Printed in *Thes. Nov. Anec.*, pp. 1230–50.
15 ibid., pp. 1237–8.
16 ibid., p. 1239.
17 ibid., pp. 1240–1.
18 ibid., p. 1245.

were aiming at the election of a malleable, and preferably French, pope; instead he proclaimed that their policy was concerned solely with the re-establishment of an undeniable legitimacy.[19] Cramaud's proposals involved some degree of conciliarism: the power to judge matters of faith resided in the church as a whole since, although the pope received his authority from God, he exercised it only with the consent of his electors, who were the representatives of the *ecclesia*. Thus, where the papal authority was abused to support heresy, the pontiffs became accountable to the whole church which could, if it saw fit, depose them.[20]

Despite such counter-proposals, the Romanist universities remained loyal to their pope throughout the period of the French subtraction of obedience, and sent numerous *rotuli* to Boniface IX.[21] But the subtle alterations in the opinions of the Oxford masters on conciliarism suggest that the steadfastness of the academics was starting to be undermined. Similar indications of such developments appear in Italy, in the works of Baldus de Ubaldis. His growing sense of disillusion with the rivals revealed itself in his legal commentaries of the period, which contained bitter attacks on the popes and demanded the summoning of a council. His ideas, however, do not seem to have been particularly well developed. Nevertheless, in contrast with the views which he had expressed in the summer of 1378, he now suggested that the summons might be issued by the cardinals, and although he denied that the emperor should be involved in the actual assembly of the council, he fully accepted that the secular princes would have a role to fulfil. Even so, he would not permit any suggestion of deposition, which suggests that his conciliarism remained within the framework of the theory of the 1380s.[22]

This foreign discussion of the schism was all peripheral to the

[19] ibid., p. 1246.
[20] ibid., pp. 1247–8.
[21] There are suggestions that the English universities may have prepared *rotuli c.* 1399 and in 1403 (*Calendar of Patent Rolls, 1395–9* (London, 1909), pp. 547, 561; *Calendar of Patent Rolls, 1401–5* (London, 1907), p. 325; Jacob, *Essays*, pp. 229–30). Vienna discussed a roll in 1401 and sent one in 1403 (Uiblein, *Acta*, pp. 180, 221–4). The University of Heidelberg also sent a *rotulus* to Rome in 1401 (Winkelmann, *Urkundenbuch*, vol. 1, no. 54, vol. 2, nos. 129–30), while the University of Cologne despatched one in 1403 (Swanson, 'Cologne', p. 7).
[22] On Baldus' conciliarism at this time, see Wahl, 'Baldus de Ubaldis', pp. 26–9; Tierney, *Foundations*, pp. 216, 217 n. 3.

main debates, which were continuing in France. The subtraction of obedience had fulfilled all the worst expectations of its opponents, without the good effects which had been proclaimed by its supporters.[23] Consequently, there soon grew up a party seeking the restoration of obedience to Benedict XIII. Indeed, given the strength of the opposition to the policy of withdrawing obedience prior to July 1398, it is possible that moves for restitution began almost immediately after subtraction was implemented.[24] These restitutionist forces, however, did not assume any real importance until the start of the new century. Initially, the party calling for restoration of obedience seems to have been strongest in the provincial universities, Orléans being apparently the first to take positive action. Although that university had originally obeyed the subtraction ordinances, dating documents by the regnal years of Benedict XIII, 'the last elected to the papacy',[25] by 1401 opposition to this situation was mounting. On 5 September 1401 the university lodged an official protest against royal claims that it had supported subtraction, those who had represented it at the council of 1398 agreeing that they had voted only in their individual capacities.[26] After a further debate on 26 February 1402, the university reiterated that it had not accepted subtraction, decided to press for the restoration of obedience to Benedict XIII, and agreed to send envoys to the Duke of Orléans to discuss the matter.[27] Elsewhere, similar steps were being taken. By June 1402 the University of Angers had concluded that the subtraction was ineffective, and the nations there all advocated that letters be sent to the king and his council, urging restitution.[28] At Toulouse, that centre of Benedictine loyalty, a similar programme was also formulated.[29]

[23] *Chron. S. Den.*, vol. 2, pp. 746–7; *Valois*, vol. 3, pp. 305–23; Salembier, *Pierre d'Ailly*, pp. 170–1.
[24] See the restitutionist tract produced *c.* 1399 in *Thes. Nov. Anec.*, pp. 1177–93; *Bulaeus*, vol. 5, pp. 56–63.
[25] Fournier, *Statuts*, nos. 238–9, 243.
[26] *BN*, MS Lat. 1479, fo. 37r; *Valois*, vol. 3, p. 257 n. 1.
[27] MS cit., fo. 37r: 'a maiori parte conclusit, quod dicte universitati expediebat se declarare, quod numquam . . . consensserat obediencie substractioni . . . eciam quod eidem expediebat universitati prosequi restitutionem obediencie fiendum . . . eciam erga . . . dominum ducem legatos mittere'. See also *Valois*, vol. 3, p. 257; Martin, *Origines*, vol. 1, p. 293.
[28] Martin, *Origines*, vol. 1, p. 293; *Valois*, vol. 3, p. 269.
[29] See below, pp. 140–1.

Despite these signs of growing provincial opposition, many members of the University of Paris remained firmly attached to the policy of subtraction, a determination in which they were led by Simon de Cramaud. About 1400, he repeated the arguments of his *De subtractione obedientie* in a series of glosses to the defence of Benedict XIII which had been drawn up by Martin de Salva.[30] These glosses Cramaud submitted 'correccioni sedis apostolice et non benedicti'.[31]

But the growing opposition to subtraction could not long be ignored. The most direct challenge was offered by the University of Toulouse, which in 1402 presented a letter to the king, setting out its views at length.[32] However, the representative nature of the opinions expressed is uncertain – it was later to be claimed that the Toulouse statements were merely the views of a group of fanatical supporters of Benedict XIII,[33] but as this retraction was made against the background of a concerted attack on the University of Toulouse by the crown in conjunction with the University of Paris, its own validity is itself questionable. Given the activities of the university's representatives at the French national councils of 1395–98, the opinions expressed in the letter may be taken as indicative of the attitudes of a large section of the university's membership, even if not exactly a majority. In the letter, Toulouse declared its loyalty to Benedict XIII, proclaiming that the university had never accepted subtraction as valid.[34] The letter also contained a pointed attack on the University of Paris, with Toulouse declaring that a council summoned without papal authorisation was incompetent to decide the issue of the schism. They also complained that the procedures which had been adopted were unjust, as the justice which every peasant could expect had been

30 *BN*, MS Lat. 1475, fos. 33r–53r.
31 ibid., fo. 33v.
32 Printed in *Bulaeus*, vol. 5, pp. 4–24. See *Valois*, vol. 3, pp. 260–1. The speech made to the king by the Toulouse envoys is in *BN*, MS Lat. 1479, fos 118r–122v; see also *Valois*, vol. 3, p. 265.
33 See the remarks of an anonymous commentator on a copy of the letter in the British Library, London, MS Add. 10020, fos 70r–77v, declaring that after the condemnation of the letter (which is here dated as having occurred in September 1405), 'audivi pro certo quod hac Epistola . . . non Ab ipse Studio, sed Ab aliquibus de studio, quj favorabiles erant suo benedicto xiij°, processit' (ibid., fo. 77v).
34 *BN*, MS Lat. 1479, fo. 122r. The speech was submitted for the pope's correction (fo. 118r).

denied to the Vicar of Christ.[35] Moreover, the Toulouse masters
pointed out that the compulsive element in subtraction could
prove a dangerous precedent, possibly leading to rebellion against
the secular princes, and causing considerable difficulties within the
church, which could only further complicate the schism rather
than aid progress towards a solution.[36] Parisian reliance on
epieikeia was bluntly rejected: where the attainment of good
ends was uncertain, the adoption of undeniably bad means was
quite unjustified.[37] Subtraction of obedience, according to the
University of Toulouse, had been a total failure – a mistake from
the beginning, and counter-productive in effect – and ought to be
rescinded as soon as possible.[38]

The Parisian reaction to this provocative letter and the speech
which accompanied its presentation to the king was, understand-
ably, hostile, although the formal total condemnation of the letter
was delayed until 1405-6.[39] The immediate opposition found
voice in a series of tracts, which included one by the Prior of
Roncy addressed to Philip of Burgundy,[40] two Parisian statements,[41] and a series of glosses on the letter prepared by Simon de
Cramaud for the king's perusal.[42] The University of Toulouse
itself became the object of a concerted campaign of vilification,
which culminated in the arrest of the university's representatives
at Paris by the Duke of Berry who, as governor of Guyenne,
complained that they had publicly defended Benedict XIII without seeking official permission.[43]

Neither of the two anonymous Parisian statements added much
to the debates on the letter, both being rather defensive and
unconvincing (in marked contrast with the zeal with which Simon
de Cramaud turned to the task), giving a most direct and damaging response. His aim throughout was to urge Charles VI not to
give way to the demands of the restitutionists, likening the

[35] *Bulaeus*, vol. 5, pp. 8–9.　　　[36] ibid., vol. 5, pp. 10–11.
[37] ibid., vol. 5, pp. 13–14.
[38] ibid., vol. 5, pp. 15–19.　　　[39] See below, p. 163.
[40] BN, MS Lat. 14644, fos 212r–230r.
[41] One is reproduced in Jean Gerson's *Trilogus de schismate* (*Glorieux*, vol. 6, pp. 76–
84; *Bulaeus*, vol. 5, pp. 25–30), the other is in *Bulaeus*, vol. 5, pp. 30–53.
[42] BN, MSS Lat. 17585; N.A. Lat. 1793, fos 97r–159v; Lat. 1480A2 (a late copy),
pp. 667ff; Archives Nationales, Paris, J.518, fos 500r–555v.
[43] *Valois*, vol. 3, pp. 267–8; *Chron. S. Den.*, vol. 3, pp. 24–5.

subtraction of obedience from Benedict XIII to the earlier withdrawal of recognition from Urban VI by Charles V.[44] The crown, Cramaud asserted, did have the authority, power and obligation to act, his justification for this summarising arguments derived from his earlier *De subtractione obediente*.[45] But Cramaud recognised that it would be the crown which would make the effective decision on the issue. He therefore presented the king with the stark choice between subtraction and restitution, the decision 'quorum oppinio est maioris auctoritatis: vel istorum dominorum qui hanc epistolam scripserunt, vel collegii dominorum Cardinalium et prelatorum francie et castelle et universitatis parisiensis et magistrorum et doctorum aliarum universitatum regni francie et castelle qui in consiliis super hoc congregatis interfuerunt?'[46]

Cramaud's hostility to restitution was maintained throughout the glosses: at one stage he rather picturesquely likened the policy to a dog returning to its own vomit.[47] He demanded punishment for the authors of the Toulouse letter,[48] expressing disbelief that such statements could possibly reflect the views of the whole university there.[49] In his references to the university itself, Cramaud adopted a highly sarcastic tone as when, for example, he contrasted the university's present stubborn refusal to desert Benedict XIII with the alacrity with which it had defected from Urban VI to Clement VII.[50]

The political arguments advanced in the glosses were not particularly new, many of them having appeared earlier in Cramaud's other writings, especially the *De subtractione obediente*. This lack of novelty aptly reflects the relative sterility of the debates on ecclesiastical reunification at this stage of the schism. Nevertheless, the glosses were not without their occasional striking points. Arbitration was rejected,[51] chiefly because of the partisanship of the people who would be nominated by the rivals – Cramaud here borrowing from the letter sent by the King of Castile to his

---

[44] *BN*, MS N.A. Lat. 1793, fo. 115r.   [45] ibid., fo. 117r.
[46] ibid., fo. 158r.
[47] ibid., fo. 140r.
[48] ibid., fo. 101r.
[49] ibid., fo. 136v. On Toulouse's continued allegiance to Benedict XIII and opposition to the *via cessionis*, Cramaud remarks: 'multum stupeo et magis doleo de istorum admiracione non bene digesta' (ibid., fo. 147v).
[50] ibid., fo. 102r.   [51] ibid., fos 149v–151v, 152v–153r.

Aragonese cousin in 1398 when he asserted that Benedict would nominate the Cardinal of Pamplona to act for him, while his Roman opponent would be represented by Baldus de Ubaldis or some similarly partisan doctor.[52] The *via concilii* was also rejected, as being impracticable [53] – although it seems probable that Cramaud was already considering the possibility of finding a way round the constitutional impasse blocking the use of that method, to judge from the vehemence of his condemnation of the Toulousain defence of the papal monopoly of the prerogative of summons. This was attacked as a view which could only lead ultimately to the total destruction of the church.[54]

It was, however, Toulouse's restitutionist arguments which were the main object of Cramaud's attacks. Despite his defence of action by the French crown, he was not prepared to accept the view that the activities of other monarchs could be taken as exemplars: Toulouse's citation of the actions of Richard II of England and Wenceslas of Bohemia was dismissed, on the grounds that if their lead had been followed at the start of the schism, France would now be subject to an intrusive pope.[55] Toulouse's analogy between Benedict XIII and Pope Symmachus was also rejected – Symmachus had been an undoubted pope, but Benedict's claims were by no means certain.[56] Against restitution, Cramaud also argued the practical case that, if Benedict died without a successor, only Boniface IX would remain to be dealt with, whereas if restitution were effected the Avignonese line would continue, and so would the schism.[57] As in earlier works, Cramaud advocated double cession, recognising that abdication by Benedict alone would be pointless.[58] The reasoning behind this illustrates, yet again, the peculiar ambivalence of Cramaud's attitude towards the Avignonese pope; for unilateral abdication by Benedict was to be rejected on the grounds that this would leave the French 'sub bonifacio in scismatica tempestate'.[59] Cramaud certainly detested the Roman line, producing a virulent attack on Roman promotions,[60] and yet so intense was his adherence to the

---

[52] ibid., fo. 149v.
[54] ibid., fo. 111r.
[55] ibid., fo. 130v.
[57] ibid., fo. 155r.
[59] ibid., fo. 114r.

[53] ibid., fo. 152r.
[56] ibid., fo. 144v.
[58] ibid., fo. 114r.
[60] ibid., fos 109v–110v.

policy of subtraction of obedience that he was quite prepared to treat Benedict as a heretic and schismatic.[61]

Apart from the works already mentioned, the controversy which surrounded the publication of the Toulouse letter may also have provided the background for the appearance of Johannes Fiot's *Dialogus*,[62] a two-part tract dealing with subtraction and restitution, and in both instances arriving at papalist conclusions. Subtraction was rejected,[63] along with the *via facti* and the council of the individual obedience.[64] Only occasionally was there any novelty in the arguments advanced. However, Fiot did demolish the theory that Benedict's death would end all the problems, asserting that the cardinals, because they had subtracted their obedience from the pope, had made themselves schismatics and thereby deprived themselves of any rights to participate in future papal elections.[65] Fiot also denied that the subtraction decrees had been obeyed as completely as Paris liked to pretend.[66] Most importantly of all, he admirably revealed the difference in ecclesiology between the subtractionists and their opponents, differences which centred on the position of the pope within the church. The supporters of subtraction denied, but the restitutionists maintained, that there was a necessary connection between the papacy and the rest of the *ecclesia*,[67] a distinction which was of monumental implications.

Less assured in attitude was a series of works poured forth at this time by the Chancellor of Paris himself, Jean Gerson.[68] He

---

[61] ibid., fo. 111v.

[62] *BN*, MS Lat. 1481, fos 159r–207v (misbound).

[63] ibid., fo. 170r–v.

[64] ibid., fos 180r, 199v.

[65] ibid., fos 200r–v, culminating in the declaration that 'Cardinales substrahentes excommunicatos esse et scismaticos, et omni jure eleccionis privatos' (ibid., fo. 200v).

[66] ibid., fo. 171r.

[67] The subtractionist view appears ibid., fo. 175r: 'Papa non est caput ecclesie proprie loquendo de capite, nec est necessaria connexio membrorum ecclesie ad ipsum; igitur potest ab eo licite fierj subtraccio causis racionabilibus . . . quia, si contra Christum qui est verum caput ecclesie peccare seu ab eo deviare deprehendatur, sibi non est obediendum, quia hoc esset deviare a capite Christo cum quo est neccessaria connexio'. Against this view, the opinion of the loyalists is given at fo. 186r: 'Papa . . . est . . . caput ecclesie militantis . . . sub Christo . . . et . . . connexio . . . primo non est necessaria simpliciter, deus enim possit alio modo ordinare. Dico secundo, quod non est necessaria connexio ad istud hominem qui est papam in quantum homo . . . sed taliter est ita neccessaria connexio ad papam in quantum papa, quod non licet sub pena peccati et dampnacionis perpetue hanc connexionem scienter rumpere'.

[68] The *Protestatio super statum ecclesie*, the *Replicationes*, the *Considerationes de restitutione obedientiae Benedicto*, the *De schismate*, the *De concilio unius obedientiae*,

declared that he was not writing as a defender of Benedict,[69] but nevertheless publicly dissociated himself and his adherents from any attempt to accuse the pope of heresy.[70] For Gerson, there were only two possible methods of advancing beyond the existing impasse within the Benedictine obedience: either total subtraction of obedience, or complete restitution,[71] both courses being potentially dangerous. Much of the argument – especially in the *De schismate* and the *De concilio unius obedientiae*[72] – concentrated on denying the need for a council of the Avignonese obedience to restore recognition to Benedict XIII, since that would allow the pope the opportunity to take revenge on his opponents.[73] Yet Gerson was an advocate of restitution, even if it was only conditional,[74] while his overall programme to end the schism did include a council of the obedience.[75]

Pierre d'Ailly also participated in the discussions on the restoration of obedience, his *De materia concilii generalis*[76] being composed against the background of the debate on restoration of allegiance. While advocating a council, the second part of the work considered whether or not obedience should be restored prior to the assembly of such a gathering.[77] This was, however, merely a question of timing: d'Ailly had earlier declared that a council of the obedience was not actually necessary to effect restitution.[78] Besides presenting the opposing arguments for restoration of obedience and continued subtraction,[79] d'Ailly also outlined a *via media*, which may have had his personal support.[80] This way involved restoring to the pope control of the spiritualities which necessarily appertained to the papacy, whilst withholding control of the temporalities which had been usurped from the prerogatives of the local churches – in other words maintaining

the *De restitutione obedientiae* and the *Super reformatione schismatis ecclesiae* (*Glorieux*, nos. 257–63. See also Posthumus Meyjes, *Jean Gerson*, pp. 71–80; Morrall, *Gerson*, pp. 55–63).

[69] *Glorieux*, vol. 6, p. 42.

[70] ibid., vol. 6, p. 35.   [71] ibid., vol. 6, p. 58.

[72] *Glorieux*, nos. 259–60.   [73] ibid., vol. 6, p. 47.

[74] ibid., vol. 6, pp. 60–1.   [75] ibid., vol. 6, p. 34.

[76] Printed in F. Oakley, *The political thought of Pierre d'Ailly: the voluntarist tradition* (New Haven, 1964), pp. 252–342; on the date see ibid., pp. 248–9.

[77] ibid., pp. 280–314.

[78] ibid., pp. 257–64.

[79] ibid., pp. 280–94.   [80] ibid., p. 250; but see his saving declaration ibid., p. 280.

the Gallican liberties without the inconveniences arising from the *de facto* state of schism within the Avignonese obedience.[81]

Despite the calibre of those supporting (or, at best, not opposing) the restoration of obedience, some Parisian academics continued their adherence to subtraction. On 15 April 1402, Jean Courtecuisse addressed the king in an attempt to counter the influence of delegations from Toulouse and Castile, arguing for continued withdrawal and a council of the obedience.[82] The violence of his attacks on Benedict XIII was mirrored, probably in 1403, in Guillaume Euvrie's *Invectiva in unum magnum clericum qui universitatem et eius processus ad pacem ecclesie vituperabat, quos prius laudaverat.*[83] The title of this short work sufficiently summarised its contents, although the individual thus attacked has not yet been identified.

In this situation, the intellectual and political stalemate appeared unbreakable. But the façade of unity on subtraction was visibly cracking. In August 1402, Louis II of Anjou had already restored allegiance to Benedict XIII.[84] On 13 March 1403 the pope managed to evade his guardians at Avignon, and fled to the duke's protection at Château-Reynard.[85] At the end of April, Castile returned to obedience.[86] All this took place as the background to another projected council of the French church, which had been summoned for May. This was undoubtedly influenced by the knowledge of Benedict's liberation, his case being ably presented by the Cardinal of Poitiers.[87] The provincial Universities of Montpellier, Angers, Orléans and Toulouse had already decided to press for restitution, having sent their envoys to advocate that course.[88] The University of Paris was still undecided, but its deliberations were pre-empted on 28 May 1403, when the Duke of Orléans carried through a palace revolution against the Burgundian party, persuading Charles VI to agree to the immediate restoration of obedience to Benedict XIII.[89]

---

[81] ibid., p. 294.
[82] *Valois*, vol. 3, p. 261.
[83] Printed in E. Pellegrin, 'Un humaniste normand du temps de Charles VI: Guillaume Euvrie', *Bulletin, Institut de recherche et d'histoire des textes*, **15** (1967–68), 19–20. On the date, see ibid., pp. 20–1.
[84] *Thes. Nov. Anec.*, pp. 1263–6.   [85] *Valois*, vol. 3, pp. 325–7.
[86] Suárez Fernández, *Castilla*, pp. 47, 238–43.   [87] *Chron. S. Den.*, vol. 3, pp. 88–9.
[88] ibid., vol. 3, pp. 88–91.   [89] ibid., vol. 3, pp. 90–1; *Valois*, vol. 3, pp. 337–9.

Yet again, the crown had decided, and there was little that the Parisian masters could do about it. Although the Romanist minority within the university still urged a policy of neutrality,[90] any effective opposition to restitution was impossible. The official pronouncement of the restoration of obedience to Benedict XIII was made by Pierre d'Ailly on 30 May 1403.[91] With the collapse of the policy of subtraction, the Parisians rapidly reconciled themselves to the changed circumstances, and led the rush of academic petitioning to Benedict. Among the numerous *rotuli* sent from throughout the Avignonese obedience, that from the University of Paris was the largest of all, over a thousand members being listed on the various rolls.[92] Yet the university's policy lay in ruins, condemned by its failure. Although not all the theorising of the previous decade was to prove fruitless, the time spent debating the *via cessionis* and subtraction of obedience had, in hindsight, been wasted.

---

90 *Valois*, vol. 3, pp. 340–1; *Auct. Ch.*, vol. 1, pp. 856–7; *Chron. S. Den.*, vol. 3, pp. 98–9.
91 *Chron. S. Den.*, vol. 3, pp. 96–7; Salembier, *Pierre d'Ailly*, pp. 176–9; *Bulaeus*, vol. 6, pp. 64–7.
92 Two Salamancan rolls were sent, several academics also appearing on private *rotuli* (Beltrán de Heredia, *Bulario*, nos. 314–7, 319–23, 326–30, 333, 335–8, 341–6). The University of Valladolid also sent a roll (ibid., no. 1430; Griera Gaja, *Miscelánea*, vol. 2, pp. 640–59), as did the University of Avignon (Denifle, *Les universités*, pp. 86–7). The French provincial Universities of Toulouse, Angers, Orléans and Montpellier all submitted long lists of petitions (ibid., pp. 52–8, 67–70, 80–1), while for the Parisian rolls see *Ch. Paris.*, nos. 1786–99; *Auct. Ch.*, vol. 1, p. 863 n. 1; *Valois*, vol. 3, p. 348. On the French *rotuli* of 1403 in general, see Verger, 'Le recrutement géographique', pp. 861–2, 868–74.

Chapter 8

DE MATERIA CONCILII GENERALIS

The reaction within France to the restoration of obedience to Benedict XIII is best epitomised in the euphoria of Jean Gerson's sermons *Emitte spiritum tuum* and *Benedic haereditate tuae*.[1] But the euphoria was all too soon dissipated, to be succeeded by disillusionment born of the realisation that the reunion of the church remained but a distant prospect. The restitution of obedience meanwhile produced its own difficulties: the French treated it as conditional, whereas Benedict considered it to be a complete vindication of his papalism. These conflicting attitudes were bound to clash; by January 1404 Gerson's earlier eulogies had become transformed into the animosity of his sermon *Apparuit gratia Dei*, preached before the pope himself at Tarascon.[2]

Meanwhile, both obediences remained steadfast in their loyalties. France and Spain, although once again recognising Benedict XIII, continued to urge implementation of the *via cessionis*. Benedict himself seems to have aspired to expand his obedience – attempts were made to gain the adherence of Florence in 1405,[3] while the Welsh revolt under Owain Glyndŵr was fully exploited.[4] On the other hand, the Romanist universities continued to send *rotuli* to their successive popes, Boniface IX, Innocent VII and Gregory XII.[5] A minority of Romanists continued to

[1] *Glorieux*, nos. 214, 225.

[2] ibid., no. 212; see also Posthumus Meyjes, *Jean Gerson*, pp. 93–103.

[3] L. Martines, *Lawyers and statecraft in renaissance Florence* (Princeton, 1968), p. 288; *Valois*, vol. 3, pp. 397–8.

[4] T. Matthews, *Welsh records in Paris* (Carmarthen, 1910), pp. 42–54, 85–99; J. E. Lloyd, *Owen Glendower* (Oxford, 1931), pp. 119–21.

[5] The University of Vienna sent a *rotulus* to Innocent VII (Uiblein, *Acta*, pp. 235-6, 238–47, 249–50, 255–6), and discussed sending one to Gregory XII (ibid., pp. 271–5). Heidelberg considered sending a second roll to Boniface IX in 1404, and it was presumably this which became the roll sent to his successor (Winkelmann, *Urkunden-buch*, vol. 1, no. 61, vol. 2, nos. 144, 151, 155). The University of Cologne sent a roll to Boniface in 1403 and considered sending one to Innocent (Swanson, 'Cologne',

exist at Paris, even during the reign of Gregory XII,[6] and there
are signs that similar groups remained in the provincial universities.[7] Moreover, the territorial integrity of the Roman obedience
was restored in October 1405 when the bishopric of Liège – the
only fragment of the obedience to follow the French lead and
withdraw recognition from its pope in 1399 – was brought back
safely into the fold.[8]

While all this was going on, the period was by no means one of
stagnation in the search for reunification of the church. The
University of Paris continued to send envoys on foreign missions
(some were at Cologne in 1405),[9] while persistent divisions on the
subject within France were reflected in the revival of the conflict
between the Universities of Paris and Toulouse in 1406.[10] But the
centre of activity had by then transferred from France to the
Roman obedience, which from 1400 onwards revealed a steadily
growing concern for reunion. The most significant indication of
this was the attempt by Pope Innocent VII to hold a conference
of his adherents in order to discuss the possibilities of terminating
the schism, although this gathering never actually met.[11] The
Roman cardinals were also concerned for union; at the papal
elections of 1404 and 1406 they followed the Avignonese precedent of 1394 and bound themselves and their pope to work for

p. 7). The University of Oxford petitioned Innocent VII (E. F. Jacob, *Archbishop
Henry Chichele* (London, 1967), p. 74 n. 2), while a number of royal pardons
granted to members of the University of Cambridge for accepting papal provisions
to benefices without royal permission may indicate that that university also sent a
roll (*Calendar of Patent Rolls, 1405–8* (London, 1907), pp. 169–70, 189, 210, 219).
From Italy, there are suggestions of Bolognese activity after the death of Boniface IX
(Winkelmann, *Urkundenbuch*, vol. 1, no. 61), and there also exists a fragment of
a *rotulus* sent to Innocent VII by members of the University of Florence (A. Gherardi, *Statuti della università e studio fiorentino*, Documenta di storia Italiana, vol. 7
(Florence, 1881), pp. 383–6).

6 The Anglo-German nation of the University of Paris frequently declared its adherence
to the Roman pope (e.g. *Auct. Ch.*, vol. 1, pp. 937–8), while Gregory XII seems to
have maintained contacts with at least one Italian – a theologian – at the university
(J. Vincke, *Briefe zum Pisaner Konzil*, Beiträge zur Kirchen- und Rechtsgeschichte,
vol. 1 (Bonn, 1940), pp. 56–7).

7 *ASV*, Indice 324, fo. 29v, records a lost bull of Innocent VII extending to his
adherents at Orléans, Montpellier, Angers, Toulouse and other *studia generalia* of
France those privileges enjoyed by his supporters at Paris.

8 M. Maillard-Luypaert, 'Une lettre d'Innocent VII du 2 octobre 1405 à propos du
retour de Liège à l'obédience romaine', *Revue d'histoire ecclésiastique*, 72 (1977),
54–60.

9 Swanson, 'Cologne', pp. 6–7.

10 See p. 163.   11 *Raynaldus, ann.* 1404, no. 13, *ann.* 1405, nos. 14–16.

union by all possible means, including resignation.[12] On both occasions, the French had tried to persuade the cardinals to defer an election, but the appropriate letters were not received until after the conclave had ended.[13] Of the individual Roman cardinals, Balthasar Cossa, the legate in Bologna, seems to have been the most demonstrative of his zeal for union. Not only was it at his behest that Petrus de Ancharano produced his first contribution to the debates in April 1405;[14] he was also the addressee of a tract composed by Dominicus de Sancto Geminiano in March 1409, which dealt mainly with procedural points relating to the forthcoming council at Pisa.[15] Cossa's encouragement of the search for union also earned him the praises of the Bolognese academic Matthaeus de Matasellanis, in his completion of Antonius de Butrio's final work.[16]

The activities of Innocent VII and the praise meted out to Cossa were all symptomatic of the increasing Romanist concern for union, which gradually came to concentrate on conciliarism. Although the conciliarist movement had never been totally extinguished within the Benedictine obedience, in the years after 1398 attention there had concentrated on the rather sterile possibilities of a council of the individual obedience, these discussions reaching their culmination in Pierre d'Ailly's *De materia concilii generalis*. While often discussing matters appertaining to a proper general council, the circumstances of the composition of this work fixed its applicability solely to the Benedictine obedience and a particular council of that section of the church.[17] Meanwhile, in the opposing obedience, conciliarism progressed and developed, even if somewhat erratically. The period from 1403 to 1409 divides at 1407, when the dashing of hopes for an amicable solution to the difficulties of the schism, in which both the contestants would be willing participants, made the sterility of cession unavoidably obvious. Thereafter, attention increasingly focussed on conciliar-

---

[12] Printed in Souchon, *Die Papstwahlen des grossen Schismas*, vol. 1, pp. 280–95; see also ibid., vol. 1, pp. 66–70, 94–111.

[13] *Valois*, vol. 3, pp. 420, 477, 484. Gerson summarised the Parisian arguments for deferring any election after the death of Boniface IX in his *Disputatio de schismate tollendo* (*Glorieux*, no. 266).

[14] Biblioteca Medicea Laurenziana, Florence, MS Plut. XX. 39, fo. 77r.

[15] Biblioteca Apostolica Vaticana, MS Vat. Lat. 4039, fos 243r–246r.

[16] *BN*, MS Lat. 17184, fo. 256r.   [17] Oakley, *Political thought*, p. 250.

ism, although this was vitally different in form from the conciliarism of the 1380s: now the theses of the subtractionists which
equated schism with heresy were combined with a pseudo-populist
interpretation of the ecclesiastical constitution to permit the
cardinals to act against their respective popes within a conciliarist
framework. Whereas the conciliarism of the 1380s had been essentially concerned with determining which of the then claimants
had been legitimately elected to the papacy, that of the 1400s was
more concerned with removing both rivals, thus obliterating the
schism, and establishing another pope. Nevertheless, the new
conciliarism contained features of all the previously discussed
solutions: shades of arbitration remained, in the hopes for a
meeting of the rival claimants, and the possibility of their involvement in the conciliarist process; the *via juris* was present in the
assumption of conciliar supremacy and (if necessary) power of
judgement, while the *via facti* was only slightly obscured by
threats of subtraction of obedience and invocation of the secular
authorities to coerce the popes into compliance with the plan. Most
strikingly, the new conciliarism was seen as a logical development
from, and indeed a means of implementing, the *via cessionis*, a
progression which becomes most obvious in Ludolf of Sagan's
summary of his intended discussion of the issues in his *Soliloquium
scismatis*.[18]

Although the development of this new conciliarism was rather
spasmodic, the approach to Pisa was a consistent intellectual progression, best illustrated by the successive expansions of Franciscus
de Zabarella's *Tractatus de schismate*. This work, begun in 1403
but not completed until the eve of the Council of Pisa,[19] falls into
three distinct sections yet never loses its overall coherence. In the
first part, Zabarella's conciliarism was unconditional, probably
owing something to the recent pronouncements by Baldus de

[18] F. J. P. Bliemetzrieder, 'Abt Ludolfs von Sagan Traktat, "Soliloquium scismatis"',
Studien und Mitteilungen aus dem Benedictiner- und dem Cistercienser-Orden, **26**
(1905), 35. See also a similar statement made by Pierre d'Ailly in 1403, in Ehrle,
Alpartils Chronica, p. 502.

[19] For editions, see the list in A. Kneer, *Kardinal Zabarella, 1360–1417* (Münster,
1891), p. 57 n. 2 (although this list is incomplete). I have used the version in
S. Schardius, *De iurisdictione, autoritate et praeeminentia imperiali* (Basel, 1566),
pp. 688–711. On the tract, see Kneer, *Zabarella*, pp. 57–63; Scheuffgen, *Beiträge*,
pp. 98–9, 102–20; Ullmann, *Origins*, pp. 195–229; Tierney, *Foundations*, pp. 220–47.

Ubaldis.[20] The council could judge an heretical pope, while
during a papal vacancy the universality of the church was the
ultimate respository of ecclesiastical authority.[21] The power to
summon a council, a power which was imperial in origins, had
only slowly been transferred to the pope, but when the papacy
was disputed the emperor retained his authority to request the
rivals to summon a council.[22] If the rivals refused, then the
cardinals, as the electing body which represented the universal
church, ought to exercise the power of summons, provided that
they remained united.[23] If they themselves were divided, the
imperial prerogative could be resurrected: as the law had
developed in one direction, so circumstances might necessitate
reversion to the pristine state.[24] Zabarella added other authorities
to his descending order of those capable of convening a council if
their superiors refused, but he recognised that actual exercise of
the power by them presented difficulties.[25]

In the second section of the *Tractatus*, Zabarella listed various
non-conciliar methods of attaining reunification of the church,
including double abdication and a new election, backed up by
appeals to the secular power if necessary.[26] His most original
scheme was the last suggested, providing for the rivals to oblige
their cardinals not to hold another election until both papacies
were vacant, the colleges then combining for a single election.[27]
In the interregna, the papal power was to be exercised either by
the whole college of that obedience, or by a single cardinal.[28] If
the union of colleges to perform the election was objected to on
grounds of numerical difference between the colleges, due steps
should be taken to circumvent the problem.[29] As with many other
works produced in the 1390s and 1400s which included lists of
possible solutions to the schism, Zabarella was here obviously

[20] See p. 138.   [21] Schardius, *De iurisdictione*, p. 689.
[22] ibid., pp. 689–90.
[23] ibid., p. 690.
[24] ibid., p. 691. This may suggest an alteration in Zabarella's views on the relative
superiority of pope and emperor. In 1398 he had delivered a staunch defence of papal
superiority before Pope Boniface IX, printed in T. Sartore, 'Un discorso inedito di
Francesco Zabarella a Bonifacio IX sull'autorità del papa', *Rivista di storia della
chiesa in Italia*, **20** (1966), 382–8.
[25] Schardius, *De iurisdictione*, pp. 693–4.
[26] ibid., pp. 695–8.   [27] ibid., pp. 697–8.
[28] ibid., p. 698.   [29] ibid., p. 698.

derivative, evoking shades of arguments which were presented all over Europe.

In the final part of Zabarella's work, the author reflected the situation immediately before the assembly of the Council of Pisa, justifying the withdrawal of obedience from the rivals as part of the process for enforcing cession, and turning from the idea of judgement between the claimants to mere removal of the contenders. The cardinals were obliged to excommunicate the popes, whose inveterate schism was heresy; thereafter the council was to determine the moral issue.[30] Yet Zabarella was no populist: the cardinals had to take the lead, and only after they had given the necessary sign should individuals act.[31] The electoral capitulations were declared valid; failure to implement them therefore permitted deposition of the popes by the council acting as a divine agent, such action also being justified on the basis that the plenitude of power, being effectively derived from man, could also be removed by man.[32] The cardinals, however, had no prerogative of deposition: as electors they were merely agents for the whole church, and only the totality which they represented could determine whether it was being misruled, and take appropriate action.[33] Nevertheless, necessity justified the cardinals in uniting and summoning a council, given the existing political and ecclesiastical circumstances, and all arguments against their activities were vigorously rejected.[34] But Zabarella's constant aim was merely informative, not determinative; he therefore deliberately abstained from proclaiming a judgement against either of the individual claimants.

Zabarella's tract – which, as far as the development of his own ideas is concerned, can be supplemented by a detailed *consilium* in favour of the cardinals, dating from the period shortly before the final break between them and Gregory XII [35] – epitomised the intellectual progression in Italy, where the developments revealed in the final sections of the *Tractatus de schismate* seem to have been most consistent. However, lack of information about progress in other Italian universities makes generalisation both difficult

---

[30] ibid., pp. 698–711. [31] ibid., p. 700.
[32] ibid., p. 708.
[33] ibid., p. 708.
[34] ibid., pp. 709–11. [35] Biblioteca Apostolica Vaticana, MS Vat. Lat. 3477, fos 32r–35v.

and dangerous. Only occasionally are attitudes suggested. At one stage, Pavia was mentioned as having declared for neutrality,[36] while during the proceedings of the Council of Pisa the University of Perugia was said to have been consulted by the Roman cardinals on whether they should proceed to Savona for negotiations with Benedict XIII after Gregory XII had refused to complete the journey, the masters having apparently urged them on.[37] Such evidence, little more than hearsay, is obviously of questionable value, but only Florence and Bologna provide any signs of consistent debate. However, despite this, it was from the University of Ferrara that there originated the second major Italian tract of this period, produced in 1405 by Petrus de Ancharano at the request of Cardinal Balthasar Cossa.[38] Both Ancharano and his pupil, Antonius de Butrio, were to become important figures in the academic development of the conciliarist theory in the next few years, especially after their return to Bologna, where they rapidly assumed the leadership in the university discussions.

As in the second section of Zabarella's work, Ancharano's tract dealt with a number of alternative solutions – six in all – to the problem of ecclesiastical reunification.[39] Effectively, however, these could be reduced to three, the familiar combination of arbitration, conciliarism and abdication. In the course of his dealings with the theoretical possibilities, Ancharano nevertheless revealed his recognition of the practical limitations on academic involvement in the discussions aimed at ending the schism. He dismissed the first of his suggested solutions, the *via discussionis*, as likely

[36] Martines, *Lawyers and statecraft*, p. 292.
[37] J. Vincke, 'Acta concilii Pisani', *Römische Quartalschrift*, **46** (1938), 248.
[38] For MSS, see Souchon, *Die Papstwahlen des grossen Schismas*, vol. 2, p. 243 n. 2. I have used the copy in Florence, MS cit., fos 77r–109r, which has the reference to Cossa at fo. 77r.
[39] ibid., fo. 79r:
'Prima, iuriumque [sic] utriusque per solemnes doctores diligens et matura discussio.
Secunda, sacri concilii generalis convocatio.
Tertia, per compromissum in paucis vel in multis totalis potestatis translatio.
Quarta, sanctj spiritus inspiratio in eorum cordibus.
Quinta, utriusque spontanea cessio et per utrumque cetum cardinalium nova electio.
Sexta, ad cedandum vel concordandum utriusque compulsio'.
In a copy of the text contained in the Bodleian Library, Oxford, MS Laud. misc. 249, the mechanics of this last method are clarified by the inclusion of the statement that the compulsion should be effected 'per seculares potestates vel principes' (fo. 77r).

to provide only further complications and uncertainties.[40] Academics might propose and discuss remedies, but clearly some other authority had to make a real decision about which of the various methods was to be implemented. Ironically, Ancharano's tract may itself be considered as falling within the category of the *via discussionis*, being little more than a catalogue of arguments about his various suggestions, with no explicit statement of which he felt ought to be adopted. However, given the relative length of the arguments deployed, and the slightly different standpoint revealed in their arrangement – more constructive than in his other considerations – it seems possible that his personal preference was for double resignation by the rivals, a policy to be carried out if necessary under pressure from the prelates and secular princes.[41]

But Ancharano made no overt declaration, and it seems possible that he wished the final choice of method to be left to the popes themselves, if his references to them as individuals are of any significance.[42] Others were to be involved in the process of terminating the schism only as a last resort. In 1407, it seemed possible that the popes had made their decisions; and had the projected negotiations between the rivals in that year actually been held, and proved successful, the schism would have been ended without the necessity for the Councils of Pisa and Constance. But the negotiations collapsed. Their failure, and the resulting crisis, forced a complete rethinking of the problems of allegiance within both obediences. Signs of this appear in the Florentine debates which, almost continuous from 1405 to 1409, only really showed much vitality towards the end of the period, culminating in the formal repudiation of Gregory XII.[43] Evidence of academic involvement is slight, although several individuals revealed their attitudes by subscribing a declaration of subtraction of obedience.[44] The only lengthy surviving academic contributions to the debates seem to be two *consilia* of Lorenzo di Ridolfi, the first of which was presented on 29 August 1408 as part of the communal debates,

---

40 Florence, MS cit., fos 79v–81r.
41 ibid., fos 95r–103v.
42 ibid., fos 104r–108r.
43 Martines, *Lawyers and statecraft*, pp. 289–95.
44 E. Martène, *Veterum scriptorum et monumentorum . . . amplissima collectio*, vol. 7 (Paris, 1733), pp. 949–62.

with the approval of his fellow academic Stephanus de Buonaccursus.[45] Ridolfi's tract was a long justification of the powers and
rights of the cardinals, based on law and justified by necessity.[46]
Although he admitted that the cardinals themselves were incapable of deposing the pope, Ridolfi nevertheless argued that they
had sufficient authority to convoke the assembly which was
capable of removing the rivals,[47] both of whom were scathingly
attacked for their obstruction of any united council.[48]

The activities of Buonaccursus and Ridolfi in the communal
debates continued in the early months of 1409. On 23 January,
the former urged neutrality and a council, although the latter
disagreed with some of his statements.[49] Academics also participated in the general assembly of Florentine prelates and clergy
which took place in February, and which provided the occasion
for Lorenzo di Ridolfi to produce his second *consilium*, in favour
of withdrawal of obedience and the deposition of Gregory XII.[50]
This policy met with the approval of the whole gathering.[51]
Stephanus de Buonaccursus for his part participated in the
embassy which Florence sent to Gregory XII to deliver a final
plea for him to act with the cardinals, before the withdrawal of
obedience was put into effect.[52]

Despite their continuity, the Florentine discussions were much
less important than those of the University of Bologna, where the
masters offered a constant stream of advice to the cardinals. This
activity involved diplomacy as well as writing: Antonius de
Butrio (returned from Ferrara) had acted as papal envoy in the
negotiations with Benedict XIII's ambassadors in the search for a
solution to the schism,[53] while in 1407 the university had sent its
own embassy to Gregory XII to urge him to fulfil his obligations
to work for union.[54] It even seems possible that the Bolognese

[45] Printed in J. Vincke, *Schriftstücke zum Pisaner Konzil*, Beiträge zur Kirchen- und Rechtsgeschichte, vol. 3 (Bonn, 1942), pp. 122–34.
[46] ibid., p. 132.　　　　　　　　[47] ibid., p. 133.
[48] ibid., p. 130.
[49] Martines, *Lawyers and statecraft*, p. 292.
[50] Biblioteca Apostolica Vaticana, MS Vat. Lat. 5608, fos 185r-202r.
[51] For these debates, see Martines, *Lawyers and statecraft*, pp. 294–5.
[52] Martène, *Amplissima collectio*, vol. 7, p. 945.
[53] J. F. von Schulte, *Die Geschichte der Quellen und Literatur des Canonischen Rechts von Gratian bis auf die Gegenwart*, vol. 2 (Stuttgart, 1877), pp. 290–1.
[54] Bzovius, *Annalium ecclesiasticorum*, vol. 15, p. 273.

masters hoped that if a general council was held, it would be held at Bologna.[55]

The numerous surviving Bolognese statements of the last years before Pisa indicate that this period was very much the equivalent for the Roman obedience of the traumas which had wracked the Avignonese obedience between 1394 and 1398. The parallel can be made even more specific, with the Bolognese debates which began in October 1407 – and in which most of the leading academics were involved – being seen as the Gregorian equivalent of the council held at Paris in mid-1398. The debates within the University of Bologna seem to have begun at the instigation of the Roman cardinals who, disillusioned and exasperated by the obstructive tactics of the rival popes, were already taking the first steps towards their rebellion and summons of the Pisan assembly.[56] The Bolognese attitude towards the situation was exemplified in comments made by Matthaeus de Matasellanis, a pupil of Antonius de Butrio.[57] For him, the question of Benedict XIII was largely an irrelevance: the activities of Gregory XII after his rejection of cession provided the impetus for the conciliarist procedure which was to be adopted. His case was to be the council's main concern; following his deposition the removal of Benedict XIII was the logical corollary.[58] Gregory's supposed heresy provided the basis for all the arguments. Matasellanis had no doubts about this point, arguing that the pope's actions since November 1407 had already deprived him of his papal powers.[59] The case of Benedict XIII received little attention, although Matasellanis did occasionally mention that the arguments advanced for or against Gregory XII were equally applicable to his opponent.[60]

These ideas presented by Matthaeus de Matasellanis, which date from the early months of 1409, were an extension of those which he had contributed to the Bolognese debates of late 1407

---

[55] Such was proposed by Petrus de Ancharano in one of his works, Florence, MS cit., fo. 117r.

[56] Vincke, *Schriftstücke*, pp. 29–30.

[57] von Schulte, *Geschichte*, vol. 2, p. 291.

[58] *BN*, MS Lat. 17184, fo. 242r.

[59] Thus, any excommunications which the pope had imposed since that date were to be considered null, 'quia ipse fuit ipso iure suspensus ab administratione papatus' (ibid., fo. 251v). [60] ibid., fo. 241r.

in a short submission also subscribed by Johannes de Gannetulo.[61]
Then he had argued that the cardinals, after the pope, had sufficient authority to summon a council,[62] which in turn possessed the
right of judgement because of the prevalent scandal within the
church, the uncertainties surrounding the papacy, and the perjury
of the contenders. Because they were bound by the electoral capitulation of 1406, the cardinals could not be prevented from acting to
end the schism by any prohibitions imposed by the pope,[63] who
was also incapable of dispensing them from their obligations to
work towards reunion.

Paulus de Castro's contribution to these debates concentrated
on the conclave oaths themselves,[64] concluding that they had
transferred responsibility for the search for union from the popes
to the cardinals, and arguing that the cardinals had the authority
to summon a council because the rivals were perjurers who had
scandalised the church. As this contingency of a council could be
considered a necessary part of the process towards union, it was
already covered by the provisions of the electoral capitulation, so
that those who rejected the cardinals' summons automatically
became schismatics. The council was to decide the legal issue
between the rival pontiffs, and legitimise the steps taken by the
cardinals. This last move was necessary because the cardinals,
although entitled to initiate the proceedings against the popes,
had no technical powers of judgement of their own.[65]

Further contributions to the Bolognese discussions were produced by Antonius de Butrio,[66] Bartholomaeus de Saliceto [67] and
Petrus de Ancharano.[68] Butrio generally concurred with the others
on the powers of the cardinals to summon a council, his short
declaration proving to be the first of a succession of tracts which
he produced. He was in the middle of his most ambitious contribution to the development of the conciliarist thesis when his

---

61 Bzovius, *Annalium ecclesiasticorum*, vol. 15, pp. 270–1; Paulus de Castro, *Consilia*
(3 vols., Frankfurt, 1582), vol. 1, fos 281r–v.
62 Bzovius, *Annalium ecclesiasticorum*, vol. 15, pp. 270–1.
63 ibid., vol. 15, p. 271.
64 ibid., vol. 15, pp. 266–8; Castro, *Consilia*, vol. 1, fos 216r–217r.
65 Bzovius, *Annalium ecclesiasticorum*, vol. 15, p. 267.
66 ibid., vol. 15, pp. 268–70; Castro, *Consilia*, vol. 1, fos 217r–218r.
67 Vincke, *Schriftstücke*, pp. 30–2.
68 Florence, MS cit., fos 117v–120v, dated 12 October 1407. See also Souchon, *Die
Papstwahlen des grossen Schismas*, vol. 2, pp. 247–8.

career was cut short by an untimely death only shortly before the opening of the Council of Pisa.[69]

The statement prepared by Bartholomaeus de Saliceto for the Bolognese debates of late 1407 added a few new variations to the general arguments. On the issue of the conclave oaths, he distinguished between the status of cardinal and pope, but asserted that, although Gregory was not necessarily bound by his oath taken as a cardinal, its reiteration after his election remained binding.[70] Moreover, if the pope, as pope, remained a member of the College of Cardinals, then the oath taken as a cardinal was also binding despite the alteration in Gregory's personal status, since the concept of collegiality allowed the whole body to bind even those of its number who had not sworn individually.[71] Apart from this, Saliceto's programme was typically conciliarist: the cardinals were to encourage a large attendance at the assembly and, even if Gregory refused to participate, his cardinals could unite with their Avignonese colleagues to elect another pope.[72]

Ancharano's treatment of the issues followed a very similar pattern, although he may still have wished to follow up his earlier cessionist and subtractionist programme. This was again proposed in a tract of June 1408,[73] in which he also denied the possibility of restoring obedience after it had been withdrawn since (presumably having the French experience in mind) this could only lead to further disorders.[74] This reversion to the programme outlined in 1405 seems to have been purely temporary: in his later works Ancharano revealed himself as a staunch conciliarist, eventually appearing as one of its leading champions at the Council of Pisa itself.[75]

Besides these tracts by identifiable Bolognese authors, the continuing debates also led to the production of other, anonymous,

---

[69] On this work, see O. Günther, 'Zur Vorgeschichte des Konzils von Pisa', *Neues Archiv der Gesellschaft für ältere deutsche Geschichtskunde*, **41** (1917–19), 656–9.

[70] Vincke, *Schriftstücke*, p. 31.

[71] ibid.

[72] ibid., p. 32.

[73] Florence, MS cit., fos 71v–74r, and again at fos 110r–112r. Printed in Vincke, *Schriftstücke*, pp. 107–12.

[74] Florence, MS cit., fo. 72v.

[75] For some tracts, see Vincke, *Schriftstücke*, pp. 112–19; Souchon, *Die Papstwahlen des grossen Schismas*, vol. 2, pp. 249–53; with the work delivered at Pisa in Weizsäcker, *Reichstagsakten*, vol. 3, pp. 521–57.

works. These were all hostile to the Roman pope in tone, although not always quite sure of their ground.[76] The most ambitious programme advanced [77] urged the cardinals to meet their commitments and form links with other interested parties, including the antipope, laying considerable emphasis on the shared tutorial responsibilities of cardinals and pope in the administration of the church.[78]

Having been initiated by the Roman cardinals in October 1407, the debates at the University of Bologna received a further stimulus in the following month, when Gregory XII wrote to the masters with a formal repudiation of his commitment to go to Savona for the negotiations with Benedict XIII.[79] The reaction to this declaration came at the turn of the year, when the academics voted in favour of four propositions which encapsulated the ideas of the earlier individual statements.[80] Thereafter, the university advocated swift action by the cardinals, opposing schemes such as that proposed by Venetian envoys to the cardinals later in 1408 which, by seeking further negotiations with Gregory XII, and urging consultation with the secular princes on the ideal location for the projected general council, could only cause additional delays.[81] But even so, in their voting in January 1408, the Bolognese still insisted that the schism was the responsibility of the Avignon line,[82] and refused to concede to Benedict XIII any suggestion of legitimacy.[83] The purpose of these declarations is not clear, and could have been counter-productive by reducing the chances of the much needed inter-obedience cooperation. As the preliminaries to the Council of Pisa progressed, the academics could not afford to run the risk of finding themselves isolated: even though labouring under the 'protection' of Balthasar Cossa, the masters of Bologna were not immune from Gregorian counter-

---

[76] For some tracts, see F. J. P. Bliemetzrieder, 'Zwei kanonistische Traktate aus Bologna (Ende 1408) wegen des Pisanerkonziles', *Studien und Mitteilungen aus dem Benedictiner- und dem Cistercienser-Orden*, 24 (1903), 112–4; Vincke, *Schriftstücke*, pp. 32–4, 134–40.

[77] Vincke, *Schriftstücke*, pp. 34–9.

[78] ibid., pp. 35–6.

[79] The letters are mentioned by Matthaeus de Matasellanis, *BN*, MS Lat. 17184, fo. 243r.

[80] On these resolutions, including a list of printed editions, see Bliemetzrieder, 'Zwei Traktate', p. 106 n. 2.

[81] Biblioteca Apostolica Vaticana, MS Vat. Lat. 7305, fos 120v–122r.

[82] Martène, *Amplissima collectio*, vol. 7, p. 896.   [83] ibid.

attacks. Both Ancharano and Butrio had to defend themselves against accusations and threats of excommunication for supporting the cardinals' council rather than the papally summoned version which Gregory XII intended to hold at Cividale, both academics taking the opportunity presented by this defence to issue a forceful attack on the plans for separate councils of the rival obediences.[84]

For, at this point, conciliarism was proving to be something of a double-edged sword. While the main trend of contemporary theorising aimed to justify action by the cardinals without the approval or involvement of the pope, another form of conciliarism was also developing in Italy. This accepted that a council would be needed to resolve the schism, but insisted that the assembly should be convened by the legitimate pope – Gregory XII. The theory was basically that advocated by Baldus de Ubaldis in the days before the schism actually began. The best exponent of this papalist form of conciliarism was Johannes de Imola, who produced his most important work late in 1408, probably at Padua.[85] The chief distinction between the two forms of conciliarism lay in their attitude towards the pope himself, and whether or not he had effectively excluded himself from the church. For Imola, there was no doubt that Gregory retained his papal prerogatives in full; his innocence and supremacy were upheld, his supposed heresy vigorously denied. Schism was not necessarily heretical in itself,[86] while the arguments over the electoral capitulations were fairly easily rebutted: in the first place, the change in Gregory's status rendered the oaths invalid – he could not bind himself as cardinal to renounce a position which he did not hold,[87] while in the second place non-observance of the capitulation was not automatic proof of heresy, since observance of the pact was not a matter of faith.[88] In any case it was possible for Gregory to be absolved from his oath, although Imola doubted whether the pope could grant himself the necessary dispensation.[89]

[84] Vincke, *Briefe*, pp. 46–50.
[85] Printed in D. Staffa, 'Tractatus Johannis ab Imola super schismate occidentis', *Rivista di storia della chiesa in Italia*, 7 (1953), 190–224; for the date see ibid., p. 184, and D. Staffa, 'De Iohannis ab Imola vita et operibus', *Apollinaris*, 10 (1937), 86–7.
[86] Staffa, 'Tractatus', p. 200.
[87] ibid., p. 193.
[88] ibid., pp. 197–203.
[89] ibid., pp. 200–1.

Yet Imola was, undeniably, a conciliarist, seeing a council as the only possible effective solution to the problem. In many respects his attitudes paralleled those of the supporters of the cardinals, even to the extent of being prepared to concede to the cardinals the authority to summon a council if the pope proved negligent in so doing. Like many other conciliarists, he produced a list of descending authorities (his scheme including the Patriarch of Constantinople and the Holy Roman Emperor) which were capable of summoning a general council of the church if their superiors refused so to do.[90] It was only his steadfast loyalty to Gregory XII which separated Imola from the mainstream of contemporary conciliarism, arguing as he did that the best method of reunification would be for all other parties to attend Gregory's council, with him providing the necessary guarantees of safety. This would have been much better than holding three separate assemblies, and thereby merely worsening the situation.[91] But despite the papalism of his tract, Imola was prepared to envisage resignation by Gregory at the council, if such was demanded of him.[92] For Johannes de Imola, and others sharing his views, the crucial point was to legitimise the council's convocation; what actually happened once this legal assembly was in progress was quite another matter – a formulation which was strikingly similar to that actually adopted by the Gregorian obedience in its dealings with the Council of Constance in 1415.

As things stood, however, conciliarism such as Imola's had little chance of success in 1409: for many supporters of the cardinals, Gregory already stood condemned, and they therefore had no inclination to obey his summons; while throughout there remained the problem of Benedict XIII, whose supporters could advance conciliarist arguments identical to those of Imola if they so wished. However, for the conciliarism of the cardinals to achieve its ends where all else had failed, it was necessary for their plan to be supported by members of both obediences. By 1408, there were signs that this necessary inter-obedience support for a concerted attack on the schism did exist. In creating this, the decisions of the universities (especially those of Paris and Bologna) had an

90 ibid., pp. 205–6.
91 ibid., p. 220.   92 ibid., p. 224.

important influence as propaganda, being cited by Cardinal Ug-
guccione in his oration to King Henry IV of England to persuade
him to endorse the steps taken by the cardinals, as well as in
Germany and elsewhere.[93] Although the courses of their debates
had differed over the previous few years, both the Universities of
Paris and Bologna had in the end accepted the *via concilii*,
although the process which produced the Parisian decision had
been the more dramatic.

At Paris, activity on the schism had revived only with the
attempt to forestall the election of Innocent VII in 1404, and the
resulting contacts with the new pope.[94] The conciliatory tone
adopted by Innocent towards the Parisians contrasted markedly
with the hostility of the Benedictine envoys, led by Cardinal de
Challant.[95] The resulting animosity against Benedict XIII
coalesced with the disillusionment earlier felt over his refusal to
accept the conditional nature of the French restitution of obedience in 1403. In 1406 the long-delayed counter-attack on the
Toulouse letter of 1401 was but one of the steps taken by the
Parisian masters to warn the pope of their growing hostility.[96]
That the Toulousain academics were still ferociously loyal to
Benedict XIII was vividly illustrated later in the year, in the
struggle between the Benedictine and royal nominees for the
succession to the archbishopric of Toulouse, during which members of the University of Toulouse supported the pope's claimant.[97]
The Parisian masters further decided that the subtraction of
obedience proclaimed in 1398 was still legally effective, Benedict
XIII having failed to honour his side of the restitution agreement
of 1403,[98] but Jean Petit, who was meant to expound this view to

[93] For citations of university opinions in discussions of the period, see Weizsäcker,
Reichstagsakten, vol. 3, pp. 382–3; Martines, *Lawyers and statecraft*, p. 292; V. H.
Galbraith, *The St Albans chronicle, 1406–20* (Oxford, 1937), pp. 43, 147–8; Vincke,
Schriftstücke, p. 140; Vincke, 'Acta', p. 248; Bliemetzrieder, 'Abt Ludolfs Traktat',
p. 227.
[94] For these contacts, see *Valois*, vol. 3, pp. 422–3, 427–9.
[95] *Chron. S. Den.*, vol. 3, pp. 360–3.
[96] See F. Astre, 'L'université de Toulouse devant le Parlement de Paris, en 1406',
*Mémoires de l'Academie impériale des Sciences, Inscriptions, et Belles-Lettres de
Toulouse*, 7th series, I (1869), 109–24; *Valois*, vol. 3, pp. 431–41; Coville, *Petit*,
pp. 47–58.
[97] *Valois*, vol. 3, pp. 453–5; Smith, *Toulouse*, pp. 152–3; J. Puget, 'L'université de
Toulouse au XIVᵉ et au XVᵉ siècles, *Annales du Midi*, 41-2 (1929–30), 358–9.
[98] *Valois*, vol. 3, pp. 430–1.

the king, seems to have lost his nerve at the last moment.[99] However, on 6 September 1406 he did put his case to the Parlement, as part of the preparations to force through another formal withdrawal of obedience from the pope, preparations which included further attacks on Benedict's supporters.[100]

While a partial subtraction of obedience was already in force in fact,[101] the formal withdrawal required another Gallican council, which convened in November 1406.[102] The attitudes of those involved were uncertain even on the eve of the assembly: a meeting of sixty-nine theologians was held on 16 November, at which Pierre d'Ailly advocated support for a conciliarist solution to the schism, gaining the support of twenty-seven of those present.[103] These included Jean Gerson, whose personal opinion (now abandoning some of his earlier stringency in matters affecting the ecclesiastical constitution) was expressed in his *Acta quedam de schismate tollendo*,[104] suggesting several possible solutions to the impasse, including a council and a new election by the united cardinals.[105]

The events of the Paris council of 1406 mirrored the proceedings of 1398, although on a rather smaller scale. Yet again, there was no sense of purpose beyond a royally enforced subtraction of obedience, although only partial withdrawal was eventually decreed.[106] The old arguments were again rehearsed, on the validity of cession, the representative nature of the Gallican council and the nature of royal authority within the church. Yet again royal influence was important and unavoidable – Guillaume Fillastre was forced to issue a public apology for an unfortunate interpretation of the relations between earlier French kings and the popes.[107] Once more, the masters of the University of Paris

---

99 ibid., vol. 3, p. 431; Coville, *Petit*, pp. 47–8.
100 *Valois*, vol. 3, pp. 442–7; Coville, *Petit*, pp. 64–5.
101 *Valois*, vol. 3, pp. 442–3.
102 On this council see ibid., vol. 3, pp. 455–75; Coville, *Petit*, 65–81; Salembier, *Pierre d'Ailly*, pp. 195–222; Bourgeois du Chastenet, *Constance*, pp. 95–234 (this and all subsequent references are to the *preuves*); Martin, *Origines*, vol. 1, pp. 313–25.
103 *Valois*, vol. 3, pp. 457–8; Salembier, *Pierre d'Ailly*, p. 195; Coville, *Petit*, p. 79. The propositions are printed in Bourgeois du Chastenet, *Constance*, pp. 153–4.
104 *Glorieux*, no. 265; see also Posthumus Meyjes, *Jean Gerson*, pp. 113–4; Morrall, *Gerson*, pp. 70–1. 105 *Glorieux*, vol. 6, p. 98.
106 *Valois*, vol. 3, pp. 472–5.   107 Bourgeois du Chastenet, *Constance*, pp. 163–4.

seized the opportunity for self-congratulation, with Simon de Cramaud referring to its mythical Athenian origins,[108] while the customary internecine strife reappeared when d'Ailly was strongly censured for the vitality of his defence of Benedict XIII.[109] The proceedings also created their own difficulties, the Archbishop of Rheims complaining about their length, declaring that he found the whole business a great bore, and wishing that the theologians and academics would reserve their disputes for the schools.[110]

Although the provincial Universities of Angers, Orléans and Montpellier are mentioned as having been represented at the council of 1406,[111] whether all the provincial universities supported the Parisian policy is unclear. It is quite probable that Toulouse (which is not mentioned as being represented) did not, although Orléans did, even though its rector held out against subtraction.[112] In any event, after the council the University of Paris sent another letter on the *via cessionis* to Charles VI.[113] The appeal against Benedict XIII, dormant since 1403, was also revived.[114] Hereafter the Parisian attack was consistently concentrated against Benedict; the Roman pope was rarely considered. Although there had been occasional expressions of hostility to Innocent VII, this antipathy apparently evaporated when Paris was informed of the election of Gregory XII, and the new pope and his cardinals proclaimed their desire for union.[115]

It was in such delicate circumstances that the manoeuvrings intended to lead to direct negotiations between the rivals began, and eventually failed. The Parisians had distrusted the project from the start, interpreting the talks as another instance of Benedict's bad faith, meant merely to pre-empt cession by enacting the *via compromissi*. The king, however, intervened to prevent any obstruction, and sent a large embassy to both popes to encourage their activities, the envoys including several members of the university. The outcome of this was intimate French involvement in

108 ibid., pp. 123–4.
109 ibid., p. 198; Salembier, *Pierre d'Ailly*, pp. 208–10; Coville, *Petit*, pp. 73–4.
110 Bourgeois du Chastenet, *Constance*, p. 211. 111 *Thes. Nov. Anec.*, p. 1307.
112 C. M. G. B. Jourdain, *Index chronologicus chartarum pertinentem ad historiam universitatis Parisiensis* (Paris, 1862), no. CMXCII.
113 *Valois*, vol. 3, pp. 475–6; *Bulaeus*, vol. 5, pp. 134–7.
114 *Thes. Nov. Anec.*, pp. 1297–1307.
115 *Valois*, vol. 3, pp. 479–81; *Thes. Nov. Anec.*, pp. 1286–93.

the attempts to arrange a meeting of the popes.[116] The subtractionist decrees were therefore temporarily suspended, although Benedict's delaying tactics soon produced demands for their immediate enforcement. To these demands Gerson, d'Ailly and others responded with their *Rationes ad deferendam substractionem*,[117] a plea not to antagonise Benedict when the search for an end to the schism was at such a critical stage.

But, with the collapse of the project for direct negotiations, the attack on Benedict could not be prevented: the demands for implementation of the subtraction decrees and a declaration of neutrality reappeared in all their old vigour.[118] In January 1408 it was announced that such a programme would be adopted if no further progress towards union had been made by 24 May.[119] Benedict's reply was a scathing attack on his detractors,[120] provoking the University of Paris (represented by Jean Courtecuisse) to a formal denunciation of both Benedict and his bulls, which were condemned and destroyed. Benedict's activities also provoked a hastening of the French programme, subtraction of obedience from the Avignon pope being actually decreed on 14 May.[121] Once again the university celebrated its success with a purge of Benedictines,[122] and urged yet another council of the French church to continue the attack. This was held at Paris in the autumn of 1408, making appropriate arrangements for the governance of the church in France during the re-imposed subtraction of obedience, and – yet again – deciding to harry the adherents of Benedict XIII.[123] As had frequently happened, with the initiative on French policy regarding the schism once more passing to the crown, the influence of the University of Paris

116 On this activity, see *Valois*, vol. 3, pp. 499–548; *Chron. S. Den.*, vol. 3, pp. 511–721; *Thes. Nov. Anec.*, pp. 1344–77; A. Bossuat, 'Une relation inédite de l'ambassade française au pape Benoît XIII en 1407', *Moyen Age*, 55 (1949), 77–101; N. Valois, 'Jacques de Nouvion et le religieux de St-Denys', *Bibliothèque de l'Ecole des chartes*, 63 (1902), 233–62.
117 *Glorieux*, no. 267; Posthumus Meyjes, *Jean Gerson*, pp. 124–5.
118 *Valois*, vol. 3, pp. 597–8.
119 ibid., vol. 3, p. 597; Martin, *Origines*, vol. 1, p. 337.
120 Martin, *Origines*, vol. 1, pp. 338–9; *Chron. S. Den.*, vol. 4, pp. 4–9.
121 *Valois*, vol. 3, pp. 608–11; *Chron. S. Den.*, vol. 4, pp. 8–15.
122 *Valois*, vol. 4, pp. 29–30; *Chron. S. Den.*, vol. 4, pp. 14–19; Salembier, *Pierre d'Ailly*, pp. 236–8.
123 *Valois*, vol. 4, pp. 22–40; *Chron. S. Den.*, vol. 4, pp. 30–53.

declined. Thereafter, with France again neutral, university activity
until the assembly of the Council of Pisa was confined almost
exclusively to contact with other bodies, including the cardinals
and princes,[124] although in December 1408 the appeal to a future
pope was again revived.[125]

In all this, there is little real indication of any advance from
cession to conciliarism. There seems to have been no formal
university declaration approving the activities of the cardinals,
merely the condemnation of Benedict XIII. The extent to which
the University of Paris, as a corporation, remained tied to cession
is impossible to determine, although presumably the contacts
with Italy which resulted from the embassy of 1407 helped foster
the acceptance of conciliarism. Certainly, once the cardinals
announced their council, that programme was accepted by the
university without demur, while Jean Gerson and Pierre d'Ailly
soon appeared amongst the cardinals' most ardent supporters.

D'Ailly's major contribution at this stage was his *Propositiones
utiles ad extinctionem presentis schismatis per viam concilii
generalis*, issued on 1 January 1409.[126] This succinct summary of
the conciliarist viewpoint encompassed all the arguments of the
preceding few years. The pope was no longer seen as the necessary head of the church, Christ being the only indispensable leader
of the *corpus mysticum*. And, just as in natural law other bodies
could unite to prevent their destruction, so the sections of the
church should come together to carry out reunion, if necessary
without papal authorisation.[127] D'Ailly listed three instances when
he felt this should occur, including where the church was divided
by schism, with no universally accepted pope.[128] In this revised
ecclesiology the authority to summon the necessary council
belonged, ultimately, to all the faithful, rather than being
restricted to pope and cardinals.[129]

Gerson's opinions on the situation were best expressed in his

124 For examples, see *Valois*, vol. 4, pp. 56–60, 72–3.
125 Vincke, *Schriftstücke*, pp. 222–6.
126 Printed in Dupin, *Gersonii opera*, vol. 2, pp. 112–13; an English translation is in
   F. Oakley, 'The "Propositiones utiles" of Pierre d'Ailly: an epitome of conciliar
   theory', *Church History*, **29** (1960), 399–402 (reprinted in Crowder, *Unity*, pp. 52–4).
   See also Martin, *Origines*, vol. 2, pp. 79–80.
127 Dupin, *Gersonii opera*, vol. 2, p. 112.
128 ibid., vol. 2, p. 113.
129 ibid., vol. 2, p. 113.

Propositio facta coram Anglicis,[130] produced early in 1409.[131] His theories were also stated in a series of other tracts, which included the *De auctoritate concilii* and the *Tractatus de unitate ecclesiae*.[132] They received their lengthiest exposition at Paris while the Council of Pisa was actually in session, in his *De auferibilitate sponsi ab ecclesia*.[133] This repeated his concept of papal accountability to the whole church, which was applied to the depositions of Benedict XIII and Gregory XII at Pisa. When the long-hoped-for reunification of the church appeared to have been achieved with the election of Alexander V, it was therefore greeted with praise.[134]

Meanwhile, in his *Propositio*, Gerson had asserted the need for a single head of the church, which he had claimed was entitled to seek unity by means of a council, even if this meant overthrowing established traditions. In his discussion of the relationships between the various constituents of the ecclesiastical hierarchy, although not denying the papal power he made a major distinction between the transience of the individual pope and the permanence of the papacy as an institution: 'Papa fluit, papatus stabilis est'.[135] This enabled him to argue that, although the *congregatio fidelium* had no powers to affect the continuing existence of the papacy as a constituent institution of the church, nevertheless a council, as representative of the whole church, could alter the method of election and, if necessary, remove or replace the individual pope, using force if he refused to resign.[136]

The conciliarist developments of the years from 1403 to 1409 were not confined only to France and Italy; but the evidence for progress elsewhere is rather patchy, and restricted to the universities of Germany and eastern Europe. The correspondence of the University of Cologne for this period contains only scattered references to the search for union.[137] Once the preparations for the Council of Pisa had begun, the masters of Cologne did prepare a

---

[130] *Glorieux*, no. 271; see also Morrall, *Gerson*, pp. 77–81; Posthumus Meyjes, *Jean Gerson*, pp. 136–41.

[131] The date usually given for this tract is late January 1409, but Dr Margaret Harvey informs me that this is questionable.

[132] *Glorieux*, nos. 269, 272.

[133] ibid., no. 102. See also Morrall, *Gerson*, pp. 88–93; Posthumus Meyjes, *Jean Gerson*, pp. 147–55.

[134] *Glorieux*, no. 221.

[135] ibid., vol. 6, p. 132.

[136] ibid., vol. 6, p. 133.

[137] *Thes. Nov. Anec.*, pp. 1282–6.

statement of their opinions, the *Conspectus universitatis in materia unionis ecclesie*, with the intention that it should be delivered to the assembly.[138] Unfortunately, the disappearance of the work means that there remains no precise indication of just how the academics of Cologne viewed the situation at this stage. Elsewhere, Rupert of the Palatinate's conciliarist activities *c*. 1405 may indicate that there had been some debates on the subject at Heidelberg, but this is uncertain; while evidence for the involvement of Cracow in these developments appears only after the university received its summons to attend Pisa, with the programme of the cardinals being accepted.[139]

Of the German and other universities of the empire, only Prague and Vienna provide more than meagre evidence of the views of the academics in the period before the Council of Pisa. That available from the University of Prague, however, is occasionally difficult to interpret. Among the many tensions affecting that university was the division between the Germans, who were generally loyal to Gregory XII and the imperial pretensions of Rupert of the Palatinate, and the Czechs who supported Wenceslas of Bohemia and the cardinals. The various conflicts between the two national groups were only resolved in January 1409 with the publication of the decree of Kutna Hora which drastically altered the constitutional arrangements within the university, and as a result of which the Czechs gained the upper hand, and the majority of the Germans withdrew in annoyance. However, although the division between Germans and Czechs did exist, the distinction between conciliarists and supporters of Gregory XII cannot have been made purely on national grounds. Indeed, one of the main tracts produced at Prague at this time was the *Tractatus de renunciatione pape* by the German John of Falkenberg, in which Gregory XII was strongly censured as a schismatic and fomenter of heresy. Falkenberg actually went so far as to declare that Gregory XII, because of his heresy, was no longer *de iure* pope, and he urged the cardinals to proceed to the election of a single and undisputed pope for the whole church. Precisely which cardinals were to perform the election was a matter which he did not consider, but he presumably intended that both colleges would

[138] Swanson, 'Cologne', p. 9.　　[139] Vincke, *Briefe*, pp. 140–1.

unite.[140] Indications that Falkenberg was not alone among the Germans at Prague are provided by the foundation of the University of Leipzig in 1409, which acquired many of its initial members from among the Germans who left Prague in 1409. From the outset the new university recognised the papacy established at the Council of Pisa.

The University of Vienna is the only university of the empire to provide indications of consistent and definable activity on the schism throughout the years 1403–9. The issue may even have been discussed before the death of Boniface IX for, when considering the sending of a *rotulus* to Innocent VII in November 1404, the masters sought ducal action on the dispute, and agreed to try to influence other secular and ecclesiastical authorities to take action.[141] Special services were also decreed, to invoke divine assistance in the search for reunion.[142] Requests for the princes to participate in moves to terminate the schism were repeated in later years,[143] but the university itself took no positive action until late 1408, when the rebellious cardinals urged the masters to send representatives to the council which they intended to summon, and to withdraw their obedience from Gregory XII.[144] The university's response, presented orally on 11 October, and in writing on the 19th, approved of the cardinals' actions, but demanded that the university be allowed to decide the timing of its subtraction of obedience.[145] While praising the cardinals and encouraging their activities, the Viennese sought time to hold further discussions on the situation with the princes and prelates, to arrange that the withdrawal of obedience would be unanimous, peaceful and constructive.[146] Negotiations accordingly continued with the Bishops of Salzburg and Passau and with the dukes.[147] The university also tried to arrange for the financing of the

---

[140] Chaloupecký, *Prague,* pp. 105–7; P. de Vooght, *L'hérésie de Jean Huss,* Bibliothèque de la Revue d'histoire ecclésiastique, vol. 34 (Louvain, 1960), pp. 107–12. Falkenberg's tract is printed in G. Sommerfeldt, 'Johann Falkenbergs Stellung zur Papstfrage in der Zeit vor dem Pisaner Konzil (1408)', *Mitteilungen des Instituts für österreichische Geschichtsforschung,* **31** (1910), 426–37.

[141] Uiblein, *Acta,* p. 235.

[142] ibid., p. 239.

[143] ibid., p. 276.

[144] ibid., p. 296; Günther, 'Zur Vorgeschichte', pp. 659–66.

[145] Uiblein, *Acta,* pp. 297–8; Günther, 'Zur Vorgeschichte', pp. 670–1.

[146] Günther, 'Zur Vorgeschichte', p. 671.

[147] Uiblein, *Acta,* pp. 301–3, 306–9.

embassy which it wished to send to the forthcoming council.[148] In the meantime, Lambert of Guelders and Gerard Vischbeck were sent as the university's representatives to the imperial Diet held at Frankfurt in January 1409, at which the schism was a major topic of discussion.[149]

It was from this assembly that there came the main German defence of Gregory XII issued prior to the Council of Pisa, the so-called 'Heidelberg Postilla',[150] a work intended to persuade Rupert of the Palatinate – if he needed any persuasion – to reject the cardinals' summons to Pisa. Although the authorship of the work is disputed, there seems little doubt that the writer was a member of the University of Heidelberg [151] – perhaps even one of that small group of university masters who frequently appeared among Rupert's counsellors at this time. However, although important as a piece of propaganda, the tract included few notable arguments, being generally intemperate, and not at all constructive. But the work cannot be simply dismissed as the rantings of a master of an intellectual backwater: the Postilla make it plain that Heidelberg was well aware of developments among the rest of the academic community, specifically rejecting the conciliarist determinations of the Universities of Bologna and Paris.[152] The tract also reveals a knowledge of the conflicts which cession and conciliarism had generated within and between the other universities, making particular mention of the earlier Parisian disputes with the Universities of Oxford and Toulouse.[153]

The main importance of the Heidelberg Postilla derives from its impact as propaganda, especially in serving to provoke conciliarist responses. Amongst these was the most precise surviving statement of Viennese opinion, a lengthy work which may have been produced by Gerard Vischbeck himself.[154] The author

---

[148] ibid., pp. 300–1, 307.

[149] ibid., p. 302; F. J. P. Bliemetzrieder, *Ein kanonistischer Traktat für das Pisaner Konzil (1409)* (Graz, 1902), p. 73.

[150] Weizsäcker, *Reichtsagsakten*, vol. 3, pp. 387–422.

[151] ibid., vol. 3, p. 323; F. J. P. Bliemetzrieder, 'Matthäus von Krakau, der Verfasser der Postillen?', *Studien und Mitteilungen aus dem Benedictiner- und dem Cistercienser-Orden*, 25 (1904), 544–56; H. Heimpel, 'Konrad von Soest und Job Vener, Verfasser und Bearbeiter der Heidelberger Postillen (Glossen) zu der Berufung des Konzils von Pisa', *Westfalen*, 51 (1973), 115–24.

[152] Weizsäcker, *Reichtstagsakten*, vol. 3, p. 401.   [153] ibid., vol. 6, pp. 392, 406.

[154] Printed in Bliemetzrieder, *Traktat*, pp. 29–51. On the date and authorship, see ibid., pp. 73, 91; Bliemetzrieder, *Das Generalkonzil*, pp. 245, 253–5.

acknowledged that the church was in a chaotic situation,[155] one which required a full and rigorous inspection of the issues involved in order to determine the appropriate course of action. His consideration therefore ranged over several aspects of the problem, in many instances the arguments serving to synthesise the conciliarist doctrine as it had been formulated in the preceding years.

The tract began by considering the mechanics of a papal election,[156] arguing that where an election which had originally been accepted had subsequently been rejected and a new election held (as had been the case at the inception of the present schism), then the logical procedure was to declare neutrality until a council could be held to determine the issue.[157] This scheme looked back to the conciliarism which had prevailed at the start of the schism; but whereas that had generally foundered on the issue of legitimacy, most people having decided their loyalties before they turned to the question of resolving the problem of the dual papacy, the Viennese writer managed to circumvent the difficulty by producing arguments to justify the view that neither of the present rivals was in fact pope. The effect of his accusations (including one of negligence for not having acted rapidly to end the dispute by summoning a council)[158] was to deprive the rivals of their immunity from legal processes,[159] and also to make papal convocation of the council no longer necessary.

From this hypothesis, it was but a short step to denying the legitimacy of Urban VI and his successors, evidenced by the continuation of the schism and the adulterous union of popes and church. By this means the author avoided the need for any council to be summoned by Gregory XII,[160] while it followed that, as there was no true pope, a further election could be held without any reservations.[161] However, the writer seems to have recognised the difficulties of his situation: law was an ineffective weapon when there were no living witnesses to the original dispute. Nevertheless, he maintained that both the elections of 1378 were of dubious validity, arguing that Urban VI had almost certainly been elected by force.[162] Attempts to defend that pope's

[155] Bliemetzrieder, *Traktat*, pp. 50-1.
[156] ibid., pp. 29-31.
[157] ibid., p. 30.
[158] ibid., p. 32.
[159] ibid., p. 33.
[160] ibid., p. 36.
[161] ibid., p. 37.
[162] ibid., p. 37.

legitimacy were vigorously repulsed, allowing the writer to indulge in a spirited attack on one of Urban's more determined advocates, who is identified in the tract merely as 'quidem magne fame doctor', but who may have been Baldus de Ubaldis.[163]

Because of the doubts thus raised about Urban VI's election, there had been consequent error in accepting him as pope before the church had confirmed his claims.[164] And if the election of April 1378 was invalid, then so also were the papal elections of 1389, 1404 and 1406, so that discussion of Gregory XII's position was irrelevant.[165] Gregory was not pope, and the actions of the cardinals in seeking union merited praise, as they were providing the leadership which the rest of the church should follow. The cardinals were justified at length (although the writer seems to have ignored the obvious logical flaw in his own arguments; that if none of the 'popes' elected since the death of Gregory XI were truly popes, then none of the cardinals they had created could really be recognised as cardinals). Claims that the cardinals were excommunicate were denied, the Viennese writer arguing that even if they were there was no real problem, for it was not they who were to decide the issue of the schism but the whole church.[166]

Nevertheless, by this stage the author had merely admitted the possibility, not the certainty, that the election of Urban VI had been invalid. The second section of the tract therefore considered the problem from a different standpoint, supposing the election to have been valid, and debating whether Urban or his successors ought to have resigned, or could be compelled to do so.[167] The customary arguments – loyalty and the dangers of cession being set against the needs of the public good [168] – were again repeated. The electoral capitulation of 1406 was also considered, with the conclusion that Gregory's oath taken as cardinal was not valid, but that its restatement by him as pope remained binding.[169]

Despite all this discussion, there still remained the problem of translating theoretical conclusions into positive action. The author therefore produced arguments to permit the council to remove the

[163] ibid., pp. 37–8, 55 n. 1. [164] ibid., p. 38.
[165] ibid., p. 39.
[166] ibid., pp. 40–1. [167] ibid., p. 41.
[168] ibid., pp. 42–4. [169] ibid., p. 45.

rival popes and proceed to a further election acceptable to all Christians.[170] But the programme still had to be implemented; hence the appeal for support from princes and prelates which occupied the final section of the work, laying particular emphasis on the need to maintain the concept of one unified church.[171]

It is this appeal for practical assistance which highlights the problem of the pre-conciliar arguments: they were still untested theories. The universities and individual academics could devise schemes which seemed to fit the requirements of the situation, and have them adopted by ecclesiastical and secular leaders, but only the actual assembly of a council and its aftermath could provide the necessary evidence and judgement of their efficacy. When it met, therefore, the Council of Pisa would judge not merely the rival contenders for the papacy, but conciliarism itself, and by extension the universities and their claims to political and ecclesiastical significance. In some respects, however, the case was already decided against the academics and their pretensions. Their activities and theorising between 1403 and 1409 had endorsed, not a populist interpretation of conciliarism, but a minor variation of the pre-existing ecclesiastical constitution. The initiative remained with the cardinals; the descending form of ecclesiastical government, although temporarily decapitated by this version of conciliarism, still lived. Even though the academics provided the theories, it was the cardinals (acting in conjunction with the secular princes) who took the necessary steps to bring the Council of Pisa into being.

[170] ibid., pp. 45-7.   [171] ibid., pp. 47-50.

Chapter 9

HAEC SANCTA SYNODUS . . .

The Councils of Pisa and Constance had a double impact on the church, allowing the recently devised conciliarist programme to be carried out and also producing a fundamental alteration in the balance of forces at work within the *ecclesia*.[1] The opening of the first of these assemblies marked the beginning of that epoch in ecclesiastical history known as the Conciliar Period, which lasted until Pope Pius II delivered a formal condemnation of the theory of conciliarism in his bull *Execrabilis*, issued in 1460. The assembly of the Council of Pisa also to some extent marked the end of what had been the apogee of university influence in European affairs, for once the conciliar procedures were under way and ecclesiastical politicians resumed control of the machinery for directing the church, then the involvement and status of the universities were considerably reduced, almost to that of mere spectators.

But although university influence became more remote, the academics were certainly not reduced to impotence. The cardinals had requested many of the universities to send representatives to their intended council – although the Spanish universities are conspicuously absent from the list of known addressees [2] – and in most cases these summonses appear to have been complied with. This was in itself an innovation, but the control which the academics who remained behind could exert over their supposed representatives was strictly limited, largely because of the diffi-

---

[1] For events at Pisa see *Valois*, vol. 4, pp. 75–107; Vincke, 'Acta', pp. 81–323. For a select bibliography on the Council of Constance, see K. A. Fink and E. Eberloh, 'Das abendländische Schisma und die Konzilien', in *Handbuch der Kirchengeschichte*, ed. H. Jedin, vol. 3/2 (Freiburg, 1968), pp. 545–7.

[2] Letters were intended to be sent to the Universities of Vienna, Erfurt, Oxford, Cambridge, Lisbon, Prague, Cracow, Cologne, Heidelberg, Naples, Pavia, Bologna, Montpellier, Paris, Toulouse, Angers and Orléans: Vincke, *Briefe*, pp. 217, 220, 223–5, 227, 232, 234, 237.

culties of communication over long distances. The actual composition of the missions sent to the councils by the universities is
therefore of little importance in assessing the latter's reactions to
the challenges posed by the summonses.

Moreover, as far as the Council of Pisa is concerned, that
assembly has to be seen in its proper context, as only one of three
gatherings held in 1409. There were also the rival Gregorian and
Benedictine meetings, held respectively at Cividale and Perpignan
and, as Benedict XIII himself pointed out, a large section of
Latin Christendom was not represented at Pisa.[3] Among the
universities, some found the cardinals' statements unconvincing
and simply refused to attend; while others, whether for financial
or other reasons, seem to have been content to forgo their claims
to independent representation and sent their envoys as members
of the larger delegation of another authority.

Of the councils besides Pisa, only that held by Benedict XIII
at Perpignan provides any evidence of university representation,
with the Spanish Universities of Lérida, Salamanca and Perpignan
remaining loyal to their Spanish pope.[4] The absence of Valladolid
from the list was apparently due to that university's poverty: it
could not afford to send any envoys.[5] Only one non-Iberian
university was officially represented at this gathering, the University of Avignon, where Benedict still retained his temporal authority.[6] Several other academics appear in the presence list of the
Perpignan meeting, mainly from the French universities but, as
their presence was unofficial and merely a declaration of personal
loyalty, they cannot really be taken into consideration. Nevertheless, their presence did indicate that not all members of the
non-Spanish universities were convinced of the validity of the
conciliarist thesis as presented by the cardinals.

The matter of university representation at the Council of Pisa
is much less straightforward than for the Perpignan assembly.
There are massive difficulties in reconciling the several presence
lists, the reliability of which is in almost all cases suspect. Diffi-

[3] See the relevant passage of his *Replicatio*, printed in F. Ehrle, 'Die kirchenrechtlichen Schriften Peters von Luna (Benedikts XIII)', *Archiv für Literatur- und
Kirchengeschichte des Mittelalters*, **7** (1900), pp. 552–3.

[4] F. Ehrle, 'Aus den Acten des Afterconcils von Perpignan, 1408 (Schluss)', *Archiv
für Literatur- und Kirchengeschichte des Mittelalters*, **7** (1900), 681.

[5] Beltrán de Heredia, *Cartulario*, vol. 1, p. 251.

[6] Ehrle, 'Aus den Acten', p. 681.

culties with the sources also mean that it is frequently impossible to differentiate between those who attended the council as official university envoys and those who (although members of a university) were present in some other capacity but nevertheless assumed the status of university representatives when necessary.[7] But whatever the difficulties, it is clear that there was a very large academic contingent at Pisa. The universities represented included both the English *studia*, and from France the Universities of Paris, Angers, Toulouse and Montpellier. Of the Italian universities, only Bologna can be shown to have definitely sent envoys, but there are indications that members of the Universities of Pisa, Florence and Padua were also present – the academics from the last of these possibly including Franciscus de Zabarella in their number. Prague and Cracow pose problems, but even if not officially represented they did have members present in an unofficial capacity. Among the German universities, Heidelberg was still loyal to Gregory XII and was to remain so for some years,[8] while Cologne, despite its earlier activity, was apparently content to submerge its claims to independent representation in the generality of the archiepiscopal mission.[9] Erfurt appears not to have been represented, although Nicholas Lubich, the university conservator who attended the council as envoy of the margraves of Meissen, may have acted for the university when required.[10] Vienna was apparently the only university of the empire formally to nominate its own representatives, although even here they served in a dual capacity – probably for financial reasons – acting also on behalf of the Austrian dukes.[11]

[7] For the list of Pisan presence lists so far published, see J. Leinweber, 'Ein neues Verzeichniss der Teilnehmer am Konzil von Pisa, 1409', in *Konzil und Papst*, ed. G. Schwaiger (Munich, 1975), pp. 207–12, with a further list published ibid., pp. 221–46. The list in *Raynaldus, ann.* 1409, no. 45, is a shortened version of a list which is contained in full in Bodleian Library, Oxford, MS Canonici Pat. Lat. 205, fos 11–15v. I have dealt with the issue of university representation at Pisa at greater length than would be practical here in my dissertation, 'Universities, academics, and the great schism', Ph.D. thesis, University of Cambridge, 1976, vol. 1, pp. 173–5, vol. 2, pp. 183–9.

[8] Members of the university supported Rupert of the Palatinate's opposition to the Pisan gathering: Weizsäcker, *Reichstagsakten*, vol. 3, pp. 496, 514.

[9] Swanson, 'Cologne', p. 9.

[10] E. Kleineidam, *Universitas Studii Erffordensis: Überblick über die Geschichte der Universität Erfurt im Mittelalter, 1392–1521. Teil 1: 1392–1460*, Erfurter theologische Studien, vol. 14 (Leipzig, 1964), p. 84.

[11] Leinweber, 'Ein neues Verzeichniss', pp. 224, 246.

Representation was only one of the issues affecting university relations with the Council of Pisa; contacts between the universities and their envoys were also important. However, the few letters which survive from the assembly throw little light on this aspect of the situation. They consist almost exclusively of recitals of events despatched from the council to the universities, with no surviving example of correspondence in the opposite direction.[12] But they were not solely statements of events: one letter, sent from Pisa on 21 May 1409 by the emissaries of the Picard nation in the University of Paris, includes a transcript of one of the council's decrees, ordering the withdrawal of obedience from the rival popes and annulling in advance any actions they might take against anyone so subtracting.[13] There are several possible reasons for the paucity of the known contacts between the universities and the council, of which the speed with which the proceedings were concluded was perhaps the most significant. Unlike the later Council of Constance, which during the four years of its existence necessitated the development of an intricate system of communications between the universities and their envoys, the Council of Pisa completed its task within a season. As everything was apparently done smoothly and without complications, this again precluded the need for much correspondence. The aspirations apparent at the beginning of the council, especially the desire to re-establish ecclesiastical unity, were considered to be perfectly feasible within the legal framework of conciliarism as evolved in the preceding few years, and no thought appears to have been given to the possibility that the theories might prove ineffective in practice. The other main area of university interest in the council – that of self-interest [14] – was something which could safely be left to the discretion of the university representatives who were actually at the council. All that was required was notification of a papal election for the preparations for another series of *rotuli* to begin.[15] That the universities had expected the council

---

[12] For the surviving letters sent by the university representatives at Pisa back to their universities, see L. Schmitz, 'Zur Geschichte des Konzils von Pisa, 1409', *Römische Quartalschrift*, **9** (1895), 372–5; *Bulaeus*, vol. 5, pp. 192–3; British Library, London, MS Add. 10020, fos 98r–99r, 148r–v. For signs of Viennese correspondence with its envoys, see Uiblein, *Acta*, pp. 318–24; Vincke, *Briefe*, pp. 204, 207–8.

[13] London, MS cit., fos 148r–v (the letter is actually bound in reverse).

[14] For signs of this at Vienna, see Uiblein, *Acta*, p. 315.   [15] ibid., pp. 323–32.

to settle the issues without real complications seems clear from the somewhat lackadaisical response to the summonses. Not only did some universities not send their own independent representatives, but even some of those which did seem to have made their preparations without any sense of urgency. The University of Montpellier did not nominate its envoys until 15 April 1409, they being the last university delegation to arrive at Pisa, on 3 June – little more than three weeks before the election of Alexander V took place on June 26.[16]

When it was all over and the new pope had been chosen, the council had succeeded in giving the impression that the church, acting on its own authority as the *congregatio fidelium*, had at last done something about its problems. Unfortunately, the plan misfired. The Pisan settlement may have been received with euphoria – as in Jean Gerson's sermon, *Pax hominibus bonae voluntatis*, with its far-fetched scheme for a speedy reunification of the Greek and Latin churches under the newly-elected Greek-born pope [17] – but the cold reality of the threefold cleavage within the Latin obedience could not long be obscured. Pisa had failed.

The causes of this failure were inherent in the form of conciliarism which had been adopted. Far from being the spontaneous movement of the *congregatio fidelium* to restore the theological and practical unity of the *ecclesia*, the Council of Pisa had been from the first conceived as a constitutional process within the church, an assembly which in reality if not in theory would also serve a judicial purpose. And in this lay its difficulties; for the constitutional framework within which the council had to operate was still basically that of 1378, and rather than remedying the defects which the clash between Urban VI and his cardinals had revealed, the council merely compounded the problem. The Council of Pisa was not revolutionary, it was intended to be fully in line with the established constitutional order. The concession to the cardinals of the power to issue the summons for the gathering was certainly a novelty, but the legal basis for the concession was not, being merely an extension of the senatorial jurisdiction exercised by the College of Cardinals during every papal vacancy.

---

[16] Vincke, *Briefe*, pp. 187–91; J. D. Mansi, *Sanctorum conciliorum et nova et amplissima, collectio*, vol. 27 (Venice, 1784), p. 354.   [17] *Glorieux*, no. 365.

The juristic determination that inveterate schism constituted heresy meant that any obstinately schismatic pope *ipso facto* deprived himself of the papacy, thereby allowing the cardinals to step into the constitutional breach and issue the summons to a council. Moreover, the theory that *papa a nemine judicatur* could thus theoretically be left untouched, the conciliar investigation being considered not as a process of judgement and sentence but as an attempt to discover whether the papacy was in fact vacant.

Such theories might be a satisfactory sop to those more concerned with restoring ecclesiastical unity than maintaining constitutional integrity, but they could not pacify everyone, least of all the claimants to the papacy themselves. The basic trouble with the Council of Pisa was that it did not go far enough: it did not elect a successor to Gregory XI, but merely restored the church to the situation of August 1378, when Baldus de Ubaldis had called for a general council but insisted that it had to be summoned by the legitimate pope.[18] Both Benedict XIII and Gregory XII accepted this formulation in 1409 – and each held his own separate council. In the meantime the dissident cardinals of both obediences transformed Pisa into a second Anagni. The constitutional difficulty remained, and for precisely this reason the Council of Pisa was soon revealed as not only a failure but a chronological irrelevance, merely having added a further variable to an already sufficiently complex situation.

Yet the Council of Pisa was significant in marking the start of a dramatic decline in university interest in the theoretical problems posed by the schism. The death of Antonius de Butrio only a few months before the opening of the council might almost be considered symbolic of the declining university involvement in the debates. Butrio's final work was completed posthumously by his pupil, Matthaeus de Matasellanis:[19] together with Petrus de Ancharano's masterly defence of the cardinals' actions delivered at the council itself in response to the envoys of Rupert of the Palatinate,[20] this final tract by Butrio and Matasellanis effectively

---

18 See above, p. 49.
19 On this, see Günther, 'Zur Vorgeschichte', pp. 656-9. I have used an eighteenth-century transcript in *BN*, MS Lat. 17184, fos 227r-256v, in which the continuation starts at fo. 238r.
20 Printed in Weizsäcker, *Reichstagsakten*, vol. 3, pp. 521-57.

marks the termination of the development of the conciliarist theory within the universities. Thereafter considerations of the theory and its implications tended to be mere recapitulations of the established ideas. This is only too obvious from the later works of Pierre d'Ailly and Jean Gerson, which contained frequent plagiarisms from the works of others, and were in many cases little more than revisions of their own earlier contributions to the discussions.[21] Meanwhile, as the academic interest in the development of conciliarism declined, the universities and their members became increasingly concerned with the problems of ecclesiastical reformation. This issue had become entwined with the problems of the schism at an early stage, and the connection apparently persisted through to 1409. There are signs that, for individuals in both obediences, it even took priority over the pressing problem of reunion. Matthaeus de Matasellanis thus reported that some supporters of Gregory XII argued that it would be better for him to remain as pope and direct this reformation, rather than resign and allow the cardinals to elect another pontiff who would merely tolerate the continuation of the manifold abuses within the church.[22] These reformist tendencies were probably encouraged by the outcome of the Council of Pisa: when the constitutional failure became obvious in the spurious unity of a third papacy, there was no solution more obvious than a frantic appeal for reform of the church *in capite et membris*. For the academics, the question of reform was increasingly to concentrate on issues relating to their own particular problem of employment and provisions to benefices, and whether these should be left with the pope or transferred to the more local ecclesiastical authorities. With these developments, and the diversion of university attentions to other local issues as well as reform, academic involvement in the schism showed a marked decline, especially within what remained of the Gregorian obedience.

But even though academic participation declined, the intensity of the propaganda battle showed no signs of diminishing. Per-

---

21 At Constance, both Conrad of Gelnhausen and Henry of Langenstein were plagiarised, by Gerson, d'Ailly and Dietrich of Niem (Spinka, *Advocates*, p. 95). D'Ailly had earlier borrowed from Gerson in his *De materia concilii generalis*, which he used later himself as the basis for further tracts (Oakley, *Political thought*, pp. 246–7, 250–2). 22 *BN*, MS cit., fo. 240v.

haps the most important of the works produced in the aftermath of the Council of Pisa was Boniface Ferrer's vigorous defence of Benedict XIII, which included a virulent attack on the Pisan proceedings.[23] To this work, which had incorporated some rather personally directed remarks against Parisian academics, Pierre d'Ailly replied with his own *Apologia pro concilio Pisano*.[24]

Ferrer's tract was particularly important in that its author recognised and acknowledged the vital influence of the universities and their members in the development of the conciliarist thesis and in the events which had preceded the Council of Pisa itself, for both of which they were thoroughly chastised. But Benedict XIII had other defenders besides Ferrer,[25] and became involved in the discussions himself by producing a series of four tracts.[26] In the course of the arguments contained in these works, Benedict added some extremely important contributions to the debates, especially in his complete adoption of the redefinition of his own legitimacy originally propounded by Raoul d'Oulmont. Benedict indeed revised Oulmont's basic argument by adding suitable qualifications to cover all possible objections to the status of those cardinals who had participated in his election and had held their position since the pontificate of Gregory XI.[27] The dialogue aspect which characterises so much of the tractarian warfare of the schism was again revealed in this instance, when the Bishop of Cahors produced a tract in which he sought to rebut Benedict's statements. This vapid challenge, consisting of no more than pious hopes for an eventual reunification

23 *Thes. Nov. Anec.*, pp. 1435–1529.

24 Printed in Tschackert, *Peter von Ailli*, pp. [31]–[41]. See also Salembier, *Pierre d'Ailly*, pp. 257–9.

25 See, for example, an anonymous defence in Vincke, *Schriftstücke*, pp. 147–54.

26 Ehrle, 'Die kirchenrechtlichen Schriften', pp. 519–71.

27 Öffentliche Bibliothek der Universität Basel, MS A.VI.17 (a MS not cited by Ehrle, but see Bliemetzrieder, *Literarische Polemik*, pp. 21*–22*), fos 60v–68v. The most important passage comes at fos 64r–v : 'Successores Urbani fuerunt electi a solis Cardinalibus vel anticardinalibus dubijs per ipsum Urbanum promotis. Nam post eleccionem Clementis nullus Cardinalum indubitatorum adhesit Urbano, unde nullus eorum eleccionj sui successoris interfuit. Sed papa Benedictus, successor Clementis, fuit concorditer electus ab omnibus indubitatis Cardinalibus et eciam a dubitatis per dominum Clementem promotis. Licet ergo negetur eundem Benedictum potuisse eligi in papam indubium a dubijs Cardinalibus, necessario tamen opportet fateri eum per eleccionem Cardinalium indubitatorum esse papam indubium, et de Jure pro tali habendum a cunctis fidelibus pendente huius scismatis dubio'.

of the church,[28] was easily demolished by the pope in his *Replicatio*.[29]

The dialogue between papalists and conciliarists was not confined to the Benedictine party: the Roman pope also had his apologists. Although Gregory XII had issued his own justification of his actions in a letter to King Henry IV of England and Sigismund of Hungary,[30] his chief defender was Cardinal Dominici, who produced two tracts. Both of these received replies in the form of glosses, possibly all the work of the conciliarist Cardinal Orsini.[31] In a similar vein there exists an anonymous Gregorian response to a defence of the Council of Pisa which may have been produced by Franciscus de Zabarella,[32] the Gregorian attack receiving an equally anonymous conciliarist reply.[33]

In all this debate there is little sign of academic participation, the patent failure of the Council of Pisa having apparently produced an atmosphere of hopeless anticlimax. There were now three distinct parties, each determined to retain whatever obedience it had. The Benedictines and Gregorians would not concede defeat without offering the fiercest possible resistance, a task most easily undertaken by denigrating the Pisan proceedings. This is most apparent in the works of Benedict XIII, in which he constantly asserted the illegality of the Pisan assembly. He also attacked the attitude of the French towards the council, raising the spectre of a renewed Babylonish Captivity and further constitutional malpractice to engineer the election of a French puppet as pope.[34] As there is the possibility that these suggestions may have had some factual justification – throughout the fifteenth century, the French were to have hopes of re-establishing the papacy at Avignon – they presumably had a considerable impact.

---

28 ibid., fo. 86v: 'Spes est magna quod finaliter tota Christianitas paulatim ad obedientiam electi in pisis, vel successorum suorum, reducetur, maxime defuncto . . . domino gregorio qui nullum ut dicitur secum habet cardinales, et dominus B. paucos qui forssam, ipso defuncto, nolent eligere et si vellent non permitteretur eis; et isto saltim modo spero istud scisma finiri'.

29 Ehrle, 'Die kirchenrechtlichen Schriften', pp. 541-53.

30 Vincke, *Schriftstücke*, pp. 241-50.

31 The tracts and glosses are ibid., pp. 40-69, 75-104.

32 The attack is printed in Weizsäcker, *Reichstagsakten*, vol. 3, pp. 557-64. For the identification of Zabarella as the author of the conciliarist work, see Bliemetzrieder, *Das Generalkonzil*, pp. 244-5.   33 Vincke, *Schriftstücke*, pp. 235-40.

34 Cf. the section quoted in Ehrle, 'Die kirchenrechtlichen Schriften', pp. 551-2.

The continuing debates as to the validity of the Council of Pisa meant that the settlement achieved there was extremely vulnerable. The universities themselves provide evidence of the prevailing uncertainty of the period. The masters of Vienna, for example, were quite willing to recognise Alexander V immediately, but nevertheless decided not to act until their princes had announced their own decision.[35] Moreover, apart from the tractarian debates, there is also evidence of an attempted counter-attack in one university. In September 1409 Cardinal Dominici prepared a letter addressed to the University of Oxford, urging the members to ignore the events of Pisa and remain loyal to Gregory XII. The letter further asserted that the Roman pope was still prepared to implement what he considered the legal form of the *via cessionis*.[36] This letter would not have been received in time to affect the English decision to recognise Alexander V, but it nevertheless illustrates that the Gregorians had not lost hope, presumably expecting that if the Oxford masters were reconverted the rest of England would soon follow their lead.

Precisely what Oxford's response to this appeal would have been if it had been received is unclear. Indeed, university activity and sentiments throughout Europe at this time are rather obscure, although events occasionally speak for themselves. Thus, it is clear that the Benedictines were forced onto the defensive in several places, especially in the provincial universities of France where they were threatened and in some cases expelled.[37] The foundation of the University of St Andrews in Scotland by Bishop Henry Wardlaw in 1410 (although the official papal foundation was delayed until 1413) may have had some connection with these events. Certainly, apart from the driving force of nationalism, a possible concern to prevent the spread of Lollardy, and the sheer accident of a concentration of men of high intellectual calibre within the chapter of St Andrews, the establishment of the new university seems also to have been motivated by a desire on Wardlaw's part to keep Scotland firmly within the Benedictine

---

[35] Uiblein, *Acta*, p. 323.

[36] Bodleian Library, Oxford, MS Arch. Seld. B. 23, fos 58v–59r.

[37] K. Eubel, *Die avignonische Obedienz der Mendikanten-Orden, sowie der Orden der Mercedarier und Trinitarier zur Zeit des grossen Schismas*, Quellen und Forschungen aus dem Gebiete der Geschichte, vol. 1, part 2 (Paderborn, 1900), nos. 1190, 1205, 1221, 1228a.

obedience.[38] The numbers involved in these movements after the Council of Pisa is uncertain – they probably bear no comparison with the movements of the 1380s – but it may well have been the additional pressure caused by them on places in the universities of Spain which persuaded Benedict XIII to attempt to establish another university at Calataydd. There would almost certainly have been a need for such an establishment after 1411, when Charles VI of France conquered the Venaissin in the name of Pope John XXIII and expelled the Spaniards who had hitherto kept both the city and University of Avignon loyal to Benedict XIII.[39] After this conquest, and the return of the papal court to Italy, the University of Avignon suffered a marked decline; in 1413 it was necessary for John XXIII to carry out what amounted to a refoundation. The bulls granted for this may also have been intended to purchase the university's support at the next general council, which was already being mooted, and also to buy off the remaining Benedictines among the academics.[40]

The Gregorian obedience was also subjected to pressure after the Council of Pisa. Even Johannes de Imola, the pope's former defender, transferred his allegiance to the Pisan line.[41] But it was in Germany that the greatest pressure was applied, especially after the death of Rupert of the Palatinate in 1410. The greatest disappointment to Gregory XII must have been the nascent University of Leipzig which, supposedly owing its origins to the determination of the Germans at Prague to remain loyal to their Roman pope and accept exile in preference to domination by the conciliarist Czechs, actually received its papal charter of foundation from Alexander V.[42]

However, the indications of collapse in both the Benedictine and Gregorian obediences need to be treated with caution. Neither party was totally obliterated by the attempts to impose the Pisan settlement. Notwithstanding that Benedict XIII, emulating the policies of Urban VI at the beginning of the original dispute, had

---

[38] See R. N. Swanson, 'The University of St Andrews and the great schism, 1410–1419', *Journal of Ecclesiastical History*, **26** (1975), 229–30.

[39] *Valois*, vol. 4, pp. 159–72.

[40] The bulls are in Fournier, *Statuts*, nos. 1282–90.

[41] Staffa, 'De Iohannis ab Imola', pp. 87, 96 n. 191.

[42] Printed in B. Stubel, *Urkundenbuch der Universität Leipzig von 1409 bis 1555*, Codex diplomaticus Saxonicae Regiae, 2ter Haupttheil, vol. 11 (Leipzig, 1879), no. 1.

decreed the closure of the University of Paris in the immediate post-Pisan crisis – a decree which some Spaniards at least observed [43] – he continued to have supporters there, as well as at Avignon and Oxford [44] and, of course, in the Spanish universities. Even during the attempts to persuade him to resign made while the Council of Constance was in session, Benedict retained his advocates. Thus Antonius de Piscibus, a recent graduate of Padua, wrote at his behest in favour of the revised definition of legitimacy derived from the events of 1394, arguing that even if Benedict did resign to obliterate the schism thus far, he alone (as the sole surviving cardinal from the pontificate of Gregory XI) would have the power to nominate the next undeniable pope. [45] Evidence for the continuation of the Gregorian obedience is less certain. It seems a reasonable probability that the University of Heidelberg remained preponderantly in his favour, but the precise strength of the various parties there is uncertain. [46] Gregory may also have retained supporters at Bologna, where a rather obscure accusation of schism was levelled against a Netherlander in 1413. [47] It may be presumed that Ladislas of Naples bullied the university at Naples into continued allegiance to the Roman pope. However, the University of Cologne adopted a determinedly anti-Gregorian policy once it had transferred its loyalty to Alexander V, the masters thereafter engaging in a vindictive pursuit of the Gregorian loyalist Johannes Malkaw de Prussia which continued until the Council of Constance. [48] This was not the only instance of a university becoming involved in local ecclesiastical politics in order to preserve the Pisan settlement. The University of Toulouse

---

[43] H. S. Denifle, 'Der Chronist fr. Petrus de Arenijs und Papa Luna', *Archiv für Literatur- und Kirchengeschichte des Mittelalters*, **3** (1887), 647; Eubel, *Die avignonische Obedienz*, no. 1274.

[44] Swanson, 'St Andrews', pp. 228–9.

[45] C. Schmitt, 'Un défenseur attardé de Benoît XIII, Antoine "de Piscibus", O.F.M.', in *Miscellanea Melchior de Pobladura*, ed. Isidorus a Villapadierna, O.F.M.Cap., vol. 1, Biblioteca Seraphico-Capuccina cura Instituti historici Ord. Fr. Min. Capuccinorum, vol. 23 (Rome, 1964), pp. 288–9.

[46] For continued contacts between the University of Heidelberg and Gregory XII see Winkelmann, *Urkundenbuch*, vol. 1, no. 68, vol. 2, nos. 178, 184.

[47] *Chartularium studii Bononiensis*, vol. 2, pp. 218–19.

[48] J. H. Beckmann, *Studien zum Leben und literarischen Nachlass Jakobs von Soest, O.P. (1360–1440)*, Quellen und Forschungen zur Geschichte des Dominikanerordens in Deutschland, vol. 25 (Leipzig, 1929), pp. 25–33.

seems to have applied a similar policy against the Benedictine inquistor Etienne Lacombe in 1411–12.[49]

In 1410, as in the 1380s, it seemed possible that Christendom would subside into a tacit acceptance of the split within the church. Certainly, between the Councils of Pisa and Constance there was little sign of university interest in the schism as such, apart from Parisian proposals to send missions to Scotland and Spain in the hope of persuading them to desert Benedict XIII and accept the Pisan arrangements.[50] On the other hand, administrative provisions were made to allow the different obediences to co-exist within the same university; and differences of allegiance do not appear to have affected the ease of movement between universities once the immediate furore which followed Pisa had quietened down.[51] During John XXIII's abortive general council held at Rome in 1412–13 the schism does not seem to have received any consideration; but perhaps this was only to be expected, as any such discussion would have meant admitting the failure of Pisa and questioning its pope's legitimacy. The confused political situation in any case reduced the Roman assembly to insignificance. It was not until the Council of Constance was announced that university interest in the schism revived; but academic involvement in the movement for ecclesiastical reform had continued unabated. The Universities of Cologne and Paris both complained about the activities of some members of John XXIII's *curia*, who were obstructing implementation of the reform decrees approved at Pisa.[52]

The constitutional background to the Council of Constance presents almost as many difficulties as that of the Council of Pisa. Theoretically, Constance began very much within the established procedures of the ecclesiastical system, once the basic premiss of John XXIII's legitimacy was accepted. Like the gathering at Rome, it was a papally summoned council on the traditional model, just as the pope intended. But from the outset John XXIII

---

[49] G. G. Meersseman, 'Etudes sur l'ordre des frères prêcheurs au début du grand schisme', *Archivum Fratrum Praedicatorum*, **25** (1955), 243–5.

[50] *Auct. Ch.*, vol. 2, pp. 66–8; *Ch. Paris.*, no. 1964.

[51] Swanson, 'St Andrews', pp. 228–9.

[52] The Cologne letter appears in *BN*, MS Lat. 5237, fos 209r–v; the letter from the University of Paris is in Pellegrin, 'Un humaniste', pp. 23–4.

saw his authority challenged by an active group more concerned for union than an outmoded constitutionalism. Moreover, the secular political situation had changed considerably: Sigismund of Hungary was now the sole claimant to the imperial office, fully imbued with an awareness of his functions within the church, and possessing the capabilities to carry them out. The squabbles of the early months of the council – over whether it was an extension of the Pisan assembly or whether there should be a return to first principles; over the inviolability of John XXIII's position and whether he should be forced to resign;[53] together with a crisis centring on the rights of academics to participate in the proceedings in their own right (an issue striking straight at the heart of university pretensions with regard to conciliar activity)[54] – need not concern us here. Constance, even more than Pisa, was to prove itself an independent entity within the church, self-governing and self-asserting; those not actually involved in its proceedings were decidedly external to them. It was because of this independence and its domination of church affairs that the Council of Constance eventually succeeded in its task. At first it was merely an assembly of the Pisan obedience, but the flight of John XXIII on 20 March 1415 allowed for fundamental changes in the council's structure. These, though accidental and on an *ad hoc* basis, were to be the principal reasons why union was ultimately achieved, for they were due not to external theorising but to the impetus generated within the council itself. When the pope fled, a number of the envoys considered the council automatically dissolved. It was only the exertions of a French-led pressure group which kept it in existence. In this respect, Jean Gerson's sermon *Ambulate dum lucem habetis*[55] was of crucial importance, its extremist definition of the relationship between pope and council producing the final crystallisation of conciliarist thought. The council was now defined as the 'congregatio legitima auctoritate facta ad aliquem locum ex omni statu hierarchico totius ecclesiae cath-

---

53 On these early quarrels, see A. Lenné, 'Der erste literarische Kampf auf dem Konstanzer Konzil im November und Dezember 1414', *Römische Quartalschrift*, **28** (1914), 3*-40*, 61*-86*; B. Katterbach, *Der zweite literarische Kampf auf dem Konstanzer Konzil im Januar und Februar 1415* (Fulda, 1919).

54 For Pierre d'Ailly's contribution to the debates about this, see Oakley, *Political thought*, pp. 150-4; *Hardt*, vol. 2, pp. 224-7 (translated in Crowder, *Unity*, pp. 74-6).

55 *Glorieux*, no. 210 (partially translated in Crowder, *Unity*, pp. 76-82).

olicae, nulla fideli persona quae audiri requirat exclusa, ad salubriter tractandum et ordinandum ea quae debitum regimen ejusdem Ecclesiae in fide et moribus respiciunt.'[56] As a result of this, the council now became the personification or epitome of the full *ecclesia*, an entity independent of the papacy and capable of assembling without the consent or mandate of the pope, even if he had been legally elected.[57] So complete was its independence that it could itself decide the circumstances in which it should assemble.[58] The council was also capable of limiting (but not abolishing) the papal plenitude of power, and was also defined as the only effective means of securing ecclesiastical reformation.[59]

From this it was a short step to the council's formal adoption of Gerson's theses in the decree *Sacrosancta*, issued on 30 March 1415. The members of the assembly thus recorded their own view of their status and authority, identifying themselves as an assembly which 'in Spiritu sancto legitime congregata, generale concilium faciens, ecclesiam catholicam militantem repraesentans, potestatem a Christo immediate habeat, cui quilibet cuiuscumque status vel dignitatis, etiam si palpalis exsistat, obedire tenetur in his quae pertinent ad fidem et exstirpationem . . . schismatis.'[60] The approval of this decree amounted to a virtual rejection of the old ecclesiastical constitution, transforming the gathering into the closest thing the church could approach to a spontaneous meeting of the *congregatio fidelium*. This action also removed all obstacles to eventual union: unlike Pisa, where the colleges of cardinals had jointly rebelled against their popes, this new phase of the council marks the rebellion of the church against schism in general.

Although *Sacrosancta* marked merely a rebellion, and not a revolution, the steps taken were to prove temporarily effective. The council ruled the church *sui juris*, and those attending it became politicians in their own right. They became administrators

---

[56] *Glorieux*, vol. 5, p. 44.   [57] ibid., vol. 5, p. 45.

[58] ibid., vol. 5, p. 45.   [59] ibid., vol. 4, pp. 44–5.

[60] Printed in *Conciliorum oecumenicorum decreta*, 3rd edn (Bologna, 1973), p. 409. On this decree and its later influence see W. Brandmüller, 'Besitzt das Konstanzer Decret *Haec sancta* dogmatische Verbindlichkeit?', *Römische Quartalschrift*, **62** (1967), 1–17; B. Tierney, 'Hermeneutics and history: the problem of *Haec sancta*', in *Essays in medieval history presented to Bertie Wilkinson*, ed. T. A. Sandquist and M. R. Powicke (Toronto, 1969), pp. 354–70.

of the church (now, they claimed, *sede vacante*), deciding matters on their own terms until they eventually restored the church to almost complete union. John XXIII was declared deposed, Gregory XII resigned, and in time even the Spaniards were induced to desert the troublesome Benedict XIII and participate in the election of a new universal pope, Martin V. But there still remained outposts of schism which survived the death of Benedict XIII in 1423 and held out until his successor (Clement VIII) capitulated to Martin V in 1429.[61]

The transformation of the Council of Constance from a papally summoned assembly on the regular model into a semi-populistic, revolutionary and completely extra-constitutional gathering which managed to carry out a successful *coup d'église* against the papal monarchy was not something which forces external to the meeting could control. Suddenly, they found themselves confronted by conciliarism in its most rampant form, the apparently total victory of the ascending system of government, and had to face all the resulting problems. University reaction, however, seems to have been rather passive: there seems to survive only one real academic tract dealing with the council, a fragmentary Bolognese consideration by Bartholomaeus de Rudis of the problems caused by Spanish obstinacy and loyalty to Benedict XIII, written *c*.1416.[62] Yet the universities were not unaware of events, or uninvolved in them. As at Pisa they were represented at the assembly and their envoys participated in many of the council's most important activities, while numerous letters passed between the academics and their conciliar representatives.

However, as in the Pisan case there are considerable difficulties in any attempt to reconcile the statements of the few presence lists which survive for the Council of Constance in order to derive some idea of the extent of university representation.[63] The chroni-

---

[61] For these lingering remains of the schism, see E. Delaruelle, E.-R. Labande and P. Ourliac, *L'église au temps du grand schisme et de la crise conciliare*, Histoire de l'église, ed. A. Fliche and V. Martin, vol. 14 (2 vols., Paris, 1962–64), vol. 1, pp. 219–21 and references. [62] Universitní knihova, Prague, MS I.B.29, fos 21v–22v.

[63] For these, see *Hardt.*, vol. 5, pp. 11–50; M. R. Buck, *Ulrichs von Richental Chronik des Constanzer Concils, 1414 bis 1418*, Bibliothek des litterarischen Vereins in Stuttgart, vol. 158 (Stuttgart, 1882), pp. 155–215 *passim*; Bayerische Staatsbibliothek, Munich, MS Clm. 5596, fos 1r–7v. For a more detailed consideration of university representation at Constance, see my dissertation, vol. 1, pp. 190–6, vol. 2, pp. 203–10.

cler Richental is the only authority to list envoys for the Universities of Buda, Prague and Bologna, and all of his lists are highly questionable. Nevertheless, from the evidence presented by Richental and other sources, it seems clear that a large number of universities were represented at Constance – although it is often difficult (as, for example, in the case of the English universities) to determine whether the members had been officially nominated as proctors. The Universities of Paris, Angers, Montpellier, Toulouse and Orléans all sent their own official embassies, that from Paris being supported by numerous unofficial representatives, including Pierre d'Ailly.[64] Cracow and the German universities present problems, but all seem to have been officially represented. Of the universities elsewhere, those of the Iberian peninsula and Italy present little difficulty. Apart from Bologna, no Italian university is mentioned as having sent a mission to the council, although the massive preponderance of Italians at the council almost certainly included a large number of academics. For the Iberian peninsula there is similarly no indication that any of the universities sent official envoys, but there were academics among the embassies sent by the various kingdoms.[65] The outnumbering of Salamancans in the Castilian delegation by members of the University of Valladolid has been cited to explain the speed with which Castile defected from Benedict XIII.[66]

As the conciliar proceedings dragged on, so the size of the individual university delegations naturally fluctuated. The University of Erfurt, for example, seems to have withdrawn its official envoys some time during 1416;[67] but the reverse process occurred with the University of Heidelberg, which was the last university to name its representatives, in March 1416. However, this delay cannot be attributed to lingering Gregorian loyalties,[68] as the university seems to have maintained some sort of unofficial representation at Constance from the early days of the council, probably

[64] For these unofficial Parisian representatives, see *Auct. Ch.*, vol. 2, pp. 186 n. 4, 200, 203, 218–19.
[65] On Spanish academic representation at Constance, see Beltrán de Heredia, *Cartulario*, vol. 1, pp. 257–60.
[66] ibid., vol. 1, pp. 259–60.
[67] *Thes. Nov. Anec.*, p. 1668; for their presence see ibid., p. 1612.
[68] As suggested in L. Dax, *Die Universitäten und die Konzilien von Pisa und Konstanz* (Freiburg-am-Main, 1909), pp. 35–6.

among the entourage of Louis of the Palatinate.[69] The Viennese representation also fluctuated considerably, Peter of Pulkau being apparently the only member of the university who was constantly at the council.[70] The representatives of the University of Paris similarly varied in number, for apart from work undertaken by the university's envoys as members of the council – acting on diplomatic missions, and temporarily transferring their procuratorial powers to others – there is considerable evidence of travelling between the council and the university, with consequent modifications in the numbers and composition of the delegation. Thus, of the original Parisian mission, Jean de Villeneuve had returned to Paris by July 1415.[71] His departure from Constance was closely followed by that of two others, apparently acting as conciliar envoys to France.[72] Other members of the original delegation may have returned to Paris by early 1417, when more envoys were nominated to take further letters to Constance. These included four members of the group sent in October 1414,[73] and although some of them may simply have been renominated by the university without ever having left the council, others had definitely returned to Paris in the interval. These included the envoys of the English nation, who were back at Paris by May 1416.[74] They apparently stayed in Paris all year, although on their return they had clearly expected to be going back to Constance without much delay.

During all these movements the council itself remained in session, busily ordering the arrangement of Latin Christendom. This process necessarily involved contacts between the members of the council and those whom they claimed to be representing. For the universities these contacts from the beginning fell into two distinct classes: communications between the universities and the council as an independent juridical body, and the more

---

[69] *Thes. Nov. Anec.*, p. 1612.

[70] Mayselstein had returned to Vienna by May 1415 (D. Girgensohn, *Peter von Pulkau und die Wiedereinführung des Laienkelches*, Veröffentlichungen des Max-Planck-Instituts für Geschichte, vol. 12 (Göttingen, 1964), p. 196). Thereafter, Pulkau was aided by the many messengers scuttling between Vienna and the council (ibid., pp. 194–205) and by the many unofficial representatives who were present at the assembly.

[71] H. Finke, *Acta concilii Constanciensis* (4 vols., Münster, 1896–1928), vol. 4, p. 658.

[72] *Chron. S. Den.*, vol. 5, pp. 696–9.

[73] *Auct. Ch.*, vol. 2, p. 224 n. 4.　　　　　　　　　　[74] ibid., vol. 2, p. 211.

informal contacts maintained with the representatives at the proceedings – informal in the sense that the individuals from whom
the universities derived their information were not giving any
definitive statement of the situation but merely recording their
personal view of events.

So far as contacts with the council *qua* council are concerned,
these appear to have been on nothing more than an intermittent
level. There is very little indication that the universities fully
comprehended the nature of the phenomenon which confronted
them; and they seem to have been rather shocked by the sudden
changes which occurred in 1415. Indeed, the masters at Paris
may well have panicked when informed of the changes in the
council's constitution, their immediate reaction to the events of
March 1415 being a flurry of letters to all parties urging the
continuation of the work towards union and trying to effect some
sort of reconciliation.[75] But apart from this spasm of activity it
seems that contacts on this impersonal level were extremely
limited. It is perhaps significant that, after the middle of 1415,
there appear to be only two surviving letters addressed to the
council as such by a university: one a somewhat eulogistic reform
manifesto issued by the University of Cracow in 1416, and the
other an undated letter from the University of Cologne concerning the heresy of Johannes Malkaw de Prussia.[76] Similarly, there
is very little sign of letters being sent to the universities, apart
from circulars such as that justifying the continuation of the
council after the flight of John XXIII.[77] Conciliarism had won its
victory, and now it was to some extent irrelevant precisely how
the council treated the universities and their representatives.

Yet there was obviously some sort of indirect dialogue between
the universities and the council, particularly on such issues as
provisions to benefices which directly affected the interests of the
academics. This dialogue was conducted on the secondary level
of communication, in contacts with individual university members
present at Constance. Apart from the reports presented to congre-
gations of the universities by their returning envoys, and occasional travellers' tales, the most important source of information

[75] *Chron. S. Den.*, vol. 5, pp. 630–41; *Hardt*, vol. 4, pp. 122–5, 175–6.
[76] *Hardt*, vol. 4, pp. 873–8; *Thes. Nov. Anec.*, p. 1708.
[77] *Thes. Nov. Anec.*, pp. 1626–8.

was letters, typified by the series which still survive reflecting the contacts between the Universities of Vienna and Cologne and their members at the council.[78] Much of this correspondence consisted merely of informative recitals of events; but more significant than these in the development of a dialogue between the universities and the council was the practice of sending various enclosures with the letters. These enclosures included transcripts of documents circulating at the council, and also copies of letters written by other universities – the Parisian letters of April 1415 found their way to Cologne by this route.[79] Indeed, Constance may almost be considered as the clearing house for much of the news which circulated in Europe during the years that the council was in session.

That Cologne and Vienna were not the only universities to engage in such correspondence is clear from several sources. The University of Paris certainly maintained official and unofficial contact with the its envoys,[80] and Oxford also had its informants – or at least the Warden of Merton College had, probably in the person of Henry Abendon.[81] It was by these means that the universities were kept informed of events at Constance and were capable of debating such issues as the Spanish claims to separate national status or the dispute over provisions to benefices. Although probably still unaware of the precise complexities of the debates – and in any case basing their comments on information which was already out of date because of the time it took letters to traverse Europe [82] – the academics could offer some sort of advice to their representatives at the council, and could also

---

[78] For the Cologne letters see ibid., pp. 1609–1712 *passim*; H. Keussen, *Regesten und Auszüge zur Geschichte der Universität Köln, 1388–1559*, Mitteilungen aus dem Stadtarchiv von Köln, vol. 15, part 36 (Cologne, 1918), nos. 213–318 *passim*. For the Viennese letters see F. Firnhaber, 'Petrus de Pulka, Abgesandter der Wiener Universität am Concilium zu Constanz', *Archiv für Kunde österreichischer Geschichts-Quellen*, **15** (1856), 12–70; Girgensohn, *Peter von Pulkau*, pp. 180–91. Three of the Viennese letters are translated in Crowder, *Unity*, pp. 130–8.

[79] For the transmission of documents to Cologne, see *Thes. Nov. Anec.*, pp. 1619, 1625, 1629, 1639, 1654, 1657, 1694.

[80] *Auct. Ch.*, vol. 2, pp. 192, 197–9, 213–14, 227–9, 232, 234–7; Finke, *Acta*, vol. 3, pp. 244–6, vol. 4, pp. 657–9.

[81] C. M. D. Crowder, 'Constance Acta in English libraries', in *Das Konzil von Konstanz*, ed. A. Franzen and W. Müller (Vienna, 1964), p. 505.

[82] For the time-lags as they affected the correspondence between Vienna and the council, see Girgensohn, *Peter von Pulkau*, p. 205.

reach their own conclusions as to the nature and state of the proceedings. It is from this that the changes in university attitudes towards the council can be assessed.

Even before the arrangements had been made for the Council of Constance the universities had been making their aspirations from any such assembly quite clear. Almost immediately after the end of the Roman council of 1412-13, John XXIII had sent letters throughout Europe suggesting that a further gathering could be held in the near future. The universities were among those circularised, Toulouse receiving its notification in May 1413 and other universities at later dates throughout the year. Cologne received the letters in December.[83] But the Council of Constance did not actually begin until November 1414, thus giving over a year in which the various interests could marshal their forces and prepare for the expected battle. The most drawn-out struggle was that between John XXIII and the prospective emperor Sigismund, a fitful conflict for supremacy in which the former sought to avoid calling the council while the latter worked to ensure its assembly. Sigismund was the more determined, eventually forcing the pope into a position where he was left with no option but to fulfil his promises. Early in 1414, Sigismund contacted Charles VI of France to arrange a meeting in Provence to arrange the agenda for the projected council, the University of Paris also being urged to send envoys to the meeting in a letter dated 27 March.[84] Sigismund clearly appreciated the potential influence of the academic contingent at a council, and his letters to the French princes indicate that he expected them to pressurise the masters into attending the Provençal meeting if necessary.[85] The Parisian reply to Sigismund, sent on 7 May 1414, agreed to send representatives if the king did likewise.[86] However, although Charles VI did send an embassy to Provence, there is no evidence of direct university involvement in the negotiations.[87]

Meanwhile, the months after March 1414 provide evidence of

---

[83] Finke, *Acta*, vol. 1, pp. 165-6; Girgensohn, *Peter von Pulkau*, p. 192; Swanson, 'Cologne', p. 10.

[84] G. Williams, *Official correspondence of Thomas Bekynton*, Rolls Series, vol. 56 (2 vols., London, 1872), vol. 2, pp. 122-3; Finke, *Acta*, vol. 1, pp. 366-7.

[85] *Valois*, vol. 4, pp. 238-9; Finke, *Acta*, vol. 1, pp. 358-65.

[86] *Valois*, vol. 4, p. 241; *Bulaeus*, vol. 5, p. 267.

[87] *Valois*, vol. 4, p. 242.

preparations being made for the general council at the University of Vienna, which was suggesting topics for discussion and resolution both at that assembly and the preliminary provincial synods.[88] The preparations for the council even affected the Benedictine adherents within the universities. In August 1414 those who remained at Paris sent an envoy to their pope, bearing supplications which are a useful indication of the extent of his obedience there at this time. The envoy also reported to the pope on the prospects for the envisaged council.[89] Benedict replied on 8 September: fearing that some of his supporters might be tempted to attend Constance he issued a strict ban on any participation. The council was to be treated as an illegal gathering and was to be ignored until it recognised that the proceedings at Pisa had been illegal and abandoned John XXIII.[90]

By now it was clear that some sort of *dénouement* was imminent. Perhaps the most typical aspirations expressed by any university – and certainly the clearest – were those of the University of Cologne. Even at the election of their envoys in December 1414, the masters already obviously considered another papal election a distinct possibility,[91] and this willingness to speculate on the removal of John XXIII was not uncommon. The English nation at Paris, with characteristic haste, had actually begun preparations for another *rotulus* late in 1413,[92] and there are signs from the early days of the council that several of the German universities had been making similar plans.[93] The University of Vienna had also commissioned its representatives to work for union,[94] which presumably indicates that they considered John XXIII disposable. But the revolutionary developments which actually occurred at the council were quite unexpected. The initial conflict there concerned papal acceptance of the *via cessionis*, and the part played by the universities in that suggests that what they had initially envisaged was a peaceful transfer of power to the new pope of a united Christendom.[95]

Further university aspirations with regard to the Council of Constance were revealed in a sermon delivered at Cologne by

[88] Uiblein, *Acta*, p. 418.
[89] Finke, *Acta*, vol. 1, pp. 343-50.
[90] ibid., vol. 1, pp. 350-2.
[91] Swanson, 'Cologne', p. 10.
[92] *Auct. Ch.*, vol. 1, p. 158.
[93] *Thes. Nov. Anec.*, p. 1611.
[94] Girgensohn, *Peter von Pulkau*, pp. 52-3.
[95] *Hardt*, vol. 2, pp. 238-41.

Haec sancta synodus . . .

Dietrich of Münster in November 1414, on the occasion of a visit to the city by Sigismund of Hungary.[96] In an overtly nationalistic oration the speaker laid considerable emphasis on the imperial role in the proceedings, reviving the views expressed by the imperialists at the very beginning of the schism. The almost apocalyptic imperialism which could result from this is best exemplified in the outlines of a programme for the reunification of the church and reconquest of the Holy Land drawn up by the Bolognese academic Bartholomaeus de Rudis in 1415–16.[97]

The issue of ecclesiastical reformation was the one topic obviously missing from the Cologne sermon, although the activities of the other universities make it clear that such reform was one of their chief aims. It was discussed at Vienna in September 1414,[98] and the related problem of maintaining theological purity was mentioned (with specific reference to the Hussite problem) in the instructions which the University of Paris gave to some envoys sent to Germany.[99] But ecclesiastical reform seems to have affected the universities directly only in one specific sense. While there is considerable evidence for their involvement in the general contemporary movements to secure changes within the church, revealed, for example, in the lengthy proposals prepared by the University of Oxford in 1414[100] and the shorter manifesto of the University of Cracow which was issued in 1416,[101] academic interest generally concentrated almost exclusively on the question of provisions to benefices, and whether these should remain with the pope or be transferred to the local prelates. The purpose of the debates was to ensure that the graduates received the just rewards for their studies. Although undoubtedly having some altruistic motivations, particularly a desire to raise the general standard of the clergy, the concern about provisions also at times revealed some rather mercenary attitudes. For the academic attitude towards papal provision was somewhat equivocal: although generally favouring restrictions on papal exactions from benefices

---

96 Swanson, 'Cologne', pp. 10–11.
97 Universitní knihova, Prague, MS I.B.29, fos 21v–22v.
98 D. Girgensohn, 'Die Universität Wien und das Konstanzer Konzil', in *Das Konzil von Konstanz*, ed. A. Franzen and W. Müller (Vienna, 1964), pp. 256–7.
99 *Bulaeus*, vol. 5, pp. 268–9.
100 Printed in D. Wilkins, *Concilia Magna Britanniae et Hiberniae*, vol. 3 (London, 1737), pp. 360–5.   101 See above, n. 76.

– as is evident, for example, from the records of the proceedings of the French nation at the Council of Constance [102] – and also seeking limitations on papal interference in the administration of the local churches, the academics nevertheless wished the system of papal provisions to be maintained. In the French instance, this desire was fortified by their practical experience of the effects of the transfer of provisions to the prelates during the periods of the subtraction of obedience from Benedict XIII, when the university clerks had not secured as many benefices as they had anticipated. The English universities – whose struggle over this issue was to continue for some years after the ending of the Council of Constance – may also have had similar experience as a result of the Statute of Provisors. But the universities' concern for self-interest was not restricted to the issue of benefices. The masters of Bologna, for example, exploited the discomfiture of John XXIII to gain revenge for his alleged tyrannical activities whilst papal legate in Bologna – activity which again seems to have had a mercenary aspect. [103]

Generally speaking, it is only when reflecting this concern for self-interest that the correspondence between the universities and their representatives at the Council of Constance shows any signs of vitality. The University of Cologne's views on this became apparent in September 1415, with the decision to send a *rotulus* to any pope elected at the council. [104] The decision was not quite as precocious as it at first appears. The lengthy gap between the deposition of John XXIII in May 1415 and the election of Martin V in November 1417 was not something which had originally been expected; and this unforeseen lengthening of the council's proceedings totally upset the time-scale originally adopted by the universities. They, taking Pisa as their model, seem to have expected a rapid completion of business and a swift reunification of the church. The extension of the proceedings naturally produced disillusionment, the development of which can be well traced in the correspondence of the Viennese envoy, Peter of Pulkau. After a succession of statements, each anticipating an end which never came, he finally expressed his despair at the situation

[102] *Thes. Nov. Anec.*, pp. 1551–2.
[103] Cf. the accusations levelled against him, *Hardt*, vol. 4, pp. 203–4.
[104] Swanson, 'Cologne', p. 13.

in October 1415 with the blank statement that 'De fine concilii nemo novit'.[105] His remark was echoed in an almost contemporary sermon delivered by Jean Courtecuisse at Paris: the assembly at Constance had been in session for a year, and yet union seemed to be no nearer at all.[106] Although this disillusionment would rapidly be dispelled with the eventual election of Martin V, the realities of the situation had still to be faced. The universities seem to have reconciled themselves to the position by mid-1416, and accepted that Constance would be a lengthy business at which peripheral matters (such as the dispute between the English and the French nations concerning the former's status [107]) would take up an increasing amount of time. Nevertheless, this did not prevent Peter of Pulkau complaining about such matters as distractions from the main aim of the council.[108] The University of Cologne seems to have adopted a particularly realistic approach towards the lengthening of the council, declaring its preference for a long meeting which would settle all the problems at one go, rather than piecemeal reformation in a succession of shorter assemblies.[109]

Meanwhile, throughout academic involvement in the debates of Constance, and throughout the university correspondence, the one constant factor was the concern for the acquisition of benefices. The sending of *rotuli* and the issue of provisions were repeatedly discussed, the whole process building up to the scramble for benefices which followed the election of Martin V on 11 November 1417 and the incorporation of some attempt to satisfy the demands of the academics in the several national concordats entered into by the new pope.[110] The news of Martin's election had been immediately circularised throughout Europe by the cardinals and by the new pope himself, with the universities being included among the addressees of the necessary letters.[111]

105 Firnhaber, 'Petrus de Pulka', p. 35.
106 di Stefano, *Jean Courtecuisse*, p. 200, lines 154-6.
107 Crowder, *Unity*, pp. 108-26.
108 Firnhaber, 'Petrus de Pulka', p. 43.   109 Swanson, 'Cologne', p. 13.
110 For references to provisions and a *rotulus* in the Viennese correspondence, see Firnhaber, 'Petrus de Pulka', pp. 24, 29, 32-3, 43, 57, 60-3, 65, 69-70; and for similar concerns in the Cologne letters, *Thes. Nov. Anec.*, pp. 1610-12, 1617, 1642, 1647, 1678, 1685-6, 1695, 1698-9. Both matters were also raised in Parisian correspondence, *Auct. Ch.*, vol. 2, pp. 199, 213-14.
111 *Thes. Nov. Anec.*, pp. 1688-94; Ullmann, 'Cambridge', pp. 65-8, 75-7.

Haec sancta synodus ...

However, the momentous tidings seem to have outpaced the official notification: the Parisian masters had been informed of the election of Martin V by their own envoys by early December 1417.[112] Their immediate and characteristic reaction had been to prepare a *rotulus*, which was duly presented at Constance in January 1418.[113] This was only one of a succession of such lists of petitions sent to the new pope, suggesting that his recognition had been quite peaceful, and virtually immediate.[114] There appear to have been only two exceptions to this general rule, in the reaction to events in France and Scotland.

The precipitate haste of the University of Paris in recognising Martin V produced an immediate clash with French royal policy. On 27 November 1417 the Dauphin had held an assembly at which the masters had been ordered to defer any recognition until Charles VI had been assured of the new pope's legitimacy – which in reality meant waiting until an acceptable compromise had been reached between the pope and the French crown on the issue of the Gallican liberties.[115] Further discussions had taken place in January 1418 on the conditions under which Martin V should be accepted. These had resulted in a clash between the crown and the university, during which several academics were arrested for attacking the royal power; they were released only after offering their submission.[116] Martin V was finally officially accepted as pope within France on 14 April 1418, and then only

112 *Auct. Ch.*, vol. 2, p. 235. The receipt of the official notice is recorded ibid., vol. 2, p. 238.
113 *Valois*, vol. 4, p. 422; Martin, *Origines*, vol. 2, pp. 206–7; *Ch. Paris.*, nos. 2089, 2092–3; Watt, 'University clerks and petitions', p. 227. Discussions on sending further rolls apparently continued throughout 1418–19 (Watt, p. 227 and references).
114 For Viennese discussions of a roll, see Girgensohn, 'Die Universität', pp. 263–5. On the Toulouse roll see Smith, *Toulouse*, p. 154; Denifle, *Les universités*, pp. 75–7. Other *rotuli* were constructed at Heidelberg (*Thes. Nov. Anec.*, pp. 1692–3; Winkelmann, *Urkundenbuch*, vol. 1, no. 75, vol. 2, no. 193), Salamanca (J. Goñi Gaztambide, 'Documentos pontificos sobre la universidad de Salamanca', *Anthologica Annua*, **8** (1960), p. 492) and Erfurt (Kleineidam, *Universitas Studii Erffordensis*, vol. 1, p. 85), as well as by the Spanish college at Bologna (Beltrán de Heredia, *Bulario*, no. 538). Other universities sought confirmation of privileges rather than sending *rotuli*, as occurred with the Universities of Valladolid and Cracow (Beltrán de Heredia, *Bulario*, nos. 1450–2; *Codex diplomaticus universitatis studii generalis Cracoviensis*, vol. 1 (Cracow, 1870), no. 63).
115 *Valois*, vol. 4, p. 421; Martin, *Origines*, vol. 2, p. 209.
116 *Valois*, vol. 4, pp. 422–3; Martin, *Origines*, vol. 2, pp. 206–10; *Ch. Paris.*, nos. 2096–8; *Bulaeus*, vol. 5, pp. 309–11.

in return for confirmation of the Gallican liberties.[117] However, it still seemed that the French would not be completely satisfied with the situation until the papacy itself was once more under their domination: the masters of Paris urged the new pope to establish his court in France,[118] and even in February 1419 it was still hoped that Avignon might yet again accommodate the *curia*.[119] The hope persisted, but nothing came of it.

Events in Scotland followed a rather different course. That country was the last state to remain within the Benedictine obedience; but the loyalty of the University of St Andrews was less than that of the Duke of Albany, the governor of the realm during the imprisonment of James I in England. The allegiance of the masters to the pope of Peñíscola had been considerably undermined during the years when the Council of Constance was meeting, and it was the academics of St Andrews who seem to have led the movement which culminated in a national council held at Perth in October 1418 and resulted in the formal transference of allegiance to Martin V.[120] Although the division of the church lingered on for a few more years, and although there are signs that individual academics continued to support Benedict XIII,[121] the submission of the University of St Andrews to the pope created at Constance marked, as far as the universities and a majority of their members were concerned, the effective end of the great schism.

[117] *Valois*, vol. 4, pp. 429–30; Martin, *Origines*, vol. 2, pp. 210–20.
[118] *Ch. Paris.*, no. 2108.
[119] ibid., vol. 4, p. 363.
[120] Swanson, 'St Andrews', pp. 236–43.   [121] See, e.g., *Ch. Paris.*, no. 2129.

Chapter 10

CONCLUSION

For the acceptance of Martin V as pope to be truly universal, he had to satisfy the qualifications of legitimacy in each of the obediences which had existed prior to his election: not only the areas formerly subject to the Roman and Pisan popes, but also both sections of what had been the Benedictine obedience, the part which accepted the conciliarism of Constance and the smaller group which had remained loyal to the outcast pope of Peñíscola. Only in 1429 did Martin V acquire legitimacy within this last fragment of the church – apart, that is, from the lingering phantom obedience of Benedict 'XIV' – when, following the abdication of Clement VIII, he was duly elected pope by Clement's cardinals, thus maintaining the fiction of the legitimate succession derived from the election of Benedict XIII in 1394. However, these later developments were of little immediate importance to the universities as they and the majority of the Roman church had been reunited under one pope since 1418, an achievement which marked the termination of academic involvement in the debates which had encompassed Europe since the double election of 1378.

However, the last years of the division, after the Council of Pisa, cannot help but give an impression of anticlimax in comparison with the hectic activities of the universities in the previous decades. The detachment of the universities from the conciliar proceedings at Constance, and their inability to be more than a peripheral influence on the debates which eventually produced reunion, give a retrospective tinge of failure which overshadows all their activities since the inception of the schism. The anticlimax is revealed especially in the correspondence between the universities and their representatives at Constance which, although illustrative of the dialogue which could be developed over considerable distances, serves mainly to emphasise the conspicuous insignificance of the universities in the conciliar debates about the reunification of the church. Acting as mere outsiders, the universities increasingly concentrated their involvement in the council's proceedings on discussions of their own parochial, selfish and rather mercenary problems of post-graduate employment. Despite their contacts, despite the letters and activity of the years from 1414 to 1418, the universities now gave the impression of being a spent force, no longer enjoying universal pre-eminence in the debates of the schism, and having scarcely any influence on the political and ecclesiastical decisions being taken in their name at Constance. All they could do was wait, and react.

But so simplistic an interpretation of the situation would be both unfair and invalid. The councils had been extraordinary events, and it may well be that the universities had not expected to be particularly influential in them – may well, indeed, have thought that there would be nothing which would require them to be influential. The Council of Pisa seems, once the ecclesiology and programme had been decided (before the council actually met), to have been treated almost as a routine matter, and the same seems to have applied to the initial stages of the Council of Constance. The transformation of the latter assembly surprised the academics as much as it shocked the rest of Europe, and by the time that the changes occurred it was too late for the universities to attempt to seize the initiative again.

Yet, throughout the schism, the academics never appear to have considered themselves to be the people who would actually reunite the church; their role was consistently that of advisers. All their energies had been channelled into formulating the policies which others could then put into effect, whether kings, cardinals, popes, or emperors. The necessarily political overtones of this academic involvement occasionally give the impression that the universities and their members were no better than contemporary propagandists sometimes suggested – mere pawns of their political masters – but that, again, would be a false interpretation. The theories had to be evolved before they could be endorsed and adopted (or rejected) by the politicians, and to argue that the universities were totally submissive would be to ignore the proliferation of possible solutions to the schism put forward by academics; the frequently bitter conflicts over the issues involved; and most importantly the numerous clashes between the would-be advisers and those whom they were seeking to influence – clashes which were a regular occurrence at Paris throughout the years of the schism.

The role which the universities had arrogated to themselves during the crisis had been, throughout, to provide the theories which would eventually restore the universal jurisdiction of the *ecclesia*, in a period when there was no corresponding secular authority to which the appeal could be made. As the sole surviving international and supra-national grouping, and one which, although affected by the tensions generated by the schism, nevertheless managed to stave off total fragmentation, the academics managed to produce a definition of the ecclesiastical constitution which permitted action by the whole church (or rather, by its theoretical intermediaries with the pope, the College of Cardinals, acting as representative of the whole) to restore the unity of the totality. Like the ancient constitutionalists of seventeenth-century England and eighteenth-century France, the academics did not claim to innovate, but to revive a mythical past. However, unlike their political successors, these medieval antiquarians were in no position to control the constitution which they had thus rediscovered; they did not define it to their own advantage, so that the implementation of their theories merely transferred – or, as they would have it, restored – power to others, and pushed the academics once more into the background. This occurred immediately the formula legitimising the Council of Pisa was put into effect, thereafter effectively excluding the universities from any real influence on the conciliar proceedings. This was the situation which prevailed at Constance; it was repeated to an even greater degree at the later Council of Basel, for there the separation of the council from external influences such as the universities was almost total, even though the academics sought to influence the ecclesiological developments.[1]

But despite the diminution of academic importance after 1409, it is impossible to deny the effect of university involvement in the

---

[1] A. Black, 'The universities and the Council of Basle: ecclesiology and tactics', *Annuarium Historiae Conciliorum*, **6** (1974), 348–51.

debates of the schism before that date, or to deny the impact of their legacy. From 1378 right through to 1418, politics alone – even politics directed by so powerful a personality as Sigismund of Hungary – could not have successfully reunited the church. It was the redefinition of the ecclesiastical constitution which, in conjunction with the political will favouring reunion, eventually proved successful; and it was to its academics that Europe turned to produce that redefinition. The task was completed by 1409, thereby producing the Council of Pisa. Although that council was to prove ineffective in its aims, this was through no fault of the academics: politics could not reunite the church, but they could certainly keep it divided. However, the academic legacy may still have had some influence: Sigismund's imperial activities after 1410 in working for the convening of the Council of Constance and the eventual reunification of the church may have owed something to the academic revision of the ecclesiastical constitution, according to which the failure of the cardinals to reunite the church transferred responsibility for that task to the emperor.

Throughout the academic involvement in the debates on the schism, until at least 1403, the most important university was that of Paris, the theological centre of Europe. Although many other universities became involved in the search for an end to the division of the church, it was Paris which was truly the hub of the intellectual activity, with its decisions, declarations and statements causing ripples throughout the continent. It is Paris which generally provides the overlap between the universities participating in the debates, whether by sending envoys and letters which encouraged other academics to consider the issues, or by its decisions provoking counter-proposals and thereby stimulating further discussion of the methods of reunification. This pre-eminence in the debates was lost after 1403 to the Italians, when the policy of subtraction of obedience suffered its ignominious defeat, but the importance of Paris was still recognised in the period immediately preceding the Council of Pisa. It may be that the French university also provided the bases on which the Italians completed the development of the conciliarist version of the ecclesiastical constitution; at the moment the evidence for direct connection and derivation seems too tenuous to admit of any positive statement, but it is quite inconceivable that Italy could have produced its theories whilst utterly divorced from knowledge of the French developments.

Although it was within the academic milieu that the revision of the ecclesiastical constitution was carried out, thereby fulfilling the theoretical role of the universities within the 'European community', this development occurred, paradoxically, at precisely the moment when the universities' abilities to carry out their supposedly independent functions were most under attack. The years of the schism were the focal years for the transformation of the medieval universities, as they became increasingly fragmented, politicised, laicised and diverted to other more local issues. The Parisian experience, with the frequent clashes between the crown and the masters over the politics of the schism, admirably reflects the growing tensions between central government and academic independence which could only result in restrictions on university freedom, as the universities became seen increasingly as appendages to the state structure. By the end of the fourteenth century this procedure was already well under way in the Italian universities, with Florence exerting tight control over the finances of its university, and the Visconti of Milan restricting the movement of academics by seeking to prevent their subjects from attending any other university than that of Pavia. Although there was still room for a sense of academic community throughout Europe – and still room for the individual peripatetic scholar or master – the reality of the community was even more illusory than it had been at the start of the schism. But the myth remained; after 1418, however, its exploitation became confined to political and personal matters, although still used for propaganda purposes as effectively as it had been during the schism. Thus, in the sixteenth century, Henry VIII of England appealed to the universities of Europe for support in his struggle against the pope to gain a divorce from Catherine of Aragon,[2] while what may be considered the final debasement of the international academic community came in the early seventeenth century in a purely private matter, when the head of the French family of Courtenay, seeking justification for his attempts to acquire the status of *Prince du*

---

[2] G. de C. Parmiter, *The king's great matter* (London, 1967), pp. 123–5.

sang, solicited the opinions of eminent lawyers from universities throughout the continent.[3] King Henry IV of France simply ignored their determinations.

The devaluation of the universities, although part of the legacy of the schism, had to some extent set in before the dispute began, and therefore cannot be considered as part of the outcome of academic involvement in the debates of the period. The redefinition of the ecclesiastical constitution which had been formulated was to prove to be the most important bequest. For, after the Council of Constance and the election of Martin V, the ideas which the schism had spawned remained as potent as ever. During the sixteenth and seventeenth centuries the theories of the conciliarists passed into the political armoury of the growing numbers opposed to authoritarian government, whether in church and state. But the inheritance was seen as the legacy of individuals, not of institutions: it was to the works of Gerson, d'Ailly and the fifteenth-century conciliarists that the Gallicans and Parliamentarians were to turn for inspiration, although the academic origin of the ideas was also recognised.[4] Within the church, the force of the conciliarist thesis and its unintentionally revolutionary implications remained a latent threat to the papal monarchy throughout the fifteenth century, even after the formal condemnation of the doctrine by Pius II in 1460.[5] Indeed, throughout the fifteenth century and after, the struggle between the contending ecclesiologies frequently polarised the church, the conflicts generally centring on the status of the cardinals and their position as intermediaries between the pope and the body of the church. Prior to the Reformation itself, the most serious of these conflicts occurred in 1512, almost resulting in a repetition of the events of 1378.[6] Each of these clashes can be treated as an individual phenomenon, but all of them were in the tradition derived from the

---

[3] *De stirpe et origine de domus de Courtenay* (Paris, 1607); the opinions of the lawyers are printed as appendices to the main work, each having its own pagination.

[4] Oakley, *Political thought,* pp. 211–32.

[5] For later conciliarism see especially A. Black, *Monarchy and community: political ideas in the later conciliar controversy, 1430–50,* Cambridge studies in medieval life and thought, 3rd series, vol. 2 (Cambridge, 1970). An English translation of *Execrabilis* is in Crowder, *Unity,* pp. 179–81.

[6] W. Ullmann, 'The legal validity of the papal electoral pacts', *Ephemerides iuris canonici,* **12** (1956), 253–69; W. Ullmann, 'Julius II and the schismatic cardinals', *Studies in Church History,* **9** (1972), 177–93.

academic redefinition of the ecclesiastical constitution which had been produced within the universities during the years 1378–1418 as a response to the problems posed by the rival elections of Bartholomew Prignano and Cardinal Robert of Geneva to the papacy, and resulted from the impact of the implementation of that redefinition at the Councils of Pisa and Constance in 1409 and 1414–18.

Appendix 1

NOTES ON SOME ACADEMIC PERSONALITIES

The following notes give brief details of the academic careers of some of the scholars involved in the university debates on the great schism. For several of the participants the available biographical data is limited; for others (particularly the French) there is a mass of information. I have restricted the list to those who feature most prominently in the course of the book.

PIERRE D'AILLY (1350–1420)
A member of the University of Paris throughout his academic career, becoming chancellor during the years 1389–95, d'Ailly had barely begun his theological studies when the schism broke out. In the early years of the dispute he wrote extensively on the issue, his most important contributions at this point being the tract *Utrum indoctus in jure divino posset juste praeesse in ecclesiae regno* and the *Epistola diaboli Leviathan*. He withdrew from the university to Noyon in 1381, returning in 1383. In 1395 Benedict XIII appointed him Bishop of Le Puy (exchanged for Cambrai in 1397). In the successive councils of the French church he defended the pope against his accusers, thereby acquiring several enemies. During the subtraction of obedience from the pope (1398–1403) he was one of the leaders of the restitutionist party, although absent from the university for much of the time at Cambrai. In 1403 he completed his most important academic contribution to the debates, the *De materia concilii generalis*. In 1407–8 he was one of those involved in the French embassy to Benedict XIII and Gregory XII which sought active papal involvement in the ending of the schism. When the embassy failed, he rapidly transferred to the conciliarist party, his *Propositiones utiles* being a succinct summary of the theory at the time. He attended the Council of Pisa in 1409, and in 1411 was elevated to the cardinalate. He also attended the Council of Constance.

PETRUS DE ANCHARANO (c. 1330–1416)
A layman, and a noted lawyer, Ancharano's career chiefly centred on Bologna. However, between the mid-1380s and the mid-1390s he was

briefly a teacher at Siena, and was also engaged on political matters in Venice. He remained at Bologna between 1396 and 1402, when (with Antonius de Butrio and Johannes de Imola) he transferred to the nascent University of Ferrara. It was there, in 1405, that he composed his *Tractus de schismate* at the request of Balthasar Cossa. In 1406 he returned to Bologna, and was thereafter closely involved in the development of conciliarism there, his activities culminating in his strong defence of the thesis at the Council of Pisa itself in 1409. Ancharano remained at Bologna after the council, but in 1415 was sent to the Council of Constance as an envoy of John XXIII. It was there that he died.

JOHANNES DE BRACULIS (*d.* 1385)
A German by birth, and a member of the Augustinian order, Braculis was a theologian at Prague when the schism broke out, although his academic career had started at Paris. In 1379 he made his own contribution to the debates on the schism with the *Determinatio quaestionis de canonica electione Urbani VI*, produced for the Archbishop of Prague, John of Jenstein. The allegorical form of this tract, and its extensive use of quotations from other writers, including pagans, make this one of the most extraordinary works produced during the crisis.

ANTONIUS DE BUTRIO (*c.* 1338–1408)
A layman, Butrio began his academic career at Bologna as a pupil of Petrus de Ancharano. A famed canonist and civil lawyer, he spent much of his career at Bologna, although he was at Perugia in 1390–91 and at Florence from 1393 to the end of the century. In 1402 he, along with Ancharano and Johannes de Imola, took up appointments at the recently established University of Ferrara; but in 1406 he returned to Bologna and in 1407 acted as Gregory XII's representative in the negotiations with Benedict XIII. Following the failure of these, he became an ardent conciliarist, producing several works at Bologna to support the Roman cardinals in their actions against Gregory XII. He was engaged in composing what was to be his most ambitious conciliarist work when he died, the tract being thereafter completed by his pupil Matthaeus de Matasellanis.

SIMON DE COLUMB
An Aragonese decretist and a collector of canonries, Simon de Columb was a member of the strong Spanish contingent which was established within the University of Avignon during the pontificate of Benedict XIII. He appears as an active member of the university during the

years 1393–1403, and was one of the pope's strongest defenders. His main contribution to the debates was a three-part statement produced *c.* 1396 in response to the Parisian proposals on the *via cessionis*.

SIMON DE CRAMAUD (*c.* 1345–1423)

In 1378 Cramaud had already moved to Paris from Orléans, where he had originally studied law, and had already come under the protection of the Duke of Berry. He was loyal to the Avignon line from the start of the schism, and in 1382 acquired the first of a succession of benefices, a progression which in 1392 elevated him to the titular position of Patriarch of Alexandria. His governmental involvement and activities on behalf of the duke meant that his attendance at Paris was rather intermittent. After the death of Clement VII, Cramaud appeared as one of the leaders of the group urging implementation of the *via cessionis* and the subtraction of obedience from Benedict XIII. He was an energetic participant in the French national councils of 1395–98, a period in which he also produced his most important work, the treatise *De subtractione obedientie*, which went through several versions prior to completion in 1398. Thereafter his works were largely summaries of the views contained in the tract, or glosses on the statements produced by the opposition, such as Martin de Salva's defence of Benedict XIII and the letter produced by the University of Toulouse in 1402 urging the restitution of obedience to the pope. In 1409 Cramaud achieved the high point of his career with his presidency of the Council of Pisa. Alexander V appointed him Archbishop of Rheims; but it was not until 1413 that he was at last elevated to the cardinalate, by John XXIII.

NICHOLAS DE FAKENHAM (*d.* 1407)

A theologian and a member of the University of Oxford, Fakenham was provincial minister of the Franciscans in England from *c.* 1395 to 1401–2. His known activity on the schism is concentrated in the years 1395–99, especially in 1395, when he not only produced two *questiones* on the issues involved but also (at the request of Richard II) composed his *Determinatio de schismate*, which marked the inception of the formal Oxonian discussions in response to the Parisian proposals on the *via cessionis*. He is also credited with another work, *Super unione ecclesiae*, which is now lost.

CONRAD OF GELNHAUSEN (1320–90)

A German, and a theologian at Paris when the great schism broke out, in the early years of the dispute he appeared as a leader of the conciliarist party, producing his *Epistola brevis* in 1379 and the *Epistola concordiae* in 1380. Both works were addressed to Charles V, Geln-hausen recognising the importance of princely participation in the search for an end to the schism. Gelnhausen was among the Germans who left Paris when Louis of Anjou clamped down on the university in 1382, and in 1386 became rector of the newly established University of Heidelberg.

JEAN GERSON (1363–1429)

Gerson entered the University of Paris in 1377, and remained there as scholar and master throughout his academic career, succeeding his former master Pierre d'Ailly as chancellor in April 1395. Philip the Bold of Burgundy was his patron until 1404, and by his favour Gerson acquired the deanery of St Donat at Bruges, to which he occasionally retired from Paris. Gerson's involvement in the debates on the schism may have begun in 1390 with the discussion *Utrum Parisiensis univer-sitas* . . . Certainly, he soon appeared as one of the most prolific writers on the topic, although he did not participate in the Parisian council of 1398 which decreed the subtraction of obedience from Benedict XIII. During 1398–1403 he was one of the leaders of the party remaining loyal to the pope, but the failure of the restoration of allegiance in 1403 led to further prolific writing from 1406 onwards. In 1407–8 he was involved in the French mission to the then rivals, returning as a convinced conciliarist. However, he did not attend the Council of Pisa, although he continued to produce important works at Paris, notably the *Propositio facta coram Anglicis* and his *De auferibilitate sponsi ab ecclesiae.* Following the election of Alexander V, he looked forward to the reunion of the Greek and Latin churches. He attended John XXIII's abortive Roman council in 1412–13, and also the Council of Constance from 1415–18. He was especially active at the latter, his sermon *Ambulate dum lucem habetis* being vital for the transforma-tion of the assembly following the flight of John XXIII in March 1415. He also exploited the council to pursue his attack on Jean Petit's theories on tyrannicide. He never returned to Paris after the ending of the council.

JOHANNES DE IMOLA (c. 1367/72–1436)

A layman, Imola was a student of Petrus de Ancharano, Johannes de Legnano and Antonius de Butrio, at Bologna. A distinguished canonist and civil lawyer, in 1402 he moved from Bologna to Ferrara with Ancharano and Butrio, and in 1406 moved again to Padua. While there he composed his *Tractatus de schismate*, the most effective exposition of the conciliarist views maintained by those who remained loyal to Gregory XII in the years immediately preceding the Council of Pisa. In 1410 Imola returned to Bologna, where he remained for the rest of his life.

HENRY OF LANGENSTEIN, *alias* HENRICUS DE HASSIA (*c.* 1340–1397)

A German and a theologian, Langenstein was a member of the University of Paris when the great schism broke out in 1378. In the early debates he appeared as a leader of the conciliarist party, producing his *Epistola pacis* in 1379 and the *Epistola consilii pacis* in 1381. In 1382, like other Germans, he left Paris, and from 1383 he was active at Vienna, where he took charge of the revival of the university. He remained at Vienna until his death, but his interest in the schism did not diminish. During the period he produced several works, including the *Carmen pro pace* and *Epistola de cathedra Petri*. Having been a conciliarist, and later supported imperial action to end the schism, he then turned to Rupert III of the Palatinate to work to end the dispute, and corresponded with members of the University of Paris. In contrast with his views at the start of the schism, he ended by accepting the *via cessionis*.

JOHANNES DE LEGNANO (*d.* 1383)

Renowned as a lawyer, but also something of a fourteenth-century polymath, Legnano was at the University of Bologna when the schism broke out, and remained there until his death. He produced a succession of statements on the problem which, together with the works produced at the same time by Baldus de Ubaldis, formed the basis of the Romanist case, and were to be much discussed throughout the period.

MATTHAEUS DE MATASELLANIS (*b. c.* 1377)

A layman, Matthaeus de Matasellanis was a pupil of Antonius de Butrio and, like him, a lawyer. In October 1407 he was a participant in the debates on conciliarism at the University of Bologna, producing a statement favouring the cardinals. After the death of Butrio, Matasellanis completed the conciliarist tract on which his teacher had been working, which was virtually the final definition of conciliarism within the universities prior to the opening of the Council of Pisa.

SANCHO MULIER

A member of the order of preachers and a theologian, Mulier was a member of the University of Toulouse during the most critical years of the French debates on the schism. In the mid-1390s he appeared as a defender of Benedict XIII against the attacks of the Parisian cessionists and subtractionists. Not only did he produce tracts supporting the pope, but also acted as a representative of his university at the Paris council of 1398.

RAOUL D'OULMONT

A member of the French nation of the University of Paris and a licentiate of both laws, Oulmont appears to have been active throughout the last quarter of the fourteenth century and to have held quite a high position among the lawyers. From the start of the schism he was an ardent Clementist. After the election of Benedict XIII he was a leading supporter of the pope, opposing the *via cessionis* and subtraction of obedience. His tract produced early in 1397 was very much a synthesis of the arguments put forward by the opponents of the French policy who defended the Avignon pope.

LORENZO DI RIDOLFI (1362–1443)

A canonist, Ridolfi acquired his doctorate from Bologna in 1388, but later that year moved to Florence, where he remained for the rest of his career. He was an active participant in the communal discussions of the schism in 1405–9, this involvement reaching its climax in 1408–9 with the production of two lengthy *consilia* in support of the cardinals, urging the withdrawal of recognition from Gregory XII.

BARTHOLOMAEUS DE SALICETO (*c.* 1330/40–1412)

A layman, and a noted lawyer, Saliceto spent much of his academic career at Bologna. However, there were several interruptions, including a period at Ferrara in the early 1390s, when he was involved in the attempt to establish a university there, and two periods of political exile, the longest being from 1398–1403. He held considerable political influence in Bologna, being much involved in the factional struggles of the period. His participation in the debates on the schism began with his *Consilium pro Urbano VI*, produced in 1379, which was a total vindication of the Romanist stance. He was also involved in the conciliarist debates within the University of Bologna in late 1407.

GUILLAUME DE SALVARVILLA (*c.* 1327–1385)

A native of the diocese of Rouen, Salvarvilla was a member of the Norman nation at Paris, and a leading member of the faculty of theology. Having originally supported Clement VII during the schism, he soon transferred his allegiance to Urban VI. In 1381 he produced his *Determinatio pro concilio generali*, and he has been suggested as the composer of Urbanist poems circulating at Paris during 1381. Following the Clementist clamp-down at Paris, Salvarvilla went into exile in the Netherlands, being deprived of his French benefices. However, these losses were compensated for by Urban VI.

BALDUS DE UBALDIS (*c.* 1319–1400)
One of the leading jurists of his day, Baldus was lecturing at Perugia when the schism broke out, but he later moved to the University of Padua. In July 1378 he prepared his *Allegationes primae*, the first academic discussion of the events which were threatening to produce a schism within the church. This tract, with his *Allegationes secundae* and the contemporary works of Johannes de Legnano, formed the basis of the Romanist case throughout the schism, provoking much discussion. His later comments on the problem revealed growing disillusionment at the prolongation of the schism, and a desire for a conciliarist solution rather different in form from that suggested in his *Allegationes primae*.

JOHN WYCLIF (*d.* 1384)
A member of the University of Oxford throughout his academic career, Wyclif's comments at the start of the schism reveal a profoundly Urbanist loyalty. However, his opposition to the *via facti* and to the papacy soon led to the adoption of a view which wanted to ignore the schism totally and allow the church to remain divided, a stance which became distinctive of the Lollard party in England but also had continental support.

FRANCISCUS DE ZABARELLA (*c.* 1335–1417)
One of the leading canonists of his time, Zabarella lectured at both Florence and Padua. It was at the latter that, between 1403 and 1409, he drew up the three works later moulded into his *Tractatus de schismate*, which summarised the development of Italian views on solving the schism during those years. He may have attended the Council of Pisa, but this is uncertain. In 1411 he was elevated to the cardinalate by John XXIII, and died at the Council of Constance.

Appendix 2

UNIVERSITY FOUNDATIONS, 1378–1418

The universities are recorded under the name of the pope from whom they received their bulls of foundation. Names in italics indicate that the foundation concerned proved ephemeral, and had died out by the end of the schism. In addition to these, it should be noted that there were also the peripatetic universities in each obedience which were attached to the papal court.

Urban VI:

1378	*Orvieto*	1387	*Lucca*
1385	Heidelberg	1388	Cologne
1386	*Kulm*		

Clement VII:

| 1379 | Perpignan, *Erfurt* | 1380 | Lisbon |

Boniface IX:

1391	*Ferrara*	1398	*Fermo*
1392	Erfurt	1400	Cracow
1395	*Buda*	1402	*Würzburg*

N.B. Gian Galeazzo Visconti claimed the authority, as imperial vicar, to establish a university at Piacenza in 1398. Although the institution was set up, it soon decayed (on the episode, see Rashdall, *The universities*, vol. 3, pp. 37–8).

Benedict XIII:

| 1405 | *Turin* | 1415 | *Calataydd* |
| 1413 | St Andrews | | |

Innocent VII:

| 1406 | *Rome* |

Alexander V:
    1409   Aix-en-Provence, Leipzig

John XXIII:
    1410   Buda
    1412   Turin

NOTES ON MANUSCRIPTS CITED

The following notes are provided to assist the interested reader who wishes to have some basic information on the manuscripts which have been used. As many of the manuscripts are miscellaneous codices, exact bibliographical details and location for the relevant tract or letter used from the volume have been given, as well as the title by which the work is generally known or some other indication of its nature. Where published descriptions of the manuscripts are known, these have been cited.

BASEL   Öffentliche Bibliothek der Universität

A.V.15: fos 157r–62r, P[etrus] de Muris: *Utrum scismate ut prochdolor nunc vigente iuste possit et debeat alter eorum vel uterque cogi ad cessionem papatus seu iuris quod habet vel habere se pretendit.* The volume also contains several other works on the schism.

A.VI.17: fos 1r–75r, *Tractatus subtilis dubiorum plurimorum in schismate post obitum Gregorij pape xj* [= Pedro de Luna: *Tractatus de nova subscismate*]; fos 77r–87v, [?Guillaume de Arpajon]: *Impugnatio precedentis tractatus*; fos 88r–138v, [Pedro de Luna]: *Replicatio contra tractatus, 'Licet tractatus', per a[u]ctorem tractatus, 'Quia non nulli'.* This manuscript is discussed by Bliemetzrieder, *Literarische Polemik*, pp. 21*–22*.

CAMBRIDGE   Emmanuel College

MS9: fos 134r–136r, Pierre d'Ailly: *Sermo de B. Bernardo.* [Description – M. R. James, *The western manuscripts in the library of Emmanuel College* (Cambridge, 1904), pp. 6–9.]

FLORENCE   Biblioteca Medicea Laurenziana

Plut.XX.39: fos 71v–74r, [Petrus de Ancharano]: *Declaracio cuiusdam dubij, an cardinales possent mandare subditis pape quod ab eius obediencia subtrahant*; fos 77r–109r, Petrus de Ancharano:

218

Tractatus . . . *de diversis modis et vijs ad faciendam unionem tempore scismatis*; fos 110r–112r, Petrus de Ancharano: *Declaracio cuiusdam dubij* . . . (as fos 71v–74r); fos 112r–117r, Petrus de Ancharano: *Consilium, an subtrahentes se ab obediencia dicuntur papam spoliare*; fos 117v–120v, Petrus de Ancharano: [Inc:] *Visis et inspectis* . . . [Description – A. M. Bandini, *Catalogus codicum latinorum bibliothecae Mediceae Laurentianae*, vol. 1 (Florence, 1774), pp. 645–50.]

GRENOBLE Bibliothèque municipale

MS 117 (formerly no. 987): fos 14r–19r, Aymeric Natalis: [Inc:] *Quamvis propter tam altam* . . . ; fos 20r–25v, Sancho Mulier: [Inc:] *Salva determinatione* . . . ; fos 30r–36r, Simon de Columb: *Allegationes*; fos 36v–40r, Simon de Columb: *Questiones tacite correspondentes questionibus Parisiensibus*; fos 40v–42v, Simon de Columb: [Inc:] *Devota creatura vestra* . . . ; fos 74r–77v, John Acton: *Contra viam cessionis*; fos 98r–103r, *Que sequuntur ut credo fuerunt magistri Stephanj de Labarella*. [Description – P. Fournier, E. Maignien and A. Prudhomme, *Catalogue général des manuscrits des bibliothèques publiques de France: départements*, vol. 7 (Paris, 1889), pp. 296–300.]

LONDON British Library

Add. 10020: fos 70r–77v, Letter of the University of Toulouse to Charles VI of France, 1402, with occasional comments; fos 98r–99r, Letter to the University of Paris from its envoys to the Council of Pisa, 29 April 1409; fos 148r–v, Letter to the Picard nation at the University of Paris, from Pierre de Plaoul and Eustace de Faucomberge, their envoys to the Council of Pisa, 20 May 1409. A composite work, the second half of which contains a considerable amount of material relating to the schism and the Council of Constance, some of which is unpublished. There is no printed description, but the MS is discussed in Crowder, 'Constance Acta', pp. 486–90, with the Constance material being detailed at pp. 498–501.

Royal 6.D.x: fos 277v–282v, Nicholas Radcliffe: *Questio de schismate*. [Description – Sir G. F. Warner and J. P. Gilson, *British Museum: catalogue of western manuscripts in the old Royal and King's collections* (4 vols., London, 1921), vol. 1, pp. 149–50.]

MUNICH   Bayerische Staatsbibliothek

Clm. 5596: fos 1r–7v, Presence list of the Council of Constance. [Description – *Catalogus codicum manu scriptorum bibliothecae regiae Monacensis*, vol. 3, part 3 (Munich, 1873), p. 26.]

Clm. 7006: fos 125r–127v, [Anon.]: *Utrum principes temporales sub pena dampnacionis eterne obligentur tollere scismate ecclesie militantis* (an important but neglected survey of European attitudes on the schism, c. 1395). [Description – *Catalogus . . . Monacensis*, vol. 3, part 3, p. 135; J. E. Weis-Liebersdorf, *Das Kirchenjahr in 156 gotischen Federzeichnungen*, Studien zur deutschen Kunstgeschichte, 160 (Strassbourg, 1913), p. 14.]

NAPLES   Biblioteca Nazionale

Vienn. latino 57 (formerly MS Lat. 3160 of the Österreichische Nationalbibliothek, removed from Vienna after World War I): fos 156r–v, Letter from the University of Paris to the University of Padua, 12 September 1395. [Description – *Tabulae codicum manu scriptorum praeter graecos et orientales in bibliotheca palatina Vindobonensi asservatorum*, vol. 2 (Vienna, 1868), pp. 217–20.]

OXFORD   Balliol College

MS 165B: pp. 1–99, *Allegationes in materia et facto subtractionis* [= Simon de Cramaud: *De subtractione obedientie*]; pp. 214–40, Raoul d'Oulmont: [Inc:] *In nomine patris* . . . [Description – R. A. B. Mynors, *Catalogue of the manuscripts of Balliol College, Oxford* (Oxford, 1963), pp. 164–70.]

OXFORD   Bodleian Library

Arch. Seld. B. 23: fos 58v–59r, Letter from Cardinal Dominici to the University of Oxford, September 1409. The letter book of William Swan, an Englishman resident at the papal court. Some of the letters in the compilation relate to English activity during the schism. There is no adequate published indication of the contents, the volume receiving scant attention in F. Madan and H. H. E. Craster, *A summary catalogue of western manuscripts in the Bodleian library, Oxford*, vol. 2, part 1 (Oxford, 1922), pp. 613–14. The MS receives greater consideration in E. F. Jacob, *Essays in later medieval history* (Manchester, 1968), pp. 58–78.

Canonici Pat. Lat. 205: fos 1r–15v, Presence list of the Council of Pisa. [Description – H. O. Coxe, *Catalogi codicum manuscrip-*

torum bibliothecae Bodleianae, pars tertia: codices graecos et latinos Canonicianos complectens (Oxford, 1854), p. 404.]

Laud. misc. 249: fos 76r–88v, Petrus de Ancharano: *Tractatus de schismate.* [Description – H. O. Coxe, *Catalogi . . . , partis secundae, fasiculus primus: catalogus codicum manuscriptorum Laudianorum, codices latini* (Oxford, 1858), pp. 208–11.]

PARIS Archives nationales

J.518: fos 360r–497v, Schedules presented at the termination of the Council of Paris, 1398; fos 500r–555v, *Quedam epistola missa ab universitate Tholose impugnans viam cessionis* (with glosses added by Simon de Cramaud). An extremely important collection of documents on the schism. The volume is almost completely transcribed in Paris, Bibliothèque nationale, MSS Lat. 1480A and 1480A2 (see below).

PARIS Bibliothèque nationale

Fr. 12470: fos 1r–5r, Jean Petit: *Complainte de l'église.* [Description – H. Omont and C. Couderc, *Bibliothèque nationale: catalogue général des manuscrits français*, vol. 2 (Paris, 1896), pp. 536–7.]

Lat. 1463: fos 73v–74r, Raoul d'Oulmont: Tract in favour of Clement VII. [Description – P. Lauer, *Bibliothèque nationale: catalogue général des manuscrits latins*, vol. 2 (Paris, 1940), pp. 17–18.]

Lat. 1467–8: Robertus Gervasius: *Liber vocatus Mirra electa.* (MS Lat. 1468 contains part 2 of this work only.) [Description – Lauer, *Catalogue des manuscrits latins*, vol. 2, p. 20.]

Lat. 1469: fos 42r–66v, Jean le Fèvre: *De planctu bonorum*; fos 115v–172r, Debates of the assembly of Medina del Campo, 1381, including tracts by Evrard de Tremaugen, Jean d'Aramon and Pierre de Thury. [Description – Lauer, *Catalogue des manuscrits latins*, vol. 2, pp. 20–22.]

Lat. 1470: fos 90r–148r, Debates of the assembly of Medina del Campo, 1381, including tracts by Evrard de Tremaugen, Pierre de Thury and Jean d'Aramon. [Description – Lauer, *Catalogue des manuscrits latins*, vol. 2, pp. 22–3.]

Lat. 1475: fos 33r–53r, Martin de Salva: *Allegationes domini Pampilonensis* (with glosses added by Simon de Cramaud). [Description – Lauer, *Catalogue des manuscrits latins*, vol. 2, pp. 25–6.]

Lat. 1479: fo 37r, Protest of the University of Orléans against the subtraction of obedience from Benedict XIII, 5 September 1401; fos 188r–122v, Speech of the envoy of the University of Toulouse to Charles VI, April 1402. [Description – Lauer, *Catalogue des manuscrits latins*, vol. 2, pp. 28–30.]

Lat. 1480A2: pp. 183–667, Schedules presented at the termination of the Council of Paris, 1398; pp. 667ff, Letter of the University of Toulouse favouring restitution of obedience to Benedict XIII, with glosses by Simon de Cramaud. [Description – Lauer, *Catalogue des manuscrits latins*, vol. 2, pp. 32–3.]

Lat. 1481: fos 23r–25r, *Gestorum a tempore instrusionis Bartholomei*; fos 123r–132r, *Conclusio universitatis juribus*; fos 135r–150r, [Anon.]: *Tractatus de substractione obedientie*; fos. 159r–207v, Johannes Fiot: *Dialogus substractionis*. [Description – Lauer, *Catalogue des manuscrits latins*, vol. 2, pp. 33–4.]

Lat. 5237: A composite volume, the final section of which contains various letters and other documents relating to the period of the Council of Constance, mainly derived from the University of Cologne.

Lat. 14643: fos 49r–52r, The letter of the University of Paris to Benedict XIII, 14 April 1395, with marginal notes of amendments made to transform it into the general letter of 25 August. The volume also contains several other tracts on the schism.

Lat. 14644: fos. 142r–161v, Henry of Langenstein: *Epistola pacis*; fos 212r–230r, Prior of Roncy: Tract addressed to Philip of Burgundy, on the subtraction and restitution of obedience to Benedict XIII. The volume also contains several other tracts on the schism.

Lat. 17184: fos 227r–238v, Antonius de Butrio: *Tractatus de schismate*; fos 238v–256v, Mattheus de Matasellanis: *Tractatus compositus . . . ad supplendum tractatum . . . D. Antonij de Butrio, qui morte praeventus non complevit*. A collection of transcripts of tracts, made in the eighteenth century.

Lat. 17585: A presentation copy of the Toulouse letter of 1401, with the glosses of Simon de Cramaud.

N.A. Lat. 1793: fos 71r–77v, Letter of the University of Paris to Benedict XIII, 14 April 1395; fos 97r–160v, Letter of the University of Toulouse to Charles VI, 1401, with glosses by Simon de Cramaud. [Description – L. Delisle, 'Vente de manuscrits du comte d'Ashburnham', *Journal des savants* (1899), 323–30.]

Notes on manuscripts cited

PRAGUE Universitní knihova

I.B.29: fos 21v–22v, Bartholomaeus de Rudis: *Determinatio Bononie*. [Description – J. Truhlář, *Catalogus codicum manu scriptorum latinorum qui in C.R. bibliotheca publica atque universitatis Pragensis asservantur* (2 vols., Prague, 1905–6), vol. 1, p. 26.]

XIV.C.16: fos 156r–170v, Johannes de Braculis: *Determinatio quaestionis de canonica electione Urbani sexti*. [Description – Truhlář, *Catalogus*, vol. 2, pp. 291–2.]

XIV.D.19: fos 45r–50v, 52r–60r, Johannes de Braculis: *Determinatio quaestionis de canonica electione Urbani sexti*. [Description – Truhlář, *Catalogus*, vol. 2, p. 303.]

VATICAN Archivio segreto

Indice 324: One of a number of seventeenth-century indices to the Lateran Registers (in this case, those of Popes Innocent VII and John XXIII) which contain references, in some cases calendars, of volumes which are now missing. See L. E. Boyle, *A survey of the Vatican Archives and of its medieval holdings*, Subsidia medievalia, vol. 1 (Toronto, 1972), pp. 144–5.

Arm. LIV: The volumes under this classification include the famous *Libri de schismate*, perhaps the most important accumulation of evidence on the debates of the schism. Most of the volumes are contemporary, but there are some later transcripts. There is no printed (or, for that matter, complete unprinted) catalogue; but a useful summary of the contents is to be found in M. Seidlmayer, 'Die spanischen "Libri de schismate" des vatikanischen Archivs', *Spanische Forschungen des Görresgesellschaft, Reihe 1*, **8** (1940), 199–262. The following volumes and tracts are specifically mentioned in this book: 18, fos 48r–51r, *Allegationes cuiusdam doctoris Salamantini*; 20, fos 184v–191v, *Allegationes cuiusdam doctoris Toletani* [Aymeric Natalis]; 21, fos 55r–56v, *Cedula magistri Egidij de Campis*, fos 57r–59r, *Cedula abbatis sancti Michaelis* [Pierre le Roy], fos 61r–v, *Ista sunt tacta pro patriarcham* [Simon de Cramaud]; 22, fos 70r–72r, *Allegationes fratri Sancii Mulerii*; 36, fos 99–107, An anonymous tract attacking the University of Paris, c. 1396, fos 125r–v, Letter of the University of Paris to the University of Bologna, 12 September 1395; 39, [Anon]: *Opus novum*.

VATICAN   Biblioteca Apostolica

Barb. Lat. 872: A volume of works relating to the schism. There is no printed description, but see Bliemetzrieder, *Literarische Polemik*, pp. 6*–7*.

Pal. Lat. 701: fos 408v–409r, Instructions of the ambassadors of Pope Boniface IX to the Reichstag of 1397. [Description – *Codices palatini latini bibliothecae Vaticanae*, vol. 1 (Rome, 1886), pp. 249–51.]

Vat. Lat. 3477: fos 32r–35v, Franciscus de Zabarella: *Consilium* favouring the cardinals, prior to the Council of Pisa. A volume of tracts relating to the schism.

Vat. Lat. 4039: fos 243r–246r, Dominicus de Sancto Geminiano: *Tractatus concilij*. The volume includes several other tracts on the schism, including one by Robertus de Fronzola. There is no printed description, but see Bliemetzrieder, *Literarische Polemik*, pp. 4*–5*.

Vat. Lat. 5608: fos 184r–202r, Laurentius de Ridolfis: *Allegationes facte . . . in congregacione prelatorum atque universitatis . . . celebrata Florentie de mense Februarij 1408*. [Description – del Re, 'Il "Consilium" ', pp. 223–33.]

Vat. Lat. 7305: fos 120v–122r, Letter of the University of Bologna to the cardinals, 1408. A volume of miscellaneous works on the schism.

BIBLIOGRAPHY OF WORKS CITED

N.B. In recent years, many of the following works have been reprinted in facsimile. The publication details given here are those of the original editions.

Arnold, T. *Select English Works of John Wyclif*. 3 vols. Oxford, 1869–71.

Arquillière, H.-X. 'L'appel au concile sous Philippe le Bel et la genèse des théories conciliares', *Revue des questions historiques*, **89** (1911), 23–55.

Asseldonk, G. A. van. *De Neerlanden en het westers Schisma (tot 1398)*. Utrecht, 1955.

Astre, F. 'L'université de Toulouse devant le Parlement de Paris, en 1406', *Mémoires de l'Academie impériale des Sciences, Inscriptions, et Belles-Lettres de Toulouse*, 7th series, **1** (1869), 109–24.

Baluzius, S. [ed. G. Mollat]. *Vitae paparum Avenionensium . . . ab anno Christi MCCCV usque ad annum MCCCXCIV*. 4 vols. Paris, 1914–22.

Bandini, A. M. *Catalogus codicum latinorum bibliothecae Mediceae Laurentianae*, vol. 1. Florence, 1774.

Baptista, J. C. 'Portugal e o cisma de ocidente', *Lusitania Sacra*, **1** (1956), 65–203.

Bartoš, F. M. *Tetragonus Aristotelis: konciliaristický projev s počátku velikého církevního rozkolu*. Historický archiv Česká akademie císaře Františka Josefa pro vědy, slovesnost a umění čísko, vol. 41. Prague, 1916.

—— 'Tetragonus Aristotelis', in *Abhandlungen aus dem Gebiete der mittleren und neueren Geschichte und ihrer Hilfswissenschaften*, pp. 233–9. Münster, 1925.

—— 'Das Rätsel des Tetragonus Aristotelis', *Communio viatorum*, **12** (1969), 159–64.

Beckmann, J. H. *Studien zum Leben und literarischen Nachlass Jakobs von Soest, O.P. (1360–1440)*. Quellen und Forschungen zur Geschichte des Dominikanerordens in Deutschland, vol. 25. Leipzig, 1929.

Bellaguet, M. L. *Chronique du religieux de St Denys*. 6 vols. Paris, 1839–52.

Beltrán de Heredia, V. *Bulario de la universidad de Salamanca*. Acta Salmanticensia, vols. 12–14. 3 vols. Salamanca, 1966–67.

Beltrán de Heredia, V. *Cartulario de la universidad de Salamanca (1218–1600)*, vol. 1. Acta Salmanticensia, vol. 17. Salamanca, 1970.

—— 'El estudio general de Calatayud, documentos referentes a su institución', in *Miscelánea Beltrán de Heredia*, ed. V. Beltrán de Heredia, vol. 1, pp. 235–55. Biblioteca de teologos españoles, vol. 25. Salamanca, 1971.

Black, A. *Monarchy and community: political ideas in the later conciliar controversy, 1430–50*. Cambridge studies in medieval life and thought, 3rd series, vol. 2. Cambridge, 1970.

—— 'The universities and the Council of Basle: ecclesiology and tactics', *Annuarium Historiae Conciliorum*, 6 (1974), 341–51.

Bliemetzrieder, F. J. P. *Ein kanonistischer Traktat für das Pisaner Konzil (1409)*. Graz, 1902.

—— 'Zwei kanonistische Traktate aus Bologna (Ende 1408) wegen des Pisanerkonziles', *Studien und Mitteilungen aus dem Benedictiner- und dem Cistercienser-Orden*, 24 (1903), 106–14.

—— 'Antwort der Universität in Wien an diejenige zu Paris, 12 Mai 1396, wegen der Zession der beiden Päpste'. *Studien und Mitteilungen aus dem Benedictiner- und dem Cistercienser-Orden*, 24 (1903), 100–5.

—— *Das Generalkonzil im grossen abendländischen Schisma*. Paderborn, 1904.

—— 'Matthäus von Krakau, der Verfasser der Postillen?', *Studien und Mitteilungen aus dem Benedictiner- und dem Cistercienser-Orden*, 25 (1904), 544–56.

—— 'Abt Ludolfs von Sagan Traktat, "Soliloquium scismatis" ', *Studien und Mitteilungen aus dem Benedictiner- und dem Cistercienser-Orden*, 26 (1905), 29–47, 226–38, 434–92.

—— 'Ein Aktenstück zu Beginn des abendländischen Schismas', *Studien und Mitteilungen aus dem Benedictiner- und dem Cistercienser-Orden*, 28 (1907), 30–7.

—— 'Ein Bericht des Matthäus Clementis an Urban VI (ca. 1381) über seine Arbeiten zu dessen Gunsten in Aragonien', *Studien und Mitteilungen aus dem Benedictiner- und dem Cistercienser-Orden*, 29 (1908), 580–6.

—— 'Traktat des Minoritenprovinzials von England Fr. Nikolaus de Fakenham (1395) über das grosse abendländische Schisma', *Archivum Franciscanum Historicum*, 1 (1908), 577–600, 2 (1909), 79–91.

—— 'Gutachten der juristischen Fakultät zu Padua über Urbans VI Wahl (Sommer 1378)', *Studien und Mitteilungen aus dem Benedictiner- und dem Cistercienser-Orden*, 30 (1909), 97–111.

—— *Literarische Polemik zu Beginn des grossen abendländischen Schismas*. Publikationen des Österreichischen Historischen Instituts in Rom, vol. 1. Vienna, 1910.

—— 'Conclusions de Guillaume de Salvarvilla, maître en théologie, à Paris, sur la question du concile général pendant le grand schisme d'occident (1381)', *Revue d'histoire ecclésiastique*, 11 (1910), 47–55.

Bibliography of works cited

Bliss, W. H. *Calendar of entries in the papal registers relating to Great Britain and Ireland: petitions to the pope*, vol. 1. London, 1896.

Bonney, F. 'Autour de Jean Gerson: opinions de théologiens sur les superstitions et la sorcellerie au début du XVᵉ siècle', *Moyen Age*, **77** (1971), 85–98.

Bossuat, A. 'Une relation inédite de l'ambassade française au pape Benoît XIII en 1407', *Moyen Age*, **55** (1949), 77–101.

Bourgeois du Chastenet, H. *Nouvelle histoire du concile de Constance.* Paris, 1718.

Boyle, L. E. *A survey of the Vatican Archives and of its medieval holdings*, Subsidia medievalia, vol. 1. Toronto, 1972.

Brady, I. 'The development of the doctrine on the Immaculate Conception in the C14 after Aureoli', *Franciscan Studies*, **15** (1955), 175–202.

Brandmüller, W. 'Besitzt das Konstanzer Decret *Haec sancta* dogmatische Verbindlichkeit?', *Römische Quartalschrift*, **62** (1967), 1–17.

Buck, M. R. *Ulrichs von Richental Chronik des Constanzer Concils, 1414 bis 1418.* Bibliothek des litterarischen Vereins in Stuttgart, vol. 158. Stuttgart, 1882.

Buddensieg, R. *John Wyclif's polemical works in Latin.* 2 vols. London, 1883.

Bulaeus, C. E. *Historia universitatis Parisiensis.* 6 vols. Paris, 1665–73.

Bzovius, A. *Annalium ecclesiasticorum*, vol. 15. Cologne, 1622.

Calendar of Patent Rolls, 1395–9. London, 1909.

Calendar of Patent Rolls, 1401–5. London, 1907.

Calendar of Patent Rolls, 1405–8. London, 1907.

Cartulaire de l'université de Montpellier. 2 vols. and supplement. Montpellier, 1890–1912.

Castro, Paulus de. *Consilia.* 3 vols. Frankfurt, 1582.

Catalogus codicum manu scriptorum bibliothecae regiae Monacensis, vol. 3, part. 3. Munich, 1873.

Chaloupecký, V. *The Caroline University of Prague: its foundation, character and development in the fourteenth century.* Prague, 1948.

Chaplais, P. 'Some documents regarding the fulfilment and interpretation of the Treaty of Brétigny (1360–1369)', in *Camden Miscellany*, vol. 19. Camden Society Publications, 3rd series, vol. 80. London, 1952.

Chartularium studii Bononiensis. 13 vols. Bologna, 1909–40.

Cobban, A. B. *The medieval universities: their development and organization.* London, 1975.

Codex diplomaticus universitatis studii generalis Cracoviensis. 5 vols. Cracow, 1870–1910.

Codices palatini latini bibliothecae Vaticanae, vol. 1. Rome, 1886.

Conciliorum oecumenicorum decreta. 3rd edn. Bologna, 1973.

Congar, Y. 'Quod omnes tangit, ab omnibus tractari et approbari debet', *Revue historique du droit français et étranger*, 4th series, **36** (1958), 210–59.

Connolly, J. L. *John Gerson, reformer and mystic.* Louvain, 1928.

Coville, A. 'Recherches sur Jean Courtecuisse et ses oeuvres oratoires', *Bibliothèque de l'Ecole des chartes*, **65** (1904), 469–529.
—— *Jean Petit: la question du tyrannicide au commencement du XVᵉ siècle.* Paris, 1932.
—— *La vie intellectuelle dans les domaines d'Anjou-Provence de 1380 à 1435.* Paris, 1941.
Coxe, H. O. *Catalogi codicum manuscriptorum bibliothecae Bodleianae, pars tertia: codices graecos et latinos Canonicianos complectens.* Oxford, 1854.
—— *Catalogi . . . , partis secundae, fasiculus primus: catalogus codicum manuscriptorum Laudianorum, codices latini.* Oxford, 1858.
Crowder, C. M. D. 'Constance Acta in English libraries', in *Das Konzil von Konstanz*, ed. A. Franzen and W. Müller, pp. 477–517. Vienna, 1964.
—— *Unity, heresy, and reform, 1378–1460: the conciliar response to the great schism.* Documents of medieval history, vol. 3. London, 1977.
Dahmus, J. H. *William Courtenay, Archbishop of Canterbury, 1381–1396.* University Park, Pa., 1966.
Dax, L. *Die Universitäten und die Konzilien von Pisa und Konstanz.* Freiburg-am-Main, 1909.
Delaruelle, E., Labande, E.-R. and Ourliac, P. *L'église au temps du grand schisme et de la crise conciliare.* Histoire de l'église (ed. A. Fliche and V. Martin), vol. 14. 2 vols. Paris, 1962–64.
Delisle, L. 'Vente de manuscrits du comte d'Ashburnham', *Journal des savants* (1899), 323–30.
Denifle, H. S. 'Der Chronist fr. Petrus de Arenijs und Papa Luna', *Archiv für Literatur- und Kirchengeschichte des Mittelalters*, **3** (1887), 645–50.
—— *Les universités françaises au moyen-âge: avis à M. Marcel Fournier.* Paris, 1892.
Denifle, H. S. and Chatelain, E. *Chartularium universitatis Parisiensis.* 4 vols. Paris, 1891–9.
—— *Auctarium chartularii universitatis Parisiensis*, vols. 1–3: *Liber procuratorum nationis Anglicanae (Alemanniae) in universitate Parisiensi.* 2nd edn. 3 vols. Paris, 1937.
De stirpe et origine de domus de Courtenay. Paris, 1607.
Diener, H. 'Zur Geschichte der Universitätsgründungen in Alt-Öfen (1395) und Nantes (1423)', *Quellen und Forschungen aus italienischen Archiven und Bibliotheken*, **42–43** (1963), 265–84.
Dupin, L. E. *Johannis Gersonii . . . opera omnia.* 5 vols. Antwerp, 1706.
Dupuy, P. *Histoire du differend d'entre le pape Boniface VIII et Philippes le Bel, roy de France.* Paris, 1655.
Ehrle, F. 'Neue Materialen zur Geschichte Peters von Luna (Benedicts XIII)', *Archiv für Literatur- und Kirchengeschichte des Mittelalters*, **6** (1892), 139–308.
—— 'Die kirchenrechtlichen Schriften Peters von Luna (Benedikts XIII)', *Archiv für Literatur- und Kirchengeschichte des Mittelalters*, **7** (1900), 515–75.

Ehrle, F. 'Aus den Acten des Afterconcils von Perpignan, 1408 (Schluss)', *Archiv für Literatur- und Kirchengeschichte des Mittelalters*, **7** (1900), 576–694.

—— *Martin de Alpartils Chronica actitatorum temporibus domini Benedicti XIII*. Quellen und Forschungen aus dem Gebiete der Geschichte, vol. 12. Paderborn, 1906.

Emden, A. B. *A biographical register of the University of Oxford to 1500*. 3 vols. Oxford, 1957–59.

—— *A biographical register of the University of Cambridge to 1500*. Cambridge, 1963.

Eubel, K. *Die avignonische Obedienz der Mendikanten-Orden, sowie der Orden der Mercedarier und Trinitarier zur Zeit des grossen Schismas*. Quellen und Forschungen aus dem Gebiete der Geschichte, vol. 1, part 2. Paderborn, 1900.

Fink, K. A. and Erberloh, E. 'Das abendländische Schisma und die Konzilien', in *Handbuch der Kirchengeschichte*, ed. H. Jedin, vol. 3/2, pp. 490–588. Freiburg, 1968.

Finke, H. *Acta concilii Constanciensis*. 4 vols. Münster, 1896–1928.

—— 'Drei spanische Publizisten aus den Anfängen des grossen Schismas: Matthäus Clementis, Nikolaus Eymeric, der hl. Vicente Ferrer', in *Gesammelte Aufsätze zur Kulturgeschichte Spaniens*, ed. H. Finke, K. Beyerle and G. Schreiber, pp. 147–95. Spanische Forschungen der Görresgesellschaft, erste Reihe, vol. 1. Münster, 1928.

Firnhaber, F. 'Petrus de Pulka, Abgesandter der Wiener Universität am Concilium zu Constanz', *Archiv für Kunde österreichischer Geschichts-Quellen*, **15** (1856), 1–70.

Fodale, S. *La politica napoletana di Urbano VI*. Collezione viaggi e studi, vol. 13. Rome, 1973.

Fournier, M. 'L'église et le droit romain au XIIIᵉ siècle, à propos de l'interprétation de la bulle *Super speculum* d'Honorius III, qui interdit l'enseignement du droit romain à Paris', *Nouvelle revue historique de droit français et étranger*, **14** (1890), 80–119.

—— *Les statuts et privilèges des universités françaises depuis leur fondation jusqu'en 1789*. 4 vols. Paris, 1890–94.

Fournier, P., Maignien, E. and Prudhomme, A. *Catalogue général des manuscrits des bibliothèques publiques de France: départments*, vol. 7. Paris, 1889.

Friedberg, E. *Corpus iuris canonici*. 2 vols. Leipzig, 1879.

Galbraith, V. H. *The St Albans chronicle, 1406–20*. Oxford, 1937.

Gargan, L. 'Libri di teologi agostiniani a Padova nel trecento', *Quaderni per la storia dell'Università di Padova*, **6** (1973), 1–23.

Gayet, L. *Le grand schisme d'occident d'après les documents contemporains déposés aux archives secrètes du Vatican*. 2 vols. Florence and Berlin, 1889.

Gewirth, A. 'John of Jandun and the *"Defensor Pacis"* ', *Speculum*, **23** (1948), 267–72.

Bibliography of works cited

Gewirth, A. *Marsilius of Padua: the Defender of Peace*, 2 vols. New York, 1951–56.

Gherardi, A. *Statuti della università e studio fiorentino*. Documenta di storia italiana, vol. 7. Florence, 1881.

Ghirardacci, C. *Della historia di Bologna, parte seconda*. Bologna, 1657.

Girgensohn, D. *Peter von Pulkau und die Wiedereinführung des Laienkelches*. Veröffentlichungen des Max-Planck-Instituts für Geschichte, vol. 12. Göttingen, 1964.

—— 'Die Universität Wien und das Konstanzer Konzil', in *Das Konzil von Konstanz*, ed. A. Franzen and W. Müller, pp. 252–81. Vienna, 1964.

Glorieux, P. 'L'année universitaire 1392–1393 à la Sorbonne à travers les notes d'un étudiant', *Revue des sciences religieuses*, **19** (1939), 429–82.

—— *Jean Gerson, oeuvres complètes*. 10 vols. [in 11]. Tournai, 1960–73.

Goñi Gaztambide, J. 'Documentos pontificos sobre la universidad de Salamanca', *Anthologica Annua*, **8** (1960), 481–93.

—— 'Los obispos de Pamplona del siglo XIV', *Principe de Viana*, **23** (1962), 5–194, 309–400.

—— 'Tres rótulos de la universidad de Salamanca de 1381, 1389, y 1393', *Anthologica Annua*, **11** (1963), 227–338.

Griera Gaja, A. (ed.). *Miscelánea Mons. J. Rius Serra*. Biblioteca filológica-histórica, vol. 15. 2 vols. Abadiá de San Cugat das Valles, 1964.

Griffiths, G. 'Leonardo Bruni and the restoration of the university of Rome (1406)', *Renaissance Quarterly*, **26** (1973), 1–10.

Günther, O. 'Zur Vorgeschichte des Konzils von Pisa', *Neues Archiv der Gesellschaft für ältere deutsche Geschichtskunde*, **41** (1917–19), 633–76.

Gwynn, A. O. *The English Austin friars in the time of Wyclif*. Oxford, 1940.

Hardt, H. von der. *Magnum oecumenicum Constantiense concilium*. 6 vols. Frankfurt and Leipzig, 1697–1700.

—— *Ineditum carmen antiquum Henrici de Hassia . . . pro pace . . . scriptum Viennae a. 1392*. Helmstadt, 1715.

Hartwig, O. *Henricus de Langenstein, dictus de Hassia: Zwei Untersuchungen über das Leben und Schriften Heinrichs von Langenstein*. Marburg, 1857.

Harvey, M. 'The letter of Oxford University on the schism, 5 February 1399', *Annuarium Historiae Conciliorum*, **6** (1974), 121–34.

—— 'The letters of the University of Oxford on withdrawal of obedience from Pope Boniface IX', *Studies in Church History*, **11** (1975), 187–98.

—— 'Two "Questiones" on the great schism by Nicholas Fakenham, O.F.M.', *Archivum Franciscanum Historicum*, **70** (1977), 97–127.

Heimpel, H. 'Konrad von Soest und Job Vener, Verfasser und Bearbeiter der Heidelberger Postillen (Glossen) zu der Berufung des Konzils von Pisa', *Westfalen*, **51** (1973), 115–24.

Bibliography of works cited

Henrici de Hassia de Langenstein, *Epistola pacis scripta 1379 . . . pro Urbano papa . . . programma . . . in academia Iulia Carolina.* Helmstadt, 1778–79.

Jacob, E. F. *Essays in the conciliar epoch.* 3rd edn. Manchester, 1963.

—— *Archbishop Henry Chichele.* London, 1967.

—— *Essays in later medieval history.* Manchester, 1968.

James, M. R. *The western manuscripts in the library of Emmanuel College.* Cambridge, 1904.

Jourdain, C. M. G. B. *Index chronologicus chartarum pertinentem ad historiam universitatis Parisiensis.* Paris, 1862.

Kadlec, J. *Leben und Schriften des Prager Magisters Adalbert Rankonis de Ericinio, aus dem Nachlass von Rudolf Holinka und Jan Vilikovský.* Beiträge zur Geschichte der Philosophie und Theologie des Mittelalters, N.F., vol. 4. Münster, 1971.

Kaiser, H. 'Der "Kurze Brief" des Konrad von Gelnhausen', *Historische Vierteljahrschrift,* **3** (1900), 379–94.

Kaminsky, H. *A history of the Hussite revolution.* Berkeley, 1967.

—— 'The politics of France's subtraction of obedience from Pope Benedict XIII, 27 July 1398', *Proceedings of the American Philosophical Society,* **115** (1971), 366–97.

Katterbach, B. *Der zweite literarische Kampf auf dem Konstanzer Konzil im Januar und Februar 1415.* Fulda, 1919.

Keussen, H. *Die Rotuli der Kölner Universität.* Mitteilungen aus dem Stadtarchiv von Köln, vol. 7, part 20. Cologne, 1891.

—— *Regesten und Auszüge zur Geschichte der Universität Köln, 1388– 1559.* Mitteilungen aus dem Stadtarchiv von Köln, vol. 15, part 36. Cologne, 1918.

Kleineidam, E. *Universitas Studii Erffordensis: Überblick über die Geschichte der Universität Erfurt im Mittelalter, 1392–1521. Teil 1: 1392–1460.* Erfurter theologische Studien, vol. 14. Leipzig, 1964.

Kneer, A. *Kardinal Zabarella, 1360–1417.* Münster, 1891.

—— *Die Entstehung der konziliaren Theorie: zur Geschichte des Schismas und der Kirchenpolitischen Schriftsteller Konrad von Gelnhausen (†1390) und Heinrich von Langenstein (†1397).* Rome, 1893.

Kürbis, B. 'Une université manquée: Chelmno entre le XIVᵉ et le XVIᵉ siècle', in *Les universités européennes du XIVᵉ au XVIIIᵉ siècle, aspects et problèmes: actes du colloque international à l'occasion du VIᵉ centenaire de l'université Jagellone de Cracovie, 6–8 Mai 1964,* Etudes et documents publiés par l'Institut d'histoire de la faculté des lettres de l'université de Genève, vol. 4, pp. 133–5. Geneva, 1967.

Kybal, V. and Odložilík, O. (eds), *Matěje z Janova, mistra Pařížského, 'Regulae veteris et novi testamenti'.* Sbírka pramenů českého hnutí náboženského, vols. 9–13. Innsbruck and Prague, 1908–26.

Lagarde, G. de. 'Marsile de Padoue et Guillaume d'Ockham', *Revue des sciences religieuses,* **17** (1937), 168–85, 428–54.

Bibliography of works cited

Lang, J. *Die Christologie bei Heinrich von Langenstein.* Freiburger theologische Studien, vol. 85. Freiburg-im-Breisgau, 1966.

Lauer, P. *Bibliothèque nationale: catalogue général des manuscrits latins,* vol. 2. Paris, 1940.

Leff, G. *Heresy in the later middle ages.* 2 vols. Manchester, 1967.

Leinweber, J. 'Ein neues Verzeichniss der Teilnehmer am Konzil von Pisa, 1409', in *Konzil und Papst,* ed. G. Schwaiger, pp. 207–46. Munich, 1975.

Lenné, A. 'Der erste literarische Kampf auf dem Konstanzer Konzil im November und Dezember 1414', *Römische Quartalschrift,* **28** (1914), 3*–40*, 61*–86*.

Lindner, T. 'Über Huttens Schrift, *De schismate extinguendo*', *Theologische Studien und Kritiken,* **46** (1873), 151–61.

Lloyd, J. E. *Owen Glendower.* Oxford, 1931.

Lopes, F. [ed. M. Lopes de Almeida and A. de Magalhães Basto]. *Crónica de D. João I.* 2 vols. Oporto, 1945–49.

Loserth, J. 'Beiträge zur Geschichte der husitischen Bewegung, III: Der Tractatus de longevo schismate des Abtes Ludolf von Sagan', *Archiv für Österreichische Geschichte,* **60** (1880), 343–561.

—— *Johannis Wyclif Tractatus de ecclesia.* London, 1886.

—— *Johannis Wyclif Tractatus de potestate pape.* London, 1907.

—— *Johannis Wyclif Opera minora.* London, 1913.

Luman, R. 'A conciliar suggestion', in *The impact of the church upon its culture,* ed. J. C. Brauer, Essays in Divinity, vol. 2, pp. 121–43. Chicago, 1968.

Lumby, J. R. *Chronicon Henrici Knighton.* Rolls Series, vol. 92. London, 1889–95.

Madan, F. and Craster, H. H. E. *A summary catalogue of western manuscripts in the Bodleian library, Oxford,* vol. 2, part 1. Oxford, 1922.

Maillard-Luypaert, M. 'Une lettre d'Innocent VII du 2 octobre 1405 à propos du retour de Liège à l'obédience romaine', *Revue d'histoire ecclésiastique,* **72** (1977), 54–60.

Mansi, J. D. *Sanctorum conciliorum nova et amplissima collectio,* vol. 27. Venice, 1784.

Marongiu, A. 'Q.o.t., principe fondamental de la démocratie et du consentment au XIVᵉ siècle', in *Album Helen Maud Cam,* vol. 2, pp. 101–15. Louvain, 1961.

Martène, E. *Veterum scriptorum et monumentorum . . . amplissima collectio,* vol. 7. Paris, 1733.

Martène, E. and Durand, U. *Thesaurus novus anecdotorum.* 5 vols. Paris, 1717. Vol. 2 only.

Martin, V. *Les origines du Gallicanisme.* 2 vols. Paris, 1939.

Martines, L. *Lawyers and statecraft in renaissance Florence.* Princeton, 1968.

Matthew, F. D. *The English works of Wyclif hitherto unprinted.* Early English Text Society, vol. 74. London, 1880.

Matthews, T. *Welsh records in Paris*. Carmarthen, 1910.

Meersseman, G. G. 'Etudes sur l'ordre des frères prêcheurs au début du grand schisme', *Archivum Fratum Praedicatorum*, **25** (1955), 213-57.

Meyer, P. and Valois, N. 'Poème en quatrains sur le grand schisme (1381)', *Romania*, **24** (1895), 197-218.

Mézières, Philippe de [ed. G. W. Coopland]. *Le songe du vieil pèlerin*. 2 vols. Cambridge, 1969.

Moreira de Sá, A. *Chartularium universitatis Portugalensis, 1288-1537*. Lisbon, 1966– . [In Progress.]

Morrall, J. B. *Gerson and the great schism*. Manchester, 1960.

Mynors, R. A. B. *Catalogue of the manuscripts of Balliol College, Oxford*. Oxford, 1963.

Oakley, F. 'The "Propositiones utiles" of Pierre d'Ailly: an epitome of conciliar theory', *Church History*, **29** (1960), 398-403.

—— *The political thought of Pierre d'Ailly: the voluntarist tradition*. New Haven, 1964.

Oman, C. *The great revolt of 1381*. 2nd edn. Oxford, 1969.

Omont, H. and Couderc, C. *Bibliothèque nationale: catalogue général des manuscrits français*, vol. 2. Paris, 1896.

Ouy, G. *Le recueil épistolaire autographe de Pierre d'Ailly, et les notes d'Italie de Jean de Montreuil*. Umbrae codicum occidentalium, vol. 9. Amsterdam, 1966.

—— 'Gerson et l'Angleterre: à propos d'un texte polémique retrouvé du chancelier de Paris contre l'université d'Oxford, 1396', in *Humanism in France at the end of the middle ages and in the early renaissance*, ed. A. H. T. Levi, pp. 43-81. Manchester, 1970.

Ozment, S. E. 'The university and the church; patterns of reform in Jean Gerson', *Medievalia et Humanistica*, N.S. **1** (1970), 111-26.

Palmer, J. J. N. 'English foreign policy, 1388-1399', in *The reign of Richard II: essays in honour of May McKisack*, ed. F. R. H. du Boulay and C. M. Barron, pp. 75-107. London, 1971.

—— *England, France, and Christendom, 1377-99*. London, 1972.

Parmiter, G. de C. *The king's great matter*. London, 1967.

Pascoe, L. B. 'Jean Gerson: mysticism, conciliarism, and reform', *Annuarium Historiae Conciliorum*, **6** (1974), 135-55.

Pellegrin, E. 'Un humaniste normand du temps de Charles VI: Guillaume Euvrie', *Bulletin, Institut de recherche et d'histoire des textes*, **15** (1967-68), 9-28.

Perroy, E. *L'Angleterre et le grand schisme d'occident*. Paris, 1933.

Pollard, A. W. *Johannis Wyclif Dialogus, sive Speculum ecclesie militantis*. London, 1886.

Posthumus Meyjes, G. H. M. *Jean Gerson: zijn Kerkpolitiek en Ecclesiologie*. The Hague, 1963.

Puget, J. 'L'université de Toulouse au XIVe et au XVe siècles', *Annales du Midi*, **41-2** (1929-30), 345-81.

Rashdall, H. [ed. F. M. Powicke and A. B. Emden]. *The universities of Europe in the middle ages.* 2nd edn. 3 vols. Oxford, 1936.

Raymond, I. W. 'D'Ailly's "Epistola diaboli Leviathan" ', *Church History*, **22** (1953), 181–91.

Re, N. del. 'Il "Consilium pro Urbano VI" di Bartolomeo da Saliceto', in *Collectanea Vaticana in honorem Anselmi M. Card. Albareda* [= Studi e Testi, vol. 219], pp. 213–63. Vatican City, 1962.

Reeves, M. *The influence of prophecy in the later middle ages.* Oxford, 1969.

Ritter, G. *Studien zur Spätscholastik, I: Marsilius von Inghen und die okkamistische Schule in Deutschland.* Sitzungsberichte der Heidelberger Akademie der Wissenschaften, vol. 12, part 4. Heidelberg, 1921.

Roschach, E. *Ville de Toulouse: inventaire des archives communales antérieures à 1790: I, Série AA.* Toulouse, 1891.

Rothbarth, M. *Urban VI und Neapel.* Abhandlungen zur mittleren und neueren Geschichte, vol. 49. Berlin and Leipzig, 1913.

Rotuli Scotiae in turri Londiniensi et domo capitulari Westmonsteriensi asservati, vol. 2. London, 1819.

Rubió y Lluch, A. *Documents per l'historia de la cultura Catalana migeval.* 2 vols. Barcelona, 1908–21.

Salembier, L. *Le cardinal Pierre d'Ailly*, Tourcoing, 1932.

Salomon, R. 'Eine vergessene Universitätsgründung', *Neues Archiv der Gesellschaft für ältere deutsche Geschichtskunde*, **37** (1911–12), 810–17.

Salter, H. E. *Snappe's formulary and other records.* Publications of the Oxford Historical Society, vol. 80. Oxford, 1924.

Salter, H. E., Pantin, W. A. and Richardson, H. G. *Formularies which bear on the history of Oxford, c. 1204–1420*, vol. 1. Publications of the Oxford Historical Society, N.S., vol. 4. Oxford, 1942.

Sartore, T. 'Un discorso inedito di Francesco Zabarella a Bonifacio IX sull'autorità del papa', *Rivista di storia della chiesa in Italia*, **20** (1966), 375–86.

Schardius, S. *De iurisdictione, autoritate et praeeminentia imperiali.* Basel, 1566.

Scheuffgen, F. J. *Beiträge zu der Geschichte des grossen Schismas.* Freiburg-im-Breisgau, 1889.

Schmitt, C. 'Un défenseur attardé de Benoît XIII, Antoine "de Piscibus", O.F.M.', in *Miscellanea Melchior de Pobladura*, ed. Isidorus a Villapadierna, O.F.M. Cap., vol. 1. Biblioteca Seraphico-Capuccina cura Instituti historici Ord. Fr. Min. Capuccinorum, vol. 23, pp. 267–89. Rome, 1964.

Schmitz, L. 'Die Quellen zur Geschichte des Konzils von Cividale, 1409', *Römische Quartalschrift*, **8** (1894), 217–58.

—— 'Zur Geschichte des Konzils von Pisa, 1409', *Römische Quartalschrift*, **9** (1895), 351–75.

Schulte, J. F. von. *Die Geschichte der Quellen und Literatur des Canonischen Rechts von Gratian bis auf die Gegenwart*, vol. 2. Stuttgart, 1877.

Seidlmayer, M. *Die Anfänge des grossen abendländischen Schismas*. Spanische Forschungen der Görresgesellschaft, zweite Reihe, vol. 5. Münster, 1940.

—— 'Die spanischen "Libri de schismate" des vatikanischen Archivs', *Spanische Forschungen des Görresgesellschaft, Reihe 1*, 8 (1940), 199–262.

Sigmund, P. E., Jr. 'The influence of Marsilius of Padua on XVth-century conciliarism', *Journal of the History of Ideas*, 23 (1962), 392–402.

Smith, C. E. *The University of Toulouse in the middle ages*. Milwaukee, 1958.

Sommerfeldt, G. 'Zwei politische Sermone des Heinrich von Oyta und des Nikolaus von Dinkelsbühl (1388 und 1417)', *Historisches Jahrbuch*, 26 (1905), 318–27.

—— 'Zwei Schismatraktate Heinrichs von Langenstein: Sendschreiben an König Wenzel von 1381 und Schreiben an Bischof Friedrich von Brixen um 1384', *Mitteilungen des Instituts für österreichische Geschichtsforschung*, Ergänzungsband 7 (1907), 436–69.

—— 'Die Stellung Rupprechts III von der Pfalz zur deutschen Publizistik bis zum Jahre 1400', *Zeitschrift für die Geschichte des Oberrheins*, N.F. 22 (1907), 291–317.

—— 'Die Prophetien der hl. Hildegard von Bingen in einem Schreiben des Magisters Heinrich v. Langenstein (1381) und Langensteins Trostbrief über den Tod eines Bruders des Wormser Bischofs Eckard von Ders (um 1384)', *Historisches Jahrbuch*, 30 (1909), 43–61, 297–307.

—— 'Johann Falkenbergs Stellung zur Papstfrage in der Zeit vor dem Pisaner Konzil (1408)', *Mitteilungen des Instituts für österreichische Geschichtsforschung*, 31 (1910), 421–37.

Souchon, M. *Die Papstwahlen von Bonifaz VIII bis Urban VI und die Entstehung des Schismas, 1378*. Brunswick, 1888.

—— *Die Papstwahlen in der Zeit des grossen Schismas*. 2 vols. Brunswick, 1898.

Spinka, M. *Advocates of reform*. Library of Christian classics, vol. 14. London, 1953.

Staffa, D. 'De Iohannis ab Imola vita et operibus', *Apollinaris*, 10 (1937), 76–104.

—— 'Tractatus Johannis ab Imola super schismate occidentis', *Rivista di storia della chiesa in Italia*, 7 (1953), 181–224.

Stefano, G. di. *L'oeuvre oratoire française de Jean Courtecuisse*. Università di Torino, facoltà di lettere e filosofia: filologica moderna, vol. 3. Turin, 1969.

Steuart, A. F. 'Scotland and the papacy during the great schism', *Scottish Historical Review*, 4 (1906–7), 144–58.

Stubel, B. *Urkundenbuch der Universität Leipzig von 1409 bis 1555.* Codex diplomaticus Saxonicae Regiae, 2ter Haupttheil, vol. 11. Leipzig, 1879.

Suárez Fernández, L. *Castilla, el cisma, y la crisis conciliar (1378–1440).* Estudios del consejo superior de investigaciones cientificas, escuela de estudios medievales, vol. 33. Madrid, 1960.

Swanson, R. N. 'The University of St Andrews and the great schism, 1410–1419', *Journal of Ecclesiastical History*, **26** (1975), 223–45.

—— 'Universities, academics, and the great schism', PhD thesis, University of Cambridge, 1976.

—— 'The University of Cologne and the great schism', *Journal of Ecclesiastical History*, **28** (1977), 1–15.

Tabulae codicum manu scriptorum praeter graecos et orientales in bibliotheca palatina Vindobonensi asservatorum, vol. 2. Vienna, 1868.

Theiner, A. *Caesaris S. R. E. Card. Baronii, Od. Raynaldi, et Jac. Laderchii . . . annales ecclesiastici*, vols. 26–7. Bar-le-Duc, 1872–74.

Thomas, A. 'Lettres closes de Charles VI et de Charles VII addressées à l'université de Toulouse', *Annales du Midi*, **27–8** (1915–16), 176–91.

Thorbeke, A. *Die älteste Zeit der Universität Heidelberg, 1386–1449.* Heidelberg, 1886.

Tierney, B. 'Ockham, the conciliar theory, and the canonists', *Journal of the History of Ideas*, **15** (1954), 40–70.

—— *Foundations of the conciliar theory.* Cambridge, 1955.

—— 'Hermeneutics and history: the problem of *Haec sancta*', in *Essays in medieval history presented to Bertie Wilkinson*, ed. T. A. Sandquist and M. R. Powicke, pp. 354–70. Toronto, 1969.

Truhlář, J. *Catalogus codicum manu scriptorum latinorum qui in C.R. bibliotheca publica atque universitatis Pragensis asservantur.* 2 vols. Prague, 1905–6.

Tschackert, P. *Peter von Ailli.* Gotha, 1877.

Uiblein, P. *Acta facultatis artium universitatis Vindobonensis, 1384–1416.* Publikationen des Instituts für österreichische Geschichtsforschung, 6 Reihe: Quellen zur Geschichte der Universität Wien, vol. 2. Graz, 1968.

Ullmann, W. *Medieval papalism: the political theories of the medieval canonists.* London, 1949.

—— 'The legal validity of the papal electoral pacts', *Ephemerides iuris canonici*, **12** (1956), 246–77.

—— 'The University of Cambridge and the great schism', *Journal of Theological Studies*, N.S. **9** (1958), 53–77.

—— 'De Bartoli sententia: concilium repraesentat mentem populi', in *Bartolo da Sassoferrato, studi e documenti per il VI centenario*, vol. 2, pp. 705–33. Milan, 1962.

—— 'Julius II and the schismatic cardinals', *Studies in Church History*, **9** (1972), 177–93.

—— *Origins of the great schism.* 2nd. edn. Hamden, Conn., 1972.

Ullmann, W. *A short history of the papacy in the middle ages.* 2nd edn. London, 1974.

—— *Law and politics in the middle ages.* London, 1975.

—— 'Boniface VIII and his contemporary scholarship', *Journal of Theological Studies,* N.S. **27** (1976), 58–87.

Valasek, E. *Das Kirchenverständniss der Prager Magisters Matthias von Janov (1350/55–1393).* Lateranum, N.S. vol. 37. Rome, 1971.

Valois, N. 'Un poème de circonstance composé par un clerc de l'université de Paris (1381)', *Annuaire-bulletin de la société de l'histoire de France,* **31** (1894), 211–38.

—— *La France et le grand schisme d'occident.* 4 vols. Paris, 1896–1902.

—— 'Jacques de Nouvion et le religieux de St-Denys', *Bibliothèque de l'Ecole des chartes,* **63** (1902), 233–62.

—— 'Un ouvrage inédit de Pierre d'Ailly, le *De persecutionibus ecclesiae*', *Bibliothèque de l'Ecole des chartes,* **66** (1904), 557–74.

Verger, J. 'Le recrutement géographique des universités françaises au début du XVᵉ siècle d'après les *Suppliques* de 1403', *Mélanges d'archéologie et d'histoire,* **82** (1970), 855–902.

Vieillard, J. and Avezou, R. 'Lettres originales de Charles VI conservées aux archives de la couronne d'Aragon à Barcelone', *Bibliothèque de l'Ecole des chartes,* **97** (1936), 317–73.

Vincke, J. 'Acta concilii Pisani', *Römische Quartalschrift,* **46** (1938), 81–331.

—— *Briefe zum Pisaner Konzil.* Beiträge zur Kirchen- und Rechtsgeschichte, vol. 1. Bonn, 1940.

—— *Schriftstücke zum Pisaner Konzil.* Beiträge zur Kirchen- und Rechtsgeschichte, vol. 3. Bonn, 1942.

Vooght, P. de. *L'hérésie de Jean Huss.* Bibliothèque de la Revue d'histoire ecclésiastique, vol. 34. Louvain, 1960.

Wahl, J. A. 'Baldus de Ubaldis; a study in reluctant conciliarism', *Manuscripta,* **18** (1974), 21–9.

Warner, Sir G. F. and Gilson, J. P. *British Museum: catalogue of western manuscripts in the old Royal and King's collections.* 4 vols. London, 1921.

Watt, D. E. R. 'University clerks and rolls of petitions for benefices', *Speculum,* **34** (1959), 213–29.

Weis-Liebersdorf, J. E. *Das Kirchenjahr in 156 gotischen Federzeichungen,* Studien zur deutschen Kunstgeschichte, 160. Strassbourg, 1913.

Weizsäcker, J. *Deutsche Reichstagsakten unter König Ruprecht.* Deutsche Reichstagsakten, vols. 4–6. 3 vols. Gotha, 1882–88.

Weltsch, R. E. *Archbishop John of Jenstein (1348–1400),* Studies in European history, vol. 8. The Hague, 1968.

Wilkins, D. *Concilia Magna Britanniae et Hiberniae,* vol. 3. London, 1737.

Wilks, M. *The problem of sovereignty in the later middle ages.* Cambridge studies in medieval life and thought, 2nd series, vol. 9. Cambridge, 1963.

Williams, G. *Official correspondence of Thomas Bekynton.* Rolls Series, vol. 56. London, 1872.

Winkelmann, E. *Urkundenbuch der Universität Heidelberg.* 2 vols. Heidelberg, 1886.

Workman, H. B. *John Wyclif: a study of the English medieval church.* 2 vols. Oxford, 1926.

Xiberta, B. M. *De scriptoribus scholasticis saeculi XIV ex ordine Carmelitarum.* Bibliothèque de la Revue d'histoire ecclésiastique, vol. 6. Louvain, 1931.

Ypma, E. 'Notice sur le "Studium" de Paris au début du schisme d'occident', *Augustiniana,* **18** (1968), 82–99.

INDEX

Index

Index

Cracow, University of, 11–12, 169, 175n, 177, 191, 193, 197, 200n, 216
Cramaud, Simon de, 19, 52, 93, 119–24, 128, 131, 137–8, 140–4, 165, 211
Cusa, Nicholas of, 51n

deposition, papal, 81, 133, 138, 153, 156–7, 173–4, 190
Dominican order, 68
Dominici, Cardinal, 183–4
Duc, Pierre le, 132–3

electoral capitulations: (1352) 90n; (1394) 90; (1404) 149; (1406) 149; debates on the validity of, 98–100, 102–3, 153, 158–9, 161, 173
emperor, 2, 17–18, 51–4, 56, 137–8, 152, 162, 188, 197, 205, 213; see also Charles IV; Louis of Bavaria; Rupert III, Elector Palatine; Sigismund of Hungary; Wenceslas, King of Bohemia
England, 9–12, 15, 33, 109–10, 135–6, 184, 211, 215; Kings of, see Henry IV; Richard II; universities of, 177, 191, 198; rotuli of, 138n; see also Cambridge, University of; Oxford, University of
epieikeia, 38, 61, 110–11, 141; see also necessity, doctrine of
Erfurt, University of, 12, 175n, 177, 191, 200n, 216
Estries, Nicholas d', 134
Euvrie, Guillaume, 146
Execrabilis, 175
Eymeric, Nicholas, 20–1

Fakenham, Nicholas of, 109–12, 211
Falkenberg, John of, 169–70
Ferdinand I, King of Portugal, 33–4, 47
Fermo, University of, 216
Ferrara, University of, 12, 154, 210, 212, 214, 216
Ferrer, Boniface, 19, 182
Fèvre, Jean le, 36n, 37–8
Fillastre, Guillaume, 164
Fiot, Johannes, 144
Flagellants, 19
Flanders, Count of, 29
Flandrin, Cardinal Pierre, 33, 62
Fleurie, Pierre, 133
Florence, 10, 148, 154–6; University of, 12, 155–6, 177, 206, 210, 214–15; rotuli of, 149n
force, use of, see via facti

France, 5–6, 9, 12, 15, 34–6, 47, 92–3, 108–10, 118–19, 128, 131–2, 135–40, 142–3, 146, 148–50, 166–7, 183, 192, 198, 200–1, 209, 212; councils of (1395–98), 96, 209, 211, see also under Paris; Dauphin of (Charles VII), 200; Kings of, see Charles V; Charles VI; Henry IV; Philip IV; princes of, 195, see also under individual dukes; universities of, 15, 31, 34–5, 71, 89, 93, 97, 125, 129, 142, 149, 176, 184; rotuli of, 91n, see also under individual institutions
Frankfurt, Diet of (1409), 171; Reichstag of (1397), 106
Fraticelli, 53
Fundi, Count of, 7

Gallicanism, 2, 39, 54, 56, 96–7, 99, 120, 128, 133–4, 145–6, 200–1, 207
Gannetulo, Johannes de, 158
Gascony, 72, 86
Gaunt, John of, 75–6, 86
Gelnhausen, Conrad of, 45, 54, 59–63, 66–8, 181n, 211–12
Geneva, Cardinal Robert of, 1, 8, 208; see also Clement VII, Pope
Genoa, 131
Germany, 163, 185, 197; universities of, 71, 74, 89, 168–9, 177, 191; rotuli of, 196, see also under individual institutions
Gerson, Jean, 13, 20, 77–8, 80–1, 83, 97, 104, 112–15, 144–5, 148, 164, 166–8, 179, 181, 188–9, 207, 212
Gervasius, Robertus, Bishop of Senez, 26, 28
Glyndŵr, Owain, 11, 148
Godard, Pierre, 134
Gordon, Johannes, 130
Goulain, Jean, 81
Greeks, schism of, 14, 53, 85, 136, 179, 212
Gregory VII, Pope, 6
Gregory XI, Pope, 5, 7, 180–1, 186
Gregory XII, Pope, 7–8, 148–9, 154–62, 165–6, 168–73, 177, 180–1, 183–6, 190–1, 209–10, 213–14; supporters of, 148–9, 160, 162, 169, 177, 181, 183, 185–6, 191
Grignonneria, Robertus de, 40
Guelders, Lambert of, 171
Guyenne, governor of, see Berry, John, Duke of

Hassia, Henricus de, see Langenstein, Henry of

241

Index

Muris, Petrus de, 115–16
mysticism, 19–21

Nantes, University of, 12
Naples, rulers of, *see* Charles III, Joanna
I, Ladislas, King of Naples; *see also*
Anjou, Louis I, and Louis II, dukes of
Naples, succession to, 9, 42, 47, 67, 76;
University of, 28, 175n, 186
Narbonne, Archbishop of (Cardinal), 81,
83, 87
Natalis, Aymeric, 99
nationalism; nationalist conflicts, 25, 29–
30, 37–8, 71, 74, 89, 137
Navarre, 30–1
necessity, doctrine of, 38, 63, 122, 156;
see also *epieikeia*
negotiation, see *via compromissi*
Netherlands, 47–8, 215
neutrality, 36, 41, 46, 58, 61, 137, 147,
154, 156, 166–7, 172
Nicholas V, Pope, 23
Niem, Dietrich of, 51n, 181n
Norwich, Bishop of, crusade of, 47–8, 51
Noyon, 68, 209

obedience, subtraction of, 79, 91–2, 114–
37, 139–47, 151, 153, 155–6, 159, 163–6,
170, 198, 209, 211–12, 214
Ockham, William of, 50, 51n, 58, 60, 63
Oesterzele, William of, 23
Orléans: Louis, Duke of, 76, 83, 139, 143;
University of, 15, 35, 130, 139, 146,
149n, 165, 175n, 191, 211; German
nation at, 34; *rotuli* of, 35, 72n, 147n
Orsini, Cardinal (d. 1379), 24; (d. 1438),
183
Orvieto, University of, 216
Oulmont, Raoul d', 37, 40, 116–20, 127,
136, 182, 214
Oxford, University of, 27–8, 43–4, 55, 57,
71, 109–13, 119, 135–6, 171, 175n, 184,
186, 194, 197, 211, 215; *rotuli* of, 149n
Oyta, Heinrich von, 13

Padua, Ludovicus de, 27
Padua, Marsilius of, 50, 51n, 56, 58
Padua, University of, 24, 26–7, 106, 161,
177, 212, 215
Palatinate, rulers of the, *see* Louis, Elector
Palatine; Rupert II; Rupert III
Pamplona, Cardinal of, *see* Salva, Cardinal
Martin de

papacy, 1, 5–6, 9, 17–18, 52–4, 63, 116–
18, 138, 144, 152, 159, 161, 167–8, 188–
9, 215
Paris, 35–6, 81
Bishop of, 42
Councils of, (1395) 92–3, 99, 121, 123–4,
(1396) 114, 121, (1398) 124–34, 139,
157, 212, 214, (1403) 146, (1406) 164–
5, (1408) 166
Parlement of, 43, 164
Ste Geneviève, 42–3
Paris, University of, 3, 13–15, 17, 19, 22,
34–7, 39, 42, 44–6, 48, 55, 58–69, 71–2,
74–100, 104–9, 112–16, 121, 125–6, 135–
7, 140–1, 144, 146–9, 162–8, 171, 175n,
177, 186–7, 191–7, 200–1, 204–6, 209–15
Chancellors of, *see* Ailly, Pierre d';
Blanchart, Jean; Gerson, Jean
College of Navarre, 31
faculty of arts, 41
English nation, 22–3, 35–6, 39–43, 66,
74, 92, 124 149n, 192, 196; *rotuli*
of, 74, 196
French nation, 40, 214; *rotuli* of, 40
Norman nation, 40–1, 214
Picard nation, 40–1, 178
faculty of law, 40–1, 77–8
rotuli of, 40, 105
faculty of medicine, *rotuli* of, 40
faculty of theology, 40–1, 97, 214
poetic debates of 1381, 45–7, 53, 64–6,
215
rector of, 67
rotuli of, 22–3, 36, 39–40, 72, 91, 105,
116, 147, 199n, 200
Passau, Bishop of, 13, 170
Pavia, University of, 12, 154, 175n, 206
Peasants' Revolt, 71
Pécs, University of, 11
Peñíscola, 8
Perpignan, Council of, 49, 176; University
of, 11, 13, 30–1, 43, 176, 216; *rotuli* of,
31, 91n
Perth, Council of, 201
Perugia, University of, 154, 210, 215
Peter IV, King of Aragon, 30
Petit, Jean, 82, 131, 134, 163–4, 212
Philip IV, King of France, 15–16, 35, 50
Piacenza, University of, 216
Pisa: Council of, 2, 8, 13, 49, 81, 150–1,
154–5, 157, 159–60, 168–9, 174–84, 186–7,
196, 202–5, 208–13, 215; University of,
12, 177
Piscibus, Antonius de, 186

Index

Index